W9-BYP-166

SOLITUDE
AND THE
SUBLIME

JAN'94 SX15.95

SOLITUDE
AND THE
SUBLIME

ROMANTICISM AND THE AESTHETICS OF INDIVIDUATION
FRANCES FERGUSON

ROUTLEDGE ▪ NEW YORK AND LONDON

Published in 1992 by

Routledge
An imprint of Routledge, Chapman and Hall, Inc.
29 West 35 Street
New York, NY 10001

Published in Great Britain by

Routledge
11 New Fetter Lane
London EC4P 4EE

Copyright © 1992 by Routledge, Chapman and Hall, Inc.

Printed in the United States of America

All rights reserved. No part of this book may be reprinted or reproduced or utilized in any form or by any electronic, mechanical or other means, now known or hereafter invented, including photocopying and recording, or in any information storage or retrieval system, without permission in writing from the publisher.

Library of Congress Cataloging-in-Publication Data

Ferguson, Frances.
    Solitude and the sublime : romanticism and the aesthetics of
  individuation / Frances Ferguson.
      p.   cm.
    Includes bibliographical references and index.
    ISBN 0-415-90548-6 : — ISBN 0-415-90549-4
    1. English literature—19th century—History and criticism—
  —Theory, etc. 2. English literature—18th century—History and
  criticism—Theory, etc. 3. Kant, Immanuel, 1724-1804—Aesthetics.
  4. Burke, Edmund, 1729–1797—Aesthetics. 5. Aesthetics,
  British—19th century. 6. Sublime, The, in literature.
  7. Individualism in literature. 8. Romanticism—Great Britain.
  9. Solitude in literature.   I. Title.
  PR457.F4   1992
  801'.93—dc20   92-7529
                                                            CIP
ISBN 0-415-90548-6 (HB)
ISBN 0-415-90549-4 (PB)

Contents

Preface With Acknowledgments

I should like to announce the argument and reveal the shape of this book at the outset. Beyond having an author's usual concern for candor and solicitude for being understood, I take such explicitness to be particularly enjoined by the nature of the argument of the book and because that argument runs counter to most of the criticism, whether deconstructive or New Historicist, being written today.

Briefly stated, the view of this book is that the aesthetics of the sublime, as staked out principally by Edmund Burke and Immanuel Kant at the end of the eighteenth century, resolves itself into two basic positions—empiricism and formal idealism. From my standpoint, that dispute is less a merely historical matter than a persistent debate, apparent most recently in current theoretical disputes about the nature of literary language and human agency. Thus, my accounts of Burke and Kant regularly advert to discussions of Theodor Adorno and Terry Eagleton, Jacques Derrida and Paul de Man, in addition to the primary texts. My basic contention is that criticism has enmired itself in the project of showing, from an empiricist perspective, the implausibility of a Kantian account. Such a procedure in dealing with Kant essentially collapses the two positions into one: it continually tries to explain to Kant that empiricism overcomes idealism in the end, or rather, that idealism is always ultimately a self-deluding empiricism. (This basic view of formal idealism represents the point of convergence between deconstruction and more conspicuously political accounts.) According to the common view, the formalist project not only failed to save empiricism, it also failed to see that empiricism itself (or what is seen as contingency in some accounts, social determination in others, and the inability of language to remain self-identical in still others) was bound to be disabling for it. Derrida's discussion of Kant in *La vérité en peinture* (*The Truth in Painting*) represents the most brilliant exposition of this view, and it is his tendency to see Kantian idealism as, ultimately, a failed empiricism that has prompted my questions about the deconstructive account of Kant.

As will be apparent, I am not myself even-handed in my discussion of these issues. This book seeks, I should say, to represent the claims of Romantic and specifically Kantian idealism in current critical debates. Thus, I shall repeatedly be talking about the arguments on behalf of formalism (which will be the term I most consistently use to identify formal idealism and to distinguish it from materialism). Formalism, for me, counts as a much larger and more interesting notion than what is usually, disparagingly, referred to as "mere" New Critical formalism, which is taken to be formal by virtue of its supposedly mechanical commitment to an organic textual unity and a concomitant indifference to context, conceived as anything outside the text. Although I have some reservations to register about the New Criticism,[1] I do not feel the force of that particular charge. And while many critics have taken the New Criticism to task for its excessive Kantianism, I would argue that its dramatistic interest in "tone," in miming the cadences of a human voice, considerably undercuts the formal commitments of Kantianism (and that, far from being too formalistic, the New Criticism is largely not formalistic enough).

For the purposes of this study, formalism represents the emergence of the question of individuation, in contradistinction to the notion of form as given. Understood properly, that question is not a genetic or psychological one (how someone or something got to be the way it is). Instead, it is a problem of the difficulty of saying how there can be one of anything (as against the Humean question of how there might be more than one of anything). I see the empiricist argument about the aesthetic and particularly the sublime (represented in Burke and continued in deconstructive criticism) as challenging the notion of unity on the basis of the argument that the mental images of aesthetic experience are neither purely subjective nor purely objective. What deconstruction will emphasize as the material nature of language that produces its own effects in the process of representing objects, Burke represents as the static that sensation produces by producing memories and anticipations as images—images that become objects of sensation in their own right. The empiricist account, in its Burkean or its modern forms, produces the sublime, I argue, in the form of an infinite regress, in which the representation of sensation produces representation as always something additional to be responded to.

I see Kantian formalism as mounting a challenge to such an empiricist account because empiricism, even in its most skeptical versions, is committed rather straitenedly to the testimony of the senses (even—or especially—as it is committed to a skeptical account of sensation). I focus here partic-

ularly on Kant's discussion of resemblance between natural and human pro-
ductions (in Chapters 1 and 3), on his distinction between aesthetic norms
arrived at through sensory induction and beautiful form (in Chapter 3), and
on the prominence he gives to the mathematical sublime (in Chapters 1 and
7). The tendency of my view of Kant is to see the Third Critique as particularly important for reviewing the questions of epistemology in a form
that tries to avoid taking the appearance of preexistent objects as its own
self-confirming assumption. The sublime, from this perspective, is not important because it represents formlessness but instead because it provides an
occasion for seeing aesthetics as grounding epistemological inquiry. This is
as much as to say that, by indicating how far the sublime is from an imitation of anything—be it an object or an action—Kant relocates the place
and the urgency of the aesthetic. If the aesthetic had seemed before Kant—
and has seemed to many since Kant—to further a skeptical argument by
advancing a conflation of appearances with realities, the function of the
Kantian sublime, in my view, is to suggest how actively such skepticism
avoids a more urgent question about ontology. Aesthetics thus concerns
itself less with telling differences between real and artificial things (or the
place of appearance) but, rather, with the way one determines anything as
a thing—as being a unit—without resorting to the self-confirming (and
indeed, ultimately self-comforting) movement that accompanies even the most
apparently skeptical moves of empiricism (as with the deconstructive infinite
regress of the *toujours déjà*).

I have divided the book into three sections. The first includes discussions
of Burke and Kant in terms of both the philosophical issues they raise and
the theoretical issues raised by some of the most important recent writing
on them. This involves, in the first place, an account of deconstruction that
sees it as crypto-empiricism and, in the second, an account of Adorno's reading of Kant and its pervasive influence on efforts made in recent years to
correlate the aesthetic and the political. The second includes chapters on
various phenomena in Romantic writing—the Gothic novel, the population
debate as it occurs in England at the end of the eighteenth century and the
beginning of the nineteenth, and travel literature in roughly the same period. This portion of the book will perhaps be most accessible to those with
little patience for theoretical discussion. Although the texts I discuss here
are not primarily philosophical in provenance or intent, they have seemed
to me important for representing what one could think of, quite loosely, as
the social philosophy (on the model of social history) of the period. That
is, these texts and my readings of them circle around the question of individual and society, part and whole in ways that indicate the pervasiveness
of the issues that engaged more overtly philosophical writing. (I should say,

however, that the material of these chapters demonstrates the impossibility of rendering empirical examples as if they actually embodied a formal idealist argument). The final section, consisting of only one chapter, weighs the materialist claims of recent literary criticism, particularly the New Historicism of Jerome McGann and the deconstruction of Paul de Man. Against McGann's notion of materialism as exceptionalism and against de Man's suggestion that aesthetic form represents a misguided attempt to harness material objects for human agents, I argue that aesthetic formalism (rightly) insists that the material can only count as matter at all through the operation of prior systematic articulations of human agency.

In the interests of streamlining the exposition of a very complex subject, I have used Burke and Kant as virtually the exclusive exemplars of the eighteenth-century and Romantic discussion of the philosophical issues. But what I have given with the one hand, I have needed to take away with the other. The relative clarity that I achieved by using Burke and Kant as epitomes I have in turn sacrificed in the interest of showing the way the issues of the sublime count for some of the critical and philosophical debates about literature, literary language, and language of the past twenty years or so.

This book, as I have said, presents, among other things, a critique of deconstruction. Anyone who anticipates that this amounts to laying all the world's ills of the last quarter century at the door of deconstruction or Derrida or de Man will, however, be considerably disappointed; my criticisms of deconstruction, at their most intense, amount less to a dismissal of its claims than to an acknowledgment of its intellectual importance. Further, I feel obliged to indulge in an advance reply to one (but only one) of the many objections that I anticipate receiving. Some will chastise the teleological nature of this project, that it pursues a chronological line as if there were something like connections among the various positions I trace and occasionally even something like development. However common it may be to hear such complaints about every second or third observation (including comparisons of yesterday's weather with today's, today's with tomorrow's), I want to register my sense of the fatuity of such remarks here before I have received a single review. It may be foolish to compare one day's weather with the next; it cannot be anything other than eminent good sense to talk about the inevitable interconnectedness that occurs when one philosopher responds to another, or one poet uses the work of another as an enabling model. Only the most pedantic literal-mindedness cannot grant that the philosophical and literary traditions become the material on which subsequent work works.

Because I have written, canceled, and written this book again over more than a decade, I have accumulated many more obligations than I can acknowledge in my footnotes or in the following sentences. Carol Clover, Michael Fried, Neil Hertz, Ruth Leys, and Walter Benn Michaels have, in the constancy of their intellectual friendship and in their willingness to read various pieces of this project, been particularly important to my efforts to think through these issues. Steven Knapp has given me a scrupulously close—indeed, exemplary—reading of this manuscript and has generously consti-tuted himself an audience of one. In Berkeley, I benefited from regular con-versations (about my work and that of others) with Paul Alpers, Svetlana Alpers, Leo Bersani, Howard Bloch, the late Joel Fineman, Catherine Gal-lagher, Stephen Greenblatt, Lynn Hunt, Denis Hollier, Thomas Laqueur, Robert Post, Michael Rogin, Randolph Starn, and Bernard Williams. Philip Fisher, Leo Lowenthal, Elaine Scarry, and Ruth Schorer have been impor-tant occasional presences, and Sharon Cameron, Jerome Christensen, and Ronald Paulson have been particularly helpful and stimulating colleagues during the past few years in which I have shared a departmental home with them. Rebecca Michaels and Sascha Michaels have earned my respect and gratitude for the grace with which they have borne the accidents of nature and culture.

I should also acknowledge the assistance of the National Endowment for the Humanities, which funded my research in its initial stages, and the Uni-versity of California-Berkeley, which provided me with Humanities Re-search Grants at crucial stages of this project's evolution. Participants in an NEH Summer Seminar that I taught at Berkeley in 1983 and in an NEH Institute that I taught with Ronald Paulson at Johns Hopkins in 1990 have helped me to think through the issues of this project, as have audiences at various institutions where I have lectured on this material (Berkeley, SUNY-Buffalo, the University of Pennsylvania, the Clark Memorial Library, the English Institute, the University of Zurich, and the Comparative Literature Colloquium of Switzerland). I want to thank the editors of *Glyph* for per-mission to reprint "The Sublime of Edmund Burke, or The Bathos of Ex-perience"; the editors of *Diacritics* for permission to reprint "Historicism, Deconstruction, and Wordsworth"; and The Johns Hopkins University Press for permission to reprint "Godwin, Malthus, and the Spirit of Solitude," which appeared in a collection of English Institute Essays, *Literature and the Body: Essays on Populations and Persons,* edited by Elaine Scarry.

The book I dedicate to the live presence of Walter Benn Michaels; the footnotes I dedicate to the memory of Michel Foucault.

Notes

1. See my "On the Numbers of Romanticisms," in Stephen J. Greenblatt and Giles Gunn, eds., *Redrawing the Boundaries of Literary Criticism* (New York: MLA, 1992).

1

An Introduction to the Sublime

This book will proceed, more or less simultaneously, on two fronts. In what may be alternately be regarded as indecision or a studied refusal to separate "theoretical" and "historical" issues from one another, it traces what I take to be the most significant portions of the development of the sublime. In the unequal and not-so-wide survey of this study, these are the Burkean empiricist model and the Kantian formalist (or formalist idealist) account;[1] in the more nearly equal and wider survey, these are the discernible corollaries of the Burkean and Kantian arguments about the sublime which appear in more popular or less argumentatively precise literature (the Gothic novel, the population debate in England from around the end of the eighteenth century, and the travel literature describing picturesque and sublime landscapes).

Yet the historical account has had its urgency for me because of the resurgence of the philosophical issues of the sublime in the work that has come to be identified as "theoretical." This is not to say, in some crudely idealist fashion that collapses ideas and opinions, objects and ideology, that "my theory" made me see certain things as if they were historically existent. It is, however, to announce my view that the modern historical development of the notion of the sublime encapsulates two basic positions on aesthetics and its importance, and that these positions continue to set the terms for even the most recent and superficially alien arguments on the subject.

In brief, my view is that the advent of aesthetics as a more or less distinct area of philosophical speculation marks an intensification of interest in the (mental image) and in the difficulties of assimilating it to the problems of ontology and epistemology, on the one hand, and to those of ethics, on the other. Burke's procedure, in discussing the sublime and the beautiful and our thoughts about them, is to treat mental images first as if they were the affective traces of objects and then as if they were objects themselves. At the outset of the *Philosophical Enquiry into the Origin of Our Ideas of the Sublime and Beautiful,* this makes it possible for him to classify objects as sublime or beautiful, as objects whose distinguishing features can be gauged by human responses. By the end of the *Enquiry,* the difficulty of making those classifications has come to be very nearly the foremost topic of Burke's discussion. If objects can be known, in Burke's aesthetics, only through experience, the persistence of mental images, the accumulation of previous responses to objects (which he refers to under the general rubric of "habit") of prior experience continually threatens to make present experience virtually illegible.

Representation for Burke thus revolves around images of affect, of present, past, or future (anticipated) experience. One can represent and give testimony about the existence and value of objects on the basis of sensory experience, what one has actually experienced. Yet that model of empirical testimony has extreme limitations because of its very capaciousness. As soon as an individual's affective response is taken as constitutive of aesthetic objects (i.e., as making them either beautiful or sublime), every occasion for affect becomes equally an object. A memory, provoking response, can on this account look as much like a sensory object as a noninternalized object, a thing or event in the outside world. By that token, the representation of experience makes affect an extremely unreliable index to the existence of objects, because the representations—in the form of memories and anticipations—themselves become the objects of response.

The problem that arises for Burke's *Enquiry* is, then, that the mental images of past or future objects of experience clutter the tablet of experience to such an extent that one cannot differentiate the response to objects from the response to one's representations of them. Burke's inability or refusal to make a thorough-going distinction between objects and mental objects makes the testimony of the senses its own skeptical double, and mental representations become their own opposites—the impossibility of sustaining a distinction between objects and representations.

Part of my argument here is that Burke's *Enquiry,* though employing vastly different terminology and procedures from recent deconstructive and historicist criticism, shares with them an aesthetic empiricism, a commitment to such a conflation (and indeed that deconstruction's interest in differences and distinctions is less important for insisting upon a gap between things and representations, or between signifiers and signifieds, than for making both of these equally objects of consciousness). In my view, Kantian aesthetics not only addresses such a central problem of empiricist aesthetics—the relative standing of objects and representations—but goes a long way toward resolving it by the simple argument of structure. (This is as much as to announce an apologia for Kant's account of aesthetic form as a regulative structure, and to suggest that Kantian aesthetics is especially important for making the argument for the primacy of the regulative, or for the claim that epistemology becomes parasitic on form). Whereas Burke had treated aesthetic experience as if it involved basically the pleasure and pain that one has in responding to objects, Kant assigned a much more distinct area to it. Just as in Burke, the classifications of objects were subject to change, but, differently from Burke, the Kantian aesthetic made clear the need to talk less about the reality of objects and responses than about the place of the mental image. And, though the Kantian separation of the aesthetic has repeatedly been seen as an escapist attempt to make reality less real, it seems to me that the Kantian boundaries achieve precisely the opposite effect. By means of the realm of the aesthetic, Kant is able to avoid the Burkean empiricist competition between objects and the representations through which they are known, and to advance a view of aesthetic objects as the more or less substantial versions of mental images.

Mental images may, in perfect keeping with his account, concern the most real and most urgent problems conceivable. Yet their consequences in action are less than clear. Aesthetic objects, like dreams, memories, anticipations, and so forth, have connections with real and substantial action and suffering, but a chief portion of their interest for Kant lies in their not being—and never being—identical to them.[2]

The differences between Burke's and Kant's positions become clearest perhaps on the most basic level, as the two are describing the distinguishing features of their subject matter. They both recognize categories of the beautiful and the sublime, and both link the beautiful with society and the sublime with individuals isolated either by the simple fact of their solitude or by an heroic distinction that sets them apart even as they participate in social enterprises. Yet where Burke continually suggests different possible classifications of the same items—horses, for instance, that may be considered as awe inspiring in their might or as reliably domesticated creatures—Kant makes a crucial decision to restrict the sublime: "it must be nature, or be thought of as nature."[3] Burke's account incorporates something like affect (or reception or context) into the terms of his classification, as if to anticipate what the twentieth century would describe as an identity between facts and values (or at least as an inability to sustain a fact-value distinction). Kant's identification of the sublime with nature, by contrast, conspicuously diminishes the place of affect. Affect, the viewer's or auditor's response, may be necessary to constitute the experience as aesthetic—to make it count as experience. Affect does not, however, work to constitute the identity of the object in the way it does for Burke. Rather, the point of a sublime object's being natural lies in its not being conditioned by the human viewer, in the indifference to knowing its ontological status (the "indifference to its existence"), which occurs in the very process of seeing it as an aesthetic object. If Burke argues that aesthetic experience enables one to know things and events through the modifications they effect on one's body, Kant's interest in nature as such registers the peculiarity that persons should see themselves as responding to intentionless and sensationless objects.

The Burkean interpenetration of human and natural types of beauty and sublimity assimilates itself to the kind of anthropomorphism that John Ruskin described in his brilliant discussion of the "pathetic fallacy," the illusion that inanimate objects can participate in human feelings. Indeed, that version of anthropomorphism makes a dramatistic and interpersonally imitative model look as though it applied even to relations between persons and trees, persons and stones. The ultimate use that Kantian formalism makes of nature, however, is to supplant such a dramatistic model by strictly limiting the number of speaking voices. If Burke locates aesthetic pleasure in the satisfactions that one can have in objects as extensions of one's relations with other human beings, Kant's account of the sublime continually asks what sort of value there might be in taking pleasure in objects that neither possess nor express consciousness.

This is, in my view, the crucial importance of the sublime in Kant's aesthetic theory—that it conspicuously reduces the force of the empiricist argument by making it unclear what the experience of the sublime would mean were it not for what Kant terms transcendental *a priori* principles of judgment. Thus, although he can, with Burke, include both natural and artificial objects in the category of the beautiful, he restricts the sublime to human pleasure in nature. The experience of sublime pleasure in nature is seen, in other words, as transcendental because of its not needing to be taught, and indeed because of the way in which the construction of the lesson plan for that learning is itself unimaginable. (The use of the sublime as a limit case, I would argue, explains the difficulty that writers from Friedrich Schiller to de Man and Eagleton have had with the notion of the aesthetic education because they correctly see the problems of distinguishing the formalist account of aesthetics from the art treatises—the communication of advice from one artist to another, and from artist to audience—that preceded it.) If education involves the notion of the heritability of intentions, the sublime in Kant's restricted description insists upon sublime aesthetic experience as the communication of intentionlessness.

Now it is on the score of the notion of the transcendent and transcendental that particular difficulties have repeatedly arisen for the Kantian account. For if the empirical account collects testimony from various different people's experience and tries to generalize on that basis, the critiques of Kant's transcendentalism have essentially tried to read the possibility of individual autonomy (not needing to be initiated into aesthetic experience) and the autonomy of the aesthetic from more practical knowledge as if they made excessive claims by propounding an empiricism in reverse. Thus, sublime transcendence has looked to some (most recently Derrida, Pierre Bourdieu, Barbara Herrnstein Smith, and Eagleton) like a false claim to individual distinction, or like an assertion of property rights in collective, socially induced experience.

With Adorno, they have seen the possibility of usefulness, didactic transmission, and cognition itself as an enduring compromise of the artfulness of any particular example of art. If art is to be art, it must be for its own sake. That formulation of the significance of the aesthetic has been enormously—if sometimes foolishly—productive for both art and criticism. Yet the burden of my argument is that such a version of aestheticism has scant purchase on the main portion of Kant's song in the Third Critique. Instead, it seems to me that Kant's segregation of the aesthetic judgment enables him, somewhat paradoxically, to broach an argument that will make the aesthetic crucial to the most central aspects of inquiry in the phenomenological tradition. This involves more than formulating a definition of the aesthetic that can be defended in the name of culture or in the name of individual freedom. Rather, as is borne out by Martin Heidegger's sustained interest in Kant's account of imagination, the aesthetic becomes the site for an examination of the meaningfulness of the very lack of fit between objects and the individuals that perceive them. The project of analyzing one's pleasure in an object that has no necessary relation to a previously existing object of exchange or use, the project of the Analytic of the Beautiful, accompanies an even more improbable undertaking in the Analytic of the Sublime, the project of justifying one's pleasure in objects that, by virtue of being natural rather than artificial, do not bear any obvious relation to intersubjective experience, and that, by virtue of not having clear and distinct boundaries, make the apparently objective act of cognition involve more than a mere response to objects.

To say that the debate over aesthetics and particularly over the sublime occurs between Burkean empiricism and Kantian formalist idealism in some sense states the obvious. This is a commonplace of the history of aesthetics, as is the usual expansion of it—that the discussion of art becomes less objective and more subjective, less oriented toward things and more oriented toward individual psychology (or what is disparagingly seen as self-absorption). That account is not wrong, or not simply wrong. What it fails to do, however, is to distinguish between the empiricist-formalist debates in aesthetics and those over ontology and epistemology. It fails, in other words, to suggest why Kant bothered to add a third critique to those of pure and practical reason, why the argument supplementing empiricism seemed to need to be led through aesthetic objects as well as "ordinary" objects. The *Critique of Judgment* seems, from such a perspective, to have been borne out of an unaccountable Kantian commitment to producing analyses in threes. Burke, in trying to establish an objectivity for individual consciousness on the basis of sensation, continually converts empiricism into a skeptical meditation on the vagaries of individual consciousness as it tries to translate between the language of persons and the language of objects. The empiricism and the skepticism are, however, less interesting from my perspective than the interest in psychology as a version of an interest in aesthetic objects. And the aesthetic, in the process of coming to be defined as something potentially distinct from taste as a particularly demanding version of consumption, becomes less important as a social and sociological phenomenon and more important for representing a distinct kind of experience. The aesthetic, as Kant outlines it, prefigures and justifies Heidegger's later suggestion (in *Kant and the Future of Metaphysics*) that the imagination should be promoted to the standing of a separate faculty, on the order of the reason or the understanding.[4]

The particular emphasis on mental images with which I am concerned is more circumscribed and circumspect than "imagination" in two influential senses of the word. It does not concern itself with visuality per se, as many eighteenth-century accounts of the term have been seen to do. Neither does it automatically entail a valorization of imagination like that proffered by defenses of art—that it brings "us" (whoever that might be) together, that it provides an escape from narrow utilitarianism, and so forth. Rather, the imagination suggests the interconnections between consciousness and matter (the way in which thought continually needs some version of objects in order to be thought—which can be seen as one aspect of Derrida's and de Man's interest in language). In addition, the imagination provides a very particular account of what counts as matter from a phenomenological view. In the strong sense of the word, imagination involves a focus on the impressional matter of states such as memory insofar as memory is a version of the aesthetic experience of everyday life. Thus, although the aesthetic continually has reference to objects that are external to individuals, the imagination suggests that these objects are, so to speak, only incidentally external (or rather that internality and externality themselves have no particular usefulness here). The externalized objects of the imagination that are paintings, poems, photographs are equally expressions of and analogues to internal impressional states. Neither pure replicas of objects nor pure projections of some supposedly pure consciousness, memories and aesthetic objects alike distinguish imagination from simple perception. Memories of experiences involve having a relation to a representation of one's past experience that, far from reenacting that experience, enables one to have the complete inventory of possible relations to it (embarrassment, pleasure, annoyance, and so forth) that people routinely have.

From this perspective, aesthetic objects are, like memories, dreams, and similar imaginative states, every bit as autonomous as Kant argued they were. They are autonomous, however, not because they never are influenced by an external reality or because they can compete with or substitute for reality. They are autonomous, rather, because they cannot be exclusively assigned to either subjectivity or objectivity. (It will be said, with justice, that nothing can be so exclusively assigned, but my basic point about aesthetic object and mental image is that they occupy a unique place. As against accounts of fantasy that make social induction produce individuals who see in a certain way and thus produce their society in a certain way, what interests me here is the perceptible ambivalence of aesthetic objects, their alternation between seeming to be things and seeming to be images of other things.) This point, however obvious it may sound as a remark on memories, dreams, and similar states, requires rehearsal in this discussion of the sublime, largely because of the way that the sublime has been taken in some quarters as the emblem of Romantic self-consciousness, the solipsistic engagement with one's own individual consciousness that prevents one from seeing what one "ought to see." Aesthetic autonomy, from this perspective, looks like a temporary appropriation of the natural world for the purpose of repudiating both the social and the natural worlds, or for repudiating the social world with a tendentious account of nature. Yet, even though it is doubtless the case that aesthetic objects and aesthetic experiences have a harder time justifying their existence than food, shelter, and other material necessities for survival, the autonomy of aesthetics that is surely more troublesome than such merely willful and inconsiderate behavior is its peculiar encapsulation of purposeful action and perception of objects. The aesthetic and particularly the sublime come, I argue, to represent the interest in all the intentional states that are unconcerned with the existence of objects. If the fact of there being chairs in the world is not enough to explain why one would take pleasure in a picture of a chair, it is likewise not enough to say that the picture of the chair merely represents one's pleasures. And this is likewise—and especially—the case of the aesthetic interest in nature that develops as the identifying mark of sublimity for Kant.

Virtually everyone who has ever commented on the sublime has followed Edmund Burke in lamenting the confusion that has beset the subject and

in promising some much-needed clarification. Burke delivered on his prom-
ise, writing his *Philosophical Enquiry into the Origin of Our Ideas of the Sublime
and Beautiful,* an exposition that is supremely clear in its basic outlines. The
beautiful, for him, registers human sensation as a susceptibility to all the
experiences that draw an individual into society. The sublime is, in his view,
likewise sensationist. Yet sensation here operates to produce two radically
different sorts of effects: inducing social cohesion, or a commitment to society, in the beautiful and precisely the reverse, or a commitment to self and
self-preservation, in the sublime. For while Burke presents the beautiful as
the sociable, he depicts sublime sensation as asocial (or even antisocial). In
representing a consciousness of individuality not as subjectivity per se but
as the by-product of a thought of self-preservation, he makes individuality
occur less as a power than as the failure of an individual in the face of
sensation. In so far as being overcome by one's experience feels like incapacity rather than capacity, Burke's description of sublimity makes the capacity for experience look like a liability as well as an asset. Sublime objects
create particular problems for the sensations—by presenting themselves as
too powerful or too vast or too obscure or too much a deprivation for the
senses to process them comfortably. The very intensification of the sensation
that had made society look like the logical culmination of shared human
sensations of a shared world makes society look irrelevant. Yet the sensationist model persists, even in Burke's account of the incompatibility between the senses and the experiences that are depicted as too immense for
them to process, in that the difficulties that the senses encounter become
empirical testimony to a nonsensory world that is, ultimately, continuous
with it. It produces from within a sensationist and physical account a metaphysics that would see itself grounded on experience alone. Burke's clarification of the sublime, then, develops the infinite and sublime out of the
finite and beautiful by suggesting that the psychological responses of love
or fear accompany perceptions of objects categorized as "less" or "more" in
relation to the individual perceiving subject. Perception thus, as I will argue
at greater length in the next two chapters, resolves itself into comparison
for Burke and the empiricist aesthetic. The individual subject relates to objects by turning itself into a measuring stick—albeit one that, in a psychic
version of Lewis Carroll's Alice, alters its self-estimation often enough to
necessitate continual revisions of what counts as less or more powerful than
it is. To say this is as much as to observe that the qualitative distinction on
which Burke's *Enquiry* hinges—that between the beautiful and the sublime—resolves itself into a quantitative distinction. We love what is beautiful for submitting to us, for being *less* than we are; we react with dread

and awe to what is sublime because of its appearing greater than we are, for being *more,* and making us acknowledge its power.

Burke, on the one hand, establishes aesthetic experience as subjective experience that is trying to recover its own objective origins in sensation: "People are not liable to be mistaken in their feelings, but they are very frequently wrong in the names they give them, and in their reasonings about them."[5] On the other hand, this very production of subjective experience continually puts in the foreground an insistence upon representations—names and reasoning—that subverts the possibility of imagining subjectivity as sustained and continuous over time.

Such a reading of Burke, developed at some length in the following chapter, is an account at least sympathetic to deconstruction, in that it insists upon the ways in which representations of experience come to make experience itself seem unavailable. Putting that line of argument differently, it makes the impossibility of sustaining claims for a unified and unitary self seem, paradoxically, to emerge precisely out of their basis in individual experience. The generation of the exception, or the possibility of the exception in the signifier's play, looks as though it vitiates arguments for connections. At the time I wrote that essay on Burke, with its deconstructive account of the impossibility of deriving objects from experience or a subject from objects, I thought I was discovering (with the usual ironic brackets around such a term) something about Burkean empiricism that was all the more compelling because of the implausibility that Burke would have recognized his own position as fundamentally consistent with deconstruction.

I here reconstruct my own past views of my essay on Burke less to provide a personal narrative than to acknowledge that I am reprinting that essay virtually unrevised and to insist that I am doing so because I take it to have been symptomatic. This is, obviously, to "distance" myself from that essay in the act of reprinting it. Yet the reasons for that distancing require elaboration here, for I would say now that I was less mistaken about Burke than about deconstruction and its relationship to empiricism. What I took myself to be demonstrating about Burke's *Enquiry* was that his conflation of artifacts and natural objects as occasions of aesthetic experience (either of sublimity or beauty) largely undoes the empiricist aesthetic. Continually equating images and objects, Burke comes to provide an account of the ways in which aesthetic images themselves become objects, supplanting or interfering with—in any case, not expressing—the "real" objects they might be supposed to represent.

The apparently naïve move of empiricism, to imagine that objects can be the basis for knowledge, thus, yields to a subversive conjunction of epistemology and aesthetics, in which the Burkean inability or refusal to distinguish between our experience of objects and our experience of representations of objects seems to prefigure the deconstructive account of the role of language. If the work of Derrida, de Man, and deconstructive criticism generally argues in what might seem an initially un-Burkean fashion against a connection between representations of things and the presences of things, it nevertheless draws considerable energy from what de Man late in his career identifies as "materialism." This commitment to materialism evolves from the claim that the signifier and the signified that make up any sign are not only not identical but that their relationship to one another is, in the terminology of structural linguistics, arbitrary, and in the terminology of deconstruction, indeterminate.[6] Social materialism makes the claim that meanings can be imbedded in objects to such an extent that even artifacts can come to have causality with respect to individuals. Deconstructive materialism, by contrast, would emphasize the primacy of the material signifier in both embodying and interfering with any and all such causal accounts. The impossibility of restricting causal connections to one set becomes the first, Shandean step in the account of the insufficiency of causal connections. This account, however, finds its complement in an argument for the fundamental incommensurability of linguistic materials (sounds, marks) and ideas. Thus, in Paul de Man's well-known formulation in his "Excuses (Confessions)" in *Allegories of Reading,* Rousseau's confession—that he stole a ribbon and blamed his fellow servant, Marion, for the theft—is merely a sound, and "one should resist all temptation to give any significance whatever to the sound 'Marion.'" "Marion," while it could potentially refer to the person Marion (since one can say anything that the grammar of one's language permits one to say)[7] always in any event remains radically material, the sound or noise of the utterance, the graphic inscription of the written word in the *Confessions.* Along the way to this conclusion, de Man provides two conjectural histories of the way Rousseau might have come to have spoken that name, along with an account of the auditors' reception of the sound as accusation. Those descriptions of intention, or psychology, and reception, or plausibility, however, are incidental to the process of marking the difference between noise and name, the material of the utterance and its communicated meaning. Indeed, the constitution of the argument for materialism rests upon the construction of multiple systematic transformations of "random error into injustice" (293); the production of links between utterance and referent that are "causal," "encoded," *and* "governed by any other conceivable relationship that could lend itself to systematization" (292) establishes meaning as "a determination which is, *ipso facto,* overdetermined" (293).

In this account of materialism, "reading" comes to be the term for what Cynthia Chase and Andrzej Warminski, two of de Man's most faithful commentators, describe as the "interminable process of deciding between the *meaning* and the *process* of signification"[8] and as "the decision between the thematic, referential meaning and the rhetorical, allegorical function that turns upon it."[9] Reading, that is, enables one to stop seeing both the ideological, which for de Man "is precisely the confusion of linguistic with natural reality, or reference with phenomenalism"[10] and the cognitive or thematic. It allows one to see the "material, linguistic conditions of meaning"— less the message than the handwriting on the wall, less the individual facial expression than the nose on one's face.

The point, for de Man, of identifying this materiality as materiality rather than phenomenality, taken as an orientation toward phenomena as things and also as the notion of referentiality, is to relocate the burden of Kant's argument in the Third Critique. All the transcendentalizing and universalizing that Kant has been seen to do, he claims, is precisely the reverse—the presentation of an extraordinary particularity that is so material as to be untranslatable. "From the organic, still asserted as architectonic principle in the *Critique of Pure Reason,* to the phenomenological, the rational cognition of incarnate ideas, which the best part of the Kant interpretation in the nineteenth and twentieth century will single out, we have reached, in the final analysis, a materialism that, in the tradition of the reception of the *Third Critique,* is seldom or never perceived."[11]

But if Kant's materialism has been given short shrift, the basic terrain that de Man delimits by the term "materialism" has not.[12] On the one hand, what de Man calls materialism seems to be among the most commonly observed aspects of Kantian aesthetics, in that it is in agreement with the traditions of formalism that suggest the irreducibility of the aesthetic object. In its most popular expression, this formalism pronounces that "a poem must not mean but be." On the other hand, de Man's account of Kant's materialism differs from the commonly accepted accounts of formalism in that it attends to a different unit, not the unity discerned in the manifold but the "prosaic materiality of the letter."[13]

This prosaically material letter is presumed to differ from the phenomenal because it would be the equivalent of the "noise" of the "Excuses" essay. It moves to mark, to articulate, the difference between its one occurrence and another. Or, as Warminski says, in one of the most accurate statements of this position, "A mark as mark, writing as writing, is not something to be heard or seen, it is something to be *read.* (Just as we can hear [b] and [p], but the difference between them that constitutes one as [b] and the other as [p] is not something we can hear—it is a marking that makes it possible for us to [think we] "hear" [b] and [p].)"[14] The prosaicly material letter, in a repetition that looks like motion, is the seen (and unseen) cause of an unseen effect, the indeterminable and interminable difference between it and another letter, and between its one occurrence and another.

As a point about the reception of any utterance, the success of any speech act, Derrida's position on undecidability, with which de Man's position is affiliated, has its force. "The irreducible excess of the syntactic over the semantic"[15]—the infinite number of things that one might do with words or letters—and the impossibility of saturating a context—so that one can effectively cordon off a text or a word from access to another syntax—all entail the argument that determinate meaning can never be assured, confirmed, transferred as the same. As a position that takes its place among theories of meaning, this insistence upon the inability to establish inevitable rules or predictions about reception is important. Yet the de Manian textual turn on the Derridean argument is one that insists that language disarticulates bodies—prevents individual humans from being able to present their thoughts as the inner contents of their bodies to others in apprehensible form—because language has a body of its own. If it didn't have a body, the argument goes, it wouldn't be perceptible or legible at all. Having a body, it, like material objects, has a perceptibility and opacity of its own that continually exceeds its representative function.

The linguistic-materialist position, that is, reconfigures the notion that a referential language might connect with a knowledge of the objects of reference so as to insist that the materiality of the signifier represents not merely one's inability to know those objects but also the inability to know the language that material signs have constituted as objects. Thus, the aporia that opens between the performative and the constative, or (to cite a related though not quite parallel opposition) between the speech act and the cognition, is unbreachable, because the speech act produces not merely a meaning that cannot lay claim to a cognition of any referential objects but also language as an ever-proliferating string of new material objects that are unavailable for cognition. The linguistic performance that would produce meaning does produce meaning. Yet it can do so only by language, which is defined as material, and thus as infinitely distanced from the meaning that its material would be connected with.

This concern with materialism—and, specifically, with opposing it to phenomenalism—can be seen as one answer to the question of the status of the mental image. For Edmund Husserl there had remained considerable ambiguity about the way one might distinguish between a perception and a mental image, and aesthetic objects had thus seemed to present a particularly problematic case. For if a mental image (like one of Pegasus) clearly does not correspond to a perception of an object, then an aesthetic object is, simultaneously, *perceptible* and *unreal*. Thus, as Jean-Paul Sartre says in his extraordinary little book *Imagination,* we can perceive an aesthetic object "as a thing-object or as an image-object," depending on our interpretation of "one and the same impressional matter." Yet while Sartre points to the problem that remains for Husserl of explaining "why my consciousness intends some matter as image rather than as perception," he follows Husserl in suggesting that aesthetic objects are particularly vexed cases for thinking about the status of the relationship between mind and matter.[16] The "hyletic ambivalence" of aesthetic objects lies in their similarity to memories and projections of the future. Without stating that aesthetic objects are themselves acts of recollection or of prophecy, one can see that aesthetic objects, like memories and anticipations, involve something—impressional matter— even in the absence of any reference to preexisting objects. While they can be (at the "realist" pole of analysis) thought of as "thing-objects," as objects that are meaningful to the extent that they involve copies of things available for perception, they can also be (at the phenomenological and deconstructive pole of analysis) thought of as "image-objects," as objects that are things in themselves regardless of whether they provide images of other things.

Deconstructive materialism can thus be said to be concerned with aesthetics not—or not merely—because the aesthetic does not immediately resolve itself into questions of existence and truth. Rather, deconstruction is concerned with the aesthetic because it continually exploits the "hyletic ambivalence" that had earlier been associated with "only a small number of privileged cases (paintings, photographs, copies, etc.)"[17] and identifies it as a more generalizable linguistic condition.[18] The ambivalence that had appeared in works of art—paintings, photographs, copies, etc.—to make them seem alternately image-objects and thing-objects, came to attach itself to the sentence, the word, the phoneme. From one standpoint, this perception of materialism suggests that, as for Derrida, the matter of language continually propels language so that each word moves through a process of self-division in the form of the pun, collecting what might appear to be new or more meanings as an unfolding of its various possible instances. From another, as for de Man, it provides the basis for imagining a text in hyperformalist terms that both exceed and repeat the critical doctrine of organic unity that de Man has repeatedly attacked. While the notion of organic unity, as enunciated most influentially by Goethe, Kant, Schelling, and Coleridge, had suggested the absolute interconnection of the elements that combined to create form (so that a change of one would be a change for all), de Man's notion of untranslatability suggests that in Kant, "this most inconspicuous of stylists," one cannot change a letter without losing a sense of "how decisively determining [is] the play of the letter and of the syllable, the way of saying (*Art des Sagens*) as opposed to what is being said (*das Gesagte*)."[19]

From the standpoint of the materialist claim about language, then, deconstruction has a particular interest in the sublime, that of demonstrating that the sublime was not about the advent of subjectivity or individual psychology. This represented a considerable revision of the history of aesthetics. For the dominant trajectory of literary history had identified the rise of the sublime as the rise of the individual subject, and specifically of that individual subjectivity as marked by a reception-based aesthetic that treats affect as the crucial index to the aesthetic object. The culmination of the surveys of the sublime that scholars such as Samuel Holt Monk or Walter Hipple, Jr., provided is always, with fewer or more interruptions, the Kantian idealism that Foucault takes as emblematic of the inauguration of the sciences of man.[20] The deconstructive account of the sublime involves removing the individual, removing the psychological, from the sublime by converting the sublime into endless work. Language becomes constantly torn between what is usually dismissed as its mere communicative function and its own material substantiality; it requires, in order for one to hear its rustle, more attention than any finite being has to give. Deconstructive reading, that is, may involve "the necessity to decide between signified and referent, between violence on the stage and violence in the streets,"[21] but it also makes the moment of decision, like the moment of performance, an extraordinarily finite act in a conspicuously infinite field.

This is to say that deconstructive reading ultimately involves a technology for producing sublimity—an infinity of materiality. In this sense, Chase's claims that de Man was writing a critique of aesthetics seem entirely correct, and her suggestion that this was a political gesture, entirely incorrect.[22] For the essence of the deconstructive position (particularly in de Man's handling of it) effectively counters the notion that there could be a practical politics; performatives, continually being undermined by the way the material of the communication exceeds the intentions they were designed to express, may represent action but always an action that is conspicuously deluded about its actual effects. For while actions are finite, the materialist reading sees only infinites and infinitesimals, ever-expanding contexts and ever more minutely distinguishable versions of matter. This is, if the heterogeneity that emerges in de Man's deconstructive reading bears the message of the non-identity of sign and referent, not even Warminski's quite accurate observation that de Man's work involves a "sustained, relentless meditation on history and the political"[23] can amount to the claim that it is itself political, because the notion of heterogeneity has been deployed to distinguish writing-as-mark from writing-as-reference, the material from the cognitive.

Ironically, deconstruction thus converts the analysis of the beautiful and the sublime into a modern variant of the empirical model that Burke established for it. For the sublime comes to seem merely a version of empiricism without induction, an association that makes "postmodernists"—and masochists—of us all by (as in Jean-François Lyotard's account) creating the impression that contemporary life is the process of discovering society as a collection of infinite technologies working on an individual whose information only operates in a limited field. The notion of communicable technology becomes the delimited replacement for Kantian transcendental structures of perception; and "know-how" becomes identical with the impossibility of epistemological certainty, as a knowledge of how to go on, how to continue a particular operation, becomes less a symptom of knowledge than of the blindness of action. In that sense, deconstruction reconfirms and extends accounts of the aesthetic that make aesthetic experience revolve around loss of agency. In discovering in language and in representation generally, the limits of cognitive knowledge, deconstruction suggests the impossibility of maintaining a distinction between the aesthetic and other kinds of experience;[24] but even as it does so it imagines the aesthetic as constituting a rebuke to technology, to a knowledge that is defined by its communication, by its successful transmission to another. The deconstructive account of language opposes itself to technology, understood as the appropriation of material nature, opposes itself to education, understood as a communication with other minds, as if there were regular processes of recognizing a connecting link that might make any series susceptible of orderly continuation. Yet in those moments in which it imagines a materialism or a zero that could appear as an outside to language or of number, it re-creates linguistic difference as a real that can be glimpsed but not known, that is supposed to present itself in a "linguistic moment" that makes an omnipresent feature of language—the split between its material nature and its mobilization for expression, denomination, and so forth—mysteriously punctual, occurring as a local effect.[25]

The importance, then, of recent (more and less deconstructive) accounts of the sublime is that they have generalized from a specifically literary problem (the appearance of unreal persons in literary works)[26] to a more generally linguistic one (the difficulty of locating a finite individual in relation to the infinite arbitrary system of language). Thus, the deconstructive portrayal of language has seemed to make it impossible to sustain traditional accounts of an author who has responsibility for the meaning of a literary work. Earlier histories of the sublime and of the emergence of the aesthetic saw the sublime as centrally concerned with affect, with the reception of objects rather than with the nature of the objects themselves. The movement from Burke to Kant for Samuel Holt Monk represents a progression from the view that reception involves an implicit statement about the nature of the object being perceived to the view that reception involves an implicit statement about the nature of the perceiving mind. More recent commentators—Derrida, Thomas Weiskel, Neil Hertz, and Peter de Bolla—have argued for a redefinition of the notion of psychology that seems to be represented by the sublime. Instead of providing empirical testimony about the kinds of objects that produce certain kinds of response, instead of suggesting the contours of the transcendental structures of cognition, the new criticism of the sublime has tended to focus on voluntarism and involuntarism. The sublime has seemed, therefore, to concern the establishment of a sense of individual power that criticism must expose as factitious, an illusion of power rather than a reality. Thus, for example, Weiskel combines the schemata of structural linguistics and Freudian psychoanalysis to suggest that the sublime comes into its own when it creates not merely individual objects by reference to a perceiving individual but also the individual subject as a fantasmatic producer of objects.[27]

The repudiation of closure, comprehension, and totalization escalates from one critic to the next. Weiskel combines a Freudian psychomachy with linguistics to suggest the way that the neutral structures of language can come to be invested with affect. The psychoanalytic scheme provides a development or originary schema that performs the same function as Burke's teleological argument; where Burke's Providence mandates that pleasure and pain should be added on to and implicated in perception, Weiskel's use of Freud makes perception pleasurable by its association with the gratification of the maternal principle and reason painful by its association with the paternal principle. Thus, the mathematical sublime comes to be read as a moment in which a sudden irruption of personified will imposes itself, in which "an excess on the part of the object with respect to the perceiving mind or imagination; in semiotic terms, an excess of the plane of the signifier" (103) produces actions in relation to perception. The self divides into portions that war with one another to exchange one self-object formation (the ego's fearful pleasure in a proliferation of objects) for another (the superego's demand for identification with an authority—the faculty of reason—that produces closure in the form of totality or infinity).

> To put it sequentially: the excessive object excites a wish to be inundated, which yields an anxiety of incorporation; this anxiety is met by a reaction formation against the wish which precipitates a recapitulation of the oedipus complex; this in turn yields a feeling of guilt (superego anxiety) and is resolved through identification (introjection).[105]

Having proposed such a coherent description of the negative sublime, however, Weiskel glosses his own explanatory formula as merely an attempt to account for his perception that "the rhetoric of power dominates" Kant's discussions of both the mathematical and the dynamical sublimes. As he observes, it "is not logically necessary that the reason's capacity for totality or infinity should be invariably construed as power degrading the sensible and rescuing man from 'humiliation' at the hands of nature"(106).

Weiskel portrays himself, that is, as identifying a rhetorical excess, a melodramatic effect, in Kant's language and as seeing that excess as itself the motive for schematizing. And in this he seems to conform to the pattern that Neil Hertz identifies in his discussion of Weiskel in "The Notion of Blockage in the Literature of the Sublime." While Weiskel sees himself as explaining an overdetermined and undermotivated rhetoric in Kant, Hertz sees Weiskel as largely complicit in the pattern he discerns, as participating in imposing a clarity achieved through "the sublime of conflict and structure."[28] Weiskel, in Hertz's view, does not merely describe the role of blockage in Kant's account of the sublime; he is himself, in a variation on Pope's description of Longinus as both describing and being sublimity, the great blockage he draws.

Even, that is, as Hertz is giving Weiskel "credit for dwelling as long as he did on the puzzles and anxieties of the pre-Oedipal" Weiskel becomes emblematic of the identification with the power of the father. To suggest the arbitrariness of the paternal principle of closure is to have "brought it all home to the Father" and to have abandoned (or fled) the pre-Oedipal or maternal (230). Just as anxiety occupies the place of an involuntary will, so (Hertz's reading of Weiskel could be seen to suggest) arbitrary objects replace mere perceptual objects. The standard against which Weiskel is being measured here is the commitment to treat the sublime as a version of the pre-Oedipal because the pre-Oedipal is treated as identical to affect without objects, either as objects of cognition or as subjects. As in Julia Kristeva's analysis, on which Hertz draws, the pre-Oedipal is not important for an account of relatedness or unity between mother and child (as in more directly ego-based and object-based accounts). Rather, it provides a language of ur-egos and ur-objects, versions of the subject-object relationship which would appear to be untainted by any of the negative consequences that closure, unity, and the like might seem to impose on egos and objects.

The sublime, in other words, seems most important to much recent criticism for what it is not. Undefined or indeterminate, neither subjective nor objective, it seems to represent the modern (or postmodern) version of Dickens's portrait of the imagination as the alternative to hard facts. As Jean-Luc Nancy has observed, at different moments of his discussion of the topic, "The sublime is fashionable" ("Le sublime est à la mode"), and the "sublime is the destiny of art."[29] As he has not observed, one might want to draw a connection between the fashion for sublimity and the discovery of sublime indeterminateness as the destiny for artifacts themselves.

Now the assumption that the sublime involves loss of agency and loss of determinate bounds for subjects as well as objects makes critical practice look like an extraordinarily vexed enterprise. Peter de Bolla, in his interesting recent study, *The Discourse of the Sublime: Readings in History, Aesthetics, and the Subject,* produces an uneasy account of the way he arrived at the sublime as a topic. By delimiting his field chronologically—to cover almost exclusively texts written between 1756 and 1763, the period of the Seven Years War, he is able to argue both that the notion of "the autonomous subject, a conceptualization of human subjectivity based on the self-determination of the subject and the perception of the uniqueness of every individual, is the product of a set of discourses present to the period 1756–63" and that the subject in question is not really a self but rather "a position, a space or an opening within discourse."[30] The subject thereby comes to be what a self never could be—"a conceptualization of the subject as the excess or overplus of discourse itself: as the remainder, that which cannot be appropriated or included within the present discursive network of control"(6). Moreover, while a discourse may be a "discourse on something," it may also be a "discourse of something"(9). This distinction between discourses "on" and discourses "of" underwrites de Bolla's interest in effecting the kind of collapse that we earlier observed Hertz making in relation to Weiskel; the effort to avoid making statements about any kind of consciousness on the basis of discourse eventuates in the more or less explicit claim that it is impossible to be *about* something without also being *of* it. Thus, the notion of excess, one that is in itself particularly hard to explain without reference to a notion of measure, becomes autonomous in the process of becoming what it purports to describe: "There is, then, a natural tendency for the discourse on the sublime to produce the conditions necessary for the construction of the discourse of the sublime, a discourse which produces from within itself sublime experience" (12). De Bolla distinguishes his work from others on the sublime by contrasting it with discourses "constructed upon the middle ground of a common topic for enquiry—the organizing principle of Hipple's book, for example" and by laying claim to "the recognition that the enquiry has no object"(32). The tendency to equate the sublime with excess, to make it an object by virtue of its not being an object, makes the discourse's reference to itself crucial. The discourse of the sublime, by virtue of being "self-reflexively aware, . . . produces the objects it sets out to control, determine, legislate and so on." The sublime can become an object of study, paradoxically, only by ceasing altogether to be an object or a mark of subjectivity, becoming instead a self-producing effect, "not a quantity or quality described by that discourse and located either in the world or in the mind by it"(35).

The accounts of the sublime that Weiskel, Hertz, and de Bolla offer agree in making literary or discursive self-reference the central point of the sublime. Even when Weiskel's description of the sublime looks psychological insofar as it employs a Freudian terminology, the combination of the psychoanalytic mapping with structural linguistics ultimately conduces to treat psychology as if it were language, and language regarded specifically as the incommensurability of the mind and objects in the world. Language becomes important for being a thing (or a nonthing) rather than a medium. And the self-reference that language or discourse is able to achieve by virtue of being a thing that is based neither on mind nor on objects ironically recuperates all that was earlier involved in the causal model of relationship between mind and world. Language or discourse is treated as animated matter that produces more of the same by virtue of its inability to coincide with itself (let alone mind and objects), as the spacing within language creates words as separate from one another (and therefore as excess rather than identity) and creates the individual as a subject position, "an opening within discourse."

Most recent criticism on the sublime has moved within the orbit I have just described: the rhetorical or linguistic has been denominated as excess in a move designed to defeat the notion of intention, and particularly of intention conceived as conscious aim.[31] The sublime is excess conceived as a mark of one's inability to control all the elements involved in producing a word or a sentence, much less an artistic object. One can, from this perspective, demonstrate the failure of the "great man" method of writing histories and literary histories by arguing that Shakespeare, for instance, couldn't have consciously decided on each and every one of the elements that would need to have been decided for him really to have "authored" his plays in full intentionality. And from this vantage, Paul de Man can make a joke out of a newspaper account of a study that behavioral psychologists conducted of the processes of driving a car; to the study's claim that one makes "at least thirty-six" calculations in the process of driving one block, de Man retorts that it seems a miracle that one drives at all.[32] The anecdote presents the ironic vision of an action, driving, for which one has presumably demonstrated competence (a knowledge of the traffic laws, an ability to slow at railroad crossings, to stop at red lights, and to parallel park) and for which one is held legally liable. Obeying the law becomes less a matter of following the rules as one knows them (whether or not this rote procedure is seen to involve tacit consent), and more a matter of engaging in a kind of acculturated animism, in which one's own action becomes something that one can never know. It has, that is, effects but no continuous history of intentions, motives, and calculations—in one sense, it may seem, no history *tout court*.

In the terms of deconstructive materialism, the trouble with technology is that it is always producing technology as know-how in excess of knowledge, that it presumes to go on, to constitute itself as a narrative. Technology, as the basis and product of institutions, is always a show of force in relation to the individual, precisely because it produces without being able to sustain a claim to knowledge. Deconstruction, by virtue of its insistence upon difference, is the study of what Kant called in his *Logic* the infinite judgment, the unboundedness achieved by saying "something is non-A."[33] Technological narrative, by virtue of arranging continuation on the basis on likeness, continually threatens to convert this infinite into finitude through what can be described as an act of suppression or violence. And deconstructive reading thus enjoins a challenge to the cognitive and to any narrative system that seems, from its standpoint, to involve such suppression, such "totalizing." (Hence, Warminski's hopeful suggestion that "reading" produces—or, rather, is—suspension and, in being suspension, is "not *inevitably* totalitarian" (in contradistinction from the nonsuspensive "inevitably totalitarian" determinate interpretations that fail to read by reading differently).[34] An insistence upon the process of aestheticization (as a version of deliberate resistance) would make an aesthetic reading just such a move, as when Derrida says, "I seduce it: by reading the Third Critique as a work of art, I neutralize or encrypt its existence."[35] The notion of a lack comes to serve to liberate objects from existence, because the lack is always the infinite, in the form of the nonexistent; so that Derrida can move to an account of infinity as opposed to existence on the basis of an assertion like "The ergon's lack is the lack of a *parergon*"(60), an outside to the work, a frame that will mark a between for the work and the world. For Derrida, "formalism," as the possibility of distinguishing between "material" and "formal" judgments (with "the latter alone constituting judgments of taste in the proper sense," is seen as an historical occurrence rather than a system, a contingency rather than a necessity. The task of what I am calling deconstructive materialism thus comes to be one of explaining how a framing system rather than systematic formalism creates the "formality-effect"(67). Formalism, in Derrida's treatment, thus engages less with accounts of what could count as arguments for form and more with something like the history of how the contingent came to look as if it did not have to be produced (in a variant on the Kiplingesque project of explaining such things as "how the leopard got his spots"). Derrida marks the contingency of the framing action by scattering portions of frames through his text, in an underlining that interrupts sentences with the gappings produced by portions of frames that do not meet.

Like de Man's assimilation of Kant's example of the heavens to an argument for flatness and the lack of "intellectual complication" as an argument for aesthetic materialism, so Derrida's historicizing gesture would argue, against the phenomenological tradition that Kant saw himself as grounding, that the material starts looking formal not by virtue of any formal system but rather because of the intervention of more matter. Formalism is, thus, always materialism in disguise, masquerading as something more than it can be.

The achievement of deconstructive materialism is thus to see Kantian aesthetics not so much as a contrast to Burkean empiricist aesthetics but as more of the same. And the deconstructive achievement likewise replicates certain kinds of problems that appear in the relationship between the individual and society in Burke's *Enquiry*. If one aspect of the Burkean claim is that societies are produced out of our love of comprehension and the pleasure that we take in what we take to be inferior to us, that account also leaves open the possibility that such assessments of relative power are painfully reversible. As Foucault's work forcibly demonstrates, the individual under social control does not emerge out of an imagined submission to authority but rather out of an imagined mastery of the techniques of authority. As Derrida and de Man's work argues, even the actions that one intends to commit are infinite, and can therefore never be fully willed actions.

Deconstructive materialism therefore, like Foucault's discursive analysis, commits itself to an empirical infinite that makes language and society, alternately and together, the infinite that humans can identify with only at their peril. Insofar as willed action is always insufficiently willed, insofar as it ultimately reveals its affinity with accidental motion, the finite becomes, from the deconstructive, postmodernist position, only an illusory way station to the infinite, with the infinite being defined as loss of control, loss of agency. Aesthetic objects and individuals alike seem, in this view, most effectively defined when they are discovered to be many, not autonomous but heteronomous. Adorno, Derrida, and de Man have all provided readings of the Third Critique which demonstrate that one can interpret Kant's discussion of aesthetics as so many backhanded and implicit arguments against the viability of ideas of unity and autonomy for art objects as well as for individuals. The finite comes to be, almost by the definition generated by force of habitual perspective, the infinite—the continual shifting of one's perspective and unit of measure. For Derrida, the fragility of the distinction between the finite and the infinite emerges in the very necessity of the frame as an historically determined device to set off the work of art from all that it is not—or that it might be lost in. For de Man, the possibility of the finite moves in the opposite direction—toward infinitesimals rather than infinites. The empirical infinite is always the production of an excess to one's powers of comprehension, and (as de Man's essay "Excuses" is designed to show), it can be produced in spite of the effort to specialize, to concentrate on the project of understanding a single name. The empirical infinite, therefore, demonstrates the radical difference between individuals and societies, either because, as in Foucault's work, society is a kind of violence done (by the individual) to the individual, or, as in de Man's, because language is not susceptible of the kind of communication that could ever make a legitimate social contract possible.

In some of the following pages I reexamine the relationship between Kant's turn on empiricist aesthetics in his emphasis on aesthetic construction (constructedness or systematicity). In his handling, I argue, aesthetic experience does not do away with the empirical infinite that dominates the empiricist account but rather harnesses it by coordinating it with an artificial infinite. That is, Kant uses his Analytic of the Sublime as the occasion for imagining that an empirical infinite (what specifically cannot be experienced by a finite human being) can be connected with the artificial systems of representing infinity that have no empirical correlates. What is experienced is, thus, correlated with what is past one's experience not as a part to a whole but as an equivalent answer produced by a completely different system of representation. The perception of the ocean stretching out before one cannot be a direct experience of infinity, but it can be thought—and thought on the basis of an appeal to the existence of mathematical representations of infinites and infinitesimals.

Kant, that is, escapes an empiricist aesthetics—or regrounds it—by shifting the bases of evidence, so that the very notion of psychology is itself reoriented. Affect in the Burkean scheme constituted the identities of objects, which meant, in turn, that Burke had to labor hard to claim similarities of response to make collective psychology continually bolster individual response. From this vantage, I interpret the hyperbolic language of conflict that Weiskel and others have noticed in Kant's discussions of the mathematical and the dynamical sublimes as hyperbole designed to show that even the most intense labor will never avail to make an aesthetics based in empirical psychology work. Ideas cannot be presented as if they were objects.[36] Yet once the empiricist link between affect and objects has been set aside, psychology, being formalized, involves a regulative model that is regulative not by virtue of imposing conformity but rather the reverse. As against the inductive model of norms and standards, the Kantian account of regulative pattern makes it possible to see psychology less as the story of affect than as the deduction of possibilities not necessarily available to the senses. A paradigmatic example of this process occurs in Freud's "A Child Is Being Beaten," in which the testimony of several of Freud's patients about versions of a recurrent dream of a child's being beaten becomes the basis for his extrapolation of other forms of the dream that no one claimed to have experienced. Formalized psychology may discredit certain kinds of testimony—as when Freud decides that his patients have lied to him about childhood sexual encounters; but it also produces nonexperiential evidence—the conviction of what might be predicted even in the absence of memory or direct sensation—*via* the discovery of pattern.[37]

Kant's formulation of the sublime supplants empiricism's self-vexing relationship with the senses with the possibility of evidence only incidentally within the reach of sense. And, as I will argue, the whole point of Kant's restriction of the sublime to what one feels in the face of nature is to defeat the doctrines of representation which look as if they can be built up from an empirical model. Deconstruction argues that what one might think of as the "literariness" of even factual statements—the specificity and materiality of what look like the mere means to the ends of expressing a position—continually keeps the formal constructive project from being able to close. It thus captures one version of "excess," the way in which the representation can never fully take itself into its account. The Kantian account of the importance of the aesthetic rests on a quite different assertion of "excess," namely that one should see things in nature and take shapelessness as an object in taking it as pleasing.

In the Analytic of the Beautiful Kant had presented two possible accounts of the aesthetically pleasing. The imagination might superimpose one's full set of mental images one on another to achieve the effect of visual averaging that would enable one to come up with an aesthetical norm. Or, on the other hand, we might stipulate a connection between certain moral attributes and empirical persons; having seen "the visible expression of moral ideas that rule men inwardly," we might insist upon extending this model to identify "pure ideas of reason" as an ideal of beauty. Both of these hypothetical models seemed to him unsatisfactory, the first because it produced only correctness (and thus ceased to be aesthetically pleasing), the second because it banished sensible charm (and thus ceased to be aesthetically pleasing).

It is these two failed models of the beautiful to which Kant is providing a countering response in his account of the sublime and his division of it into two distinct kinds, the mathematical and the dynamical. The mathematical sublime, as I shall argue at some length in the third chapter as I try to correlate Kant's variations on Burkean themes, adapts the procedure that Kant had outlined for the aesthetical norm of a beautiful figure by substituting the construction of a series for the imaginative superposition that had produced an imaginative average. Where the imagination had employed mental images rather than objects in the attempt to imagine what kinds of standards judgments of beauty employ, those mental images were described entirely as memory images with a continual reference to figures that had actually, at some time, been seen. The account of the mathematical sublime differs from this in using the example of the series (much as Burke had used the counting of columns or pillars) to insist upon the inevitability of exceeding the experiences that one has actually had. The mathematical sublime, therefore, differs crucially from Burke's account of sublime obscurity, which involves the dread of some unperceived power potentially concealed in darkness. Burke's obscurity, that is to say, continually occupies the role of potential experience in suspending the force of actual experience. In the terms of an empiricism divided between its sensationism and its skepticism, it registers the inability of anyone's experiences to "saturate the context" of possible experiences, and becomes emblematic of the kind of question that Hume raises about our knowledge of whether the sun will rise tomorrow (our being able to point to its having happened before not really counting as certainty).

In the notion of the mathematical series, Kant solves this problem of the opposition between actual and potential experience by indicating a more complex account of the relationship between identity and difference. Burkean empiricism made new experiences look like a potential threat to the generalizations one might have derived from one's earlier experiences, so that replicability and its contradictions look like the only possibilities. The series, however, operates not to produce random confirmation or contradiction of what has already been encountered; instead, it describes the process of generating what is, by definition, unexperienced out of the very pattern of experience. One makes progress in counting or measuring by going to higher and higher units, but the very ability to construct a next number or a next unit by seeing the "next" as $n + 1$ prevents one from arriving at a moment at which one can identify n, the number one is counting, with $n + 1$, the number that the act of counting calls on one to produce.

What commentators have repeatedly missed about the mathematical sublime is, ironically, exactly how mathematical it is. A claim about the indeterminacy of relationships between words and objects can always be maintained on the basis of the argument that one can never stabilize what is to count as the defining term (redness, tulipness, oneness, plantness, etc.). And such an argument goes some distance toward explaining the anxiety occasioned by the beautiful, which, by virtue of having a place in society, always looks like a way of using the "same thing" to mean "something else," your "redness" for my "plantness." (Manners and aesthetics repeatedly converge in this line of thought, with a Richardson maintaining the horror of the aesthete's equivocal speech and a Schiller providing something like the standard aesthete's defense of the aesthetic; the aesthetic, in his view, never risks the immorality of duping anyone because it never seems to be an object that might be exchanged or a contractual obligation: "Only a stranger to fashionable society, for example, will interpret assurances of politeness, which is a universal form, as tokens of personal attachment, and when he is disappointed will complain of hypocrisy.")[38] With the introduction of the mathematical sublime, however, Kant makes the cognition of objects far more irrelevant to the aesthetic experience (at least of the sublime) than has been acknowledged. For even if some apparently boundless space or indefinitely bounded object provoked the counting or the measuring, the contradictions that Kant uses to define the experience of the sublime all derive from mathematical representations, for which referential connection quickly becomes irrelevant, rather than from intuitive experiences of objects (*Anschauungen*).

The discussions of the mathematical sublime that seize upon Kant's terms "apprehension" and "comprehension" continually reinstate either a cognitive object or a version of it—an extent or power that might not be measured exactly but that can always be translated into a relation with the individual perceiving subject, even if that subject is divided into self-opposing elements (as with Weiskel) and even if the object retains its obscurity, its lack of clarity, by being the pretext of an object, a pre-Oedipal nonformation (as with Hertz). Similarly, de Bolla's discursive subject and discursive formation remain obscure to one another as a whole exceeds an individual part and as it becomes difficult to identify a part with exactitude on the basis of the whole. Kant's description of the sublime in terms of a mathematical representation is fundamentally different from all of these, in that it attends to mathematical representation as a system of identities sustained by contradiction. Thus, the discovery of the relationship between finitude and infinitude turns first on the fact that the series, the progressiveness in the representation of infinitude, relies on the inability to make $n + 1 = n$ (so that the series might come to an end). Second, and more important, the relationship between finitude and infinitude rests upon an assertion of the possibility of reassembling these discrete units into a unity, of insisting that a one can be made out of this many.

But now the mind listens to the voice of reason which, for every given magnitude—even for those that can never be entirely apprehended, although (in sensible representation) they are judged as entirely given—requires totality. Reason consequently desires comprehension in *one* intuition, and so that [joint] *presentation* of all these members of a progressively increasing series. It . . . renders it unavoidable to think the infinite (in the judgment of common reason) as *entirely given* (according to its totality).[39]

This account of the availability of the idea of infinity in *one* intuition has seemed emblematic of what Hegel first identified as Kant's insidious psychologism—"that is to say, he hunts through the soul's sack to see what faculties are still to be found there; and thus by merest chance he lights on Reason."[40] If this is psychology, however, it would appear to be the same kind of psychology that was involved in the perception of the relationship between mathematics of finite quantities and infinite series that had become apparent in Newton's work—namely that "the analysis by infinite series [has] the same inner consistency, and [is] subject to the same general laws, as the algebra of finite quantities."[41]

Similarly, Kant's account of the dynamical sublime, "on nature regarded as might,"[42] relies on a connection between distinct explanatory systems to restate the extensional terms of the mathematical sublime in intensional or causal terms. Nature and natural might directly oppose human (physical) might, so that Kant can adduce a host of examples that "exhibit our faculty of resistance as infinitely small in comparison with their might"(100). The Kantian opposition between nature and freedom then develops from a perspective in which it becomes possible to judge the relative might of humans and specific natural objects to a perspective that emphasizes human freedom from natural determination. Just as it is important for Kant to distance the sublime from the complications introduced by the social world of the beautiful (so as to separate the argument for aesthetic value from the question of reception per se), so it is similarly important for him to appeal to nature for mental representations that exceed natural might:

> But the sight of [such things as volcanoes, hurricanes, the boundless ocean in a state of tumult] is all the more attractive, the more fearful it is, provided only that we are in security; and we willingly call these objects sublime, because they raise the energies of the soul above their accustomed height and discover in us a faculty of resistance of a quite different kind, which gives us courage to measure ourselves against the apparent almightiness of nature.[101]

Natural might may determine human beings—may, as Kant puts it, make them "recognize [their] own [physical] impotence, considered as beings of nature"(101). Yet Kant exploits a different aspect of the notion of aesthetic distance that Burke had raised in the *Enquiry*. Whereas Burke had found distance to be a necessary but not sufficient condition of the pleasure one takes in representations of suffering (one cannot be dead and experience any pleasure in the representation of a death), Kant suggests that our very ability to achieve distance produces both the safety and the pleasure and that the distance crucially in question involves mental images rather than physical proximity. Burke continually makes all danger but the most immediate and death dealing seem to verge on the factitious and theatrical; Kant counters by suggesting that being able to escape, to achieve distance from, danger is an essentially technological action, grounded in the capacity for discerning causal relationships. Moreover, such implicitly technological perceptions become both the precondition and the by-product of aesthetic pleasure. The ability to put oneself out of danger and in security—to distance oneself from the operation of nature's might—bespeaks an intersection between the two opposed dynamical systems, the one indicating the supremacy of natural might, the other suggesting a human, "nonsensuous standard, which has that infinity itself under it as a unity, in comparison with which everything in nature is small, and thus in our mind we find a superiority to nature even in its immensity"(101).

In short, the discussion of the mathematical sublime becomes the occasion in the Third Critique for Kant to argue that the finite and infinite are not related as is a part to an unapprehensible whole but rather as are two distinct but converging systems that enable alternative forms of the functions they represent. But if the mathematical sublime puts in abeyance questions about reference (about the connections of the numbers with any objects), the dynamical sublime links the perspective of natural causality with the perspective of human causality in a way that is clearly referential.

Now Kant's discussion of the mathematical and dynamical sublimes immediately precedes his "General Remark upon the Exposition of the Aesthetic Reflective Judgment" and his "Deduction of [Pure] Aesthetic Judgments." Moreover, he asserts quite flat-footedly that his "exposition of judgments concerning the sublime in nature was at the same time their deduction"(121), so as to insist that the mere description of them involved a claim for their "universal and necessary validity." In this he is affirming that the sublime in nature which could be "regarded as quite formless or devoid of figure" may be "the object of a pure satisfaction" because *the sublime in nature does not exist*. The sublime in nature "is improperly so called" and, "properly speaking, the word should only be applied to a state of mind, or rather to its foundation in human nature"(121). The mathematical sublime and the dynamical sublime obtain not because one can claim that mathematical progressions or scientific representations of causal connections depend upon their reference to natural objects. Although science continually involves the attempt to harness mathematical progression and dynamical causation to objects, the sublime aesthetic for Kant revolves around the way that succession and causation look less like connections between persons and objects than like connections between persons. This is to say that Kant establishes his transcendental aesthetic here, in the account of the sublime. Moreover, in an extraordinary adaptation of Burke's use of the "universal testimony of languages," Kant bases his account of the way the aesthetic can mediate between the empirical and the transcendental on conspicuously artificial representational systems. One recurrent account of the difference between languages and nature is that languages contain negatives, no's and not's, and that nature doesn't.[43] Kant, however, considerably extends the argument that nature does not completely authorize language. That is, mathematics and causation become linguistic rather than nature-based or nature-directed in the moment in which their systematicity, their artificiality, emerges as the possibility—indeed, the inevitability—that one would be able to make the next move in the series. (Ludwig Wittgenstein's notion of being able to "go on" with a language game is the less—or less conspicuously—extended form of this claim.)

The *sensus communis,* that peculiar supplementary sense of which Kant gives rather cryptic descriptions, comes to seem like a sense of form per se, the ability to continue a series or a pattern, in a way that ceases to rely altogether on the existence of any object. Formality, understood in the terms of Kantian formal idealism, makes it possible to assimilate a particular to a general, an individual to a pattern. It would therefore seem to replicate the kind of problem posed by the empirical account of imagination that Kant had tried out in the Analytic of the Beautiful: even the most exact transcription of individual images of a figure arrives at an average that does not merely fail to represent all of the figures being averaged; it represents only correctness. Yet the account of the sublime movement beyond objects crucially redirects the trajectory of the movement from particulars to generals. While the *Critique of Pure Reason* links particular intuitions with general cognition and while the *Critique of Practical Reason* links particular persons with the notion of personhood in general, the *Critique of Judgment* links particular intuitions with the notion of personhood in general. The movement from particularity to generality thus involves a complete shift in what is being particularized, what is being generalized. The best picture of the human soul becomes not the human body (as in Wittgenstein's famous description),[44] but the sublime landscape. This is to say that the landscape does not so much replace portraiture as become it. The landscape can be a portrait, moreover, not because its sublime indeterminacy allows for the possibility for seeing a whale in a cloud with Hamlet or, as Lyotard insists, to make "the stake of art in the nineteenth and twentieth centuries" to be "witness to indeterminacy."[45] Rather, the portrait *is* the most determinate and determinable aspects of language, the point at which it most nearly approaches logic.[46] The artificial sublimes, mathematical and dynamical, that Kant discovers as what nature cannot supply become, then, the general form of a particular that has been chosen for its very formlessness, for the way in which its form clearly does not come with it, as part of its package.

Now the account I am giving of Kant's aesthetics suggests that in the Analytic of the Sublime he verges on what looks like an extraordinarily unaesthetic account of aesthetic pleasure, something with all the charm of logical positivism. This, however, would be mistaken. For the signal importance of Kantian aesthetics is that it resolutely declines to restrict itself to the claims that can be substantiated by the artificial language of logic. Indeed, it continually suggests that the complications—and the interest— that appear in beauty emerge as a result of the inability to reduce natural language in its peculiar combination of rule-governedness and erraticness to the regularity of the artificial languages of mathematics or logic. In fact, Kant's very notion of the aesthetic particular entails the insistence that "you have to be there," that description of the object (criticism) can never substitute for acquaintance with it (aesthetic experience).[47] Yet, as I think becomes relatively clear in the Fourth Moment of the Judgment of Taste (sects. 18–22 of the Analytic of the Beautiful), aesthetic experience as the communication of sympathy, understood as parallel responses to similar objects, ceases to exist. It becomes instead an overleaping of the movement from particular objects to general ideas and of that from particular persons to humanity in general: the particular that looks like an object proceeds directly to the general of humanity, because the formless object of the sublime can seem to have a shape only in so far as it resembles the *synthetic* a priori in the form of mathematics and the notion of physical causation.

Kant's discussion thus presents the sublime, in conformity with his account of the moral law, as a disclosure of the mental legislation involved in even the most apparently useless endeavors. It is conspicuously absurd, from one perspective, for a solitary individual to decide, without any aid from technology, to start measuring boundless nature, because its phenomenological boundlessness means that an individual can never get to the end of it. Better to search for a needle in a haystack, gold in a London dustheap. From another perspective, the arranging that one does of the natural sublime becomes the precondition for the creation of any object whatsoever: measuring the sublime is like giving a shape to Yeats's mouthful of air.

The double point of Kant's propulsion of the aesthetic in the direction of such a priori forms as mathematical and physical representation is, first, to avoid starting with an artistic social contract and, second, to insist upon the absolute equality of all persons in relation to the transcendental schemata. It therefore makes aesthetics absolutely social without making it political, susceptible to the manipulation that would enable one person to become the cause to another person's effect. Yet, even in going beyond the Burkean empiricist account, Kant does not suggest that one can speak the formal language of the synthetic a priori (that would involve taking quite literally the old joke about prisoners who had become so familiar with their stock of jokes that they had assigned numbers to them and merely called out numbers to get laughs from one another).

The order in which Kant presents the beautiful and the sublime is appropriate to the aesthetic judgment's intermediate position between the pure reason's capacity for experience and the practical reason's capacity for self-positing moral ends. Yet, from another perspective, the sublime is something like a cornerstone for the claim to aesthetic judgment in the beautiful. For the sequel to Kant's account of the sublime is the world of the beautiful in society. However much the sublime aesthetic may rely on the evenhandedness implicit in imagining that no empirical self can identify with the transcendental, the social experience of beauty hopelessly complicates the individual's relation to aesthetics by superimposing a social induction upon the sequences (number following number, effect following cause) that are so supremely egalitarian in the sublime. The beautiful falls into conflict with the idea of freedom elaborated in the sublime because it does not merely count but begins its count by making "one" start here, with the first person singular as "number one." In the empirical world of society, one should say, the numbers do not distribute themselves equally. As in the final part of the story about the numbers of jokes, a newcomer arrives, shouts out a number—only to get an answering silence, followed by the gloss, "Some people just don't know how to tell a joke." Knowing how to tell a joke becomes less a matter of what one says than of how one says it—as if the joke were itself a parable of the tendency of both detractors and defenders of aesthetic experience to distance such experience from content and to align it with rhetoric, form conceived in terms so material (as spacing, the difference of a letter, and so forth) that the ability to read it at all looks like the projection of an individual, a group of initiates, a profession, or a social class. Matter, seen so particularly, is identical with manner.

The pages that follow attempt two distinct but mutually implicated projects: a presentation of some of the primary historical arguments about the sublime and a discussion (sometimes less explicit, sometimes more) of the ways in which recent criticism has made the sublime the area of greatest contestation of the place of aesthetics. The first of these involves sketching the contours of the eighteenth- and nineteenth-century discussions of the sublime, particularly as they concern the relationships between individuals and their societies that aesthetic objects enable. Burke, in this context, represents the paradigm of the eighteenth-century version of the empirical sublime. The aesthetic project for him emerges from a demonstration of the similarities among the responses of various different individuals, so that the beautiful would seem to lead to an argument that the social contract is implicit even in perception. Yet the sublime must be invented precisely because the arena of the beautiful, of society, introduces yet another version of order, the habit, custom, and use that represent both socialization and the impossibility of socialization simultaneously. The agreement of one person with another would, Burke suggests, be consistent, were it not that custom (the empirical induction of daily life) continually provides one set of social agreements too many. The effects of objects on persons therefore no longer give reliable information about either the objects or the persons on which they impinge, so that the manifold nature of objects and the variousness of human perception become ever more conspicuous. The sublime then functions as an antidote to the beautiful, making danger stabilize objects in the process of isolating individuals, deploying the impulses of self-preservation to override the impulses toward society.

Ultimately, the subject of this book is the way in which the aesthetic discussion that emerged in the eighteenth century located an anxiety about the relationship between the individual and the type, the particular and the general, not merely as one epistemological problem among others but as *the* characteristically aesthetic epistemological problem. When Kant formulates the aesthetic as a kind of experience in which one moves from a perception of a particular thing directly to a claim about the typical human response, he only states more clearly a pervasive anxiety about it becoming difficult for any manifold object—and all objects are manifold—to avoid looking like a lying particularity, meaningful to all observers without being a basis for a social contract. My claim about Kant is that he used the mathematical sublime to install a transcendental account of essentially narrative agreement, making representative structures more important than the objects that move into and out of their particular patterns. Yet at approximately the same time at which he postulates the mathematical sublime, other kinds of discourse—such as the Gothic novel and the developing population debate in England at the end of the eighteenth century—testify to a fundamentally different view of the same problem. Like most of the writing that is currently identified as postmodern, such discussions project an empirical sublime, one in which the numbers of persons, things, and properties seemed continually increasing past the limit of individual control. As Thomas Robert Malthus redefines the population debate so that it does not merely turn on a comparison between eighteenth-century England and ancient or classical civilizations, he annexes the future to the present by presenting a fiction of social planning that has been brought into being by a preexisting sense of its own futility—the perception that one cannot count on the numbers of individuals in a society to remain constant. Malthus, that is, projects exponentially increasing numbers of persons, on the basis of the perception that one person is never one person (even as a body); one person is sometimes single, sometimes a token of a couple, sometimes a token of and producer of families. (The logic that haunts Malthus's progressions recurs in some of Russell's mathematical logic in the form of an example that claims that the population of a country is, at any given moment, infinite.)

The sublime concerns solitude not because it represents a particularly arduous version of pastoral retreat. In the empirical account, solitude comes to seem the inevitable psychological reflexiveness that creates individuation as a terror of being included in a social induction. In the formal account, solitude represents the difficulties of arriving at any account of any *one* whatever outside a process of systematic formalization.

Notes

1. I should distinguish between the way I am using "formalist" and the way in which it has come to be used, pejoratively, in relation to the American New Criticism. In the first place, I use "formal" in the most purely and almost neutrally descriptive philosophical sense to distinguish an emphasis on the a priori.

2. Stanley Cavell's important essay "Must We Mean What We Say?" is particularly effective at posing some of these questions from the opposite direction, asking, for instance, why it is that one knows not to participate in the action on a stage, or why one recognizes such an idea as either a joke—in the case of the Southern racist gentleman who supposedly rushes up to save Desdemona from her interracial relationship with Othello—or as a theatrical argument about theater—in the case of Brecht. See *Must We Mean What We Say? A Book of Essays* (New York: Charles Scribner's Sons, 1969).

3. I pick up this quotation from Kant's Deduction of Judgments of Taste (Sect. 42) in *Critique of Judgment,* trans. J. H. Bernard (New York: Hafner Publishing Co., 1951), 145. My view is that the beautiful in society, the beautiful in nature, and the sublime in nature represent a continuum. Although Kant specifically refers to the beautiful in the passage on which I am drawing, my view is that what he means here by the "beautiful as such" is the same as what he means most often by the "sublime." That is, beautiful nature presents the same problem as sublime nature does; the question of how it can be available for any kind of human use is the essential one. I find confirmation of this view in the fact that the Deduction of Judgments of Taste and its discussion of beauty as well as sublimity appear in the Analytic of the Sublime.

4. In this he is, of course, recurring to a sense of the prominence of the imagination that others before him—Hume, for instance—had shared.
5. Edmund Burke, *A Philosophical Enquiry into the Origin of Our Ideas of the Sublime and Beautiful,* ed. J. T. Boulton (Notre Dame, Ind.: University of Notre Dame Press, 1958), 32.
6. See Ferdinand de Saussure, *Course in General Linguistics,* ed. Charles Bally and Albert Sechehaye (New York: McGraw-Hill Book Company, 1966), 65 ff., for the classic structuralist linguistic account of the linguistic sign as a "double entity" that "unites, not a thing and a name, but a concept and a sound-image." See Andrzej Warminski's description of Paul de Man's position in terms of the way in which "the system of meaning and representation depends on a radically heterogeneous materiality that at one and the same time makes meaning possible and impossible—that renders it truly undecidable," "Response," *Diacritics* 17 (Winter 1987): 147–48.
7. Paul de Man, *Allegories of Reading* (New Haven: Yale University Press, 1979), 289, 293.
8. See Cynthia Chase, "Trappings of an Education" in *Responses: On Paul de Man's Wartime Journalism,* ed. Werner Hamacher, Neil Hertz, and Thomas Keenan (Lincoln: University of Nebraska Press, 1989), 44–79 (hereafter *Responses*). "We saw this undoing of the claim to determination occur with the emergence of the work as a process of reading, as the model of imitation gave way to the work of interpretation. Therewith the prospect of 'the determination of meaning' does not remain intact: instead of having to be found, uncovered, determined, meaning has to be decided, in an interminable process of deciding between the *meaning* and the *process* of signification." She goes on to connect this version of reading with "the status of the aesthetic," which is "neither an uncovery [sic] of meaning, nor determining" (62).
9. Andrzej Warminski, "Terrible Reading (preceded by 'Epigraphs')," in *Responses,* 385–96. Warminski, specifically directing himself to the question of de Man's wartime journalism, is advocating a model of reading as indeterminacy and suspension: "Of course, everything changes as soon as we begin reading, the texts—that is, begin reading *as* text—even the newspapers. For as soon as we begin to do so, we lose the possibility of using the referential moment inscribed in the newspapers as a reliable model for a cognition on the basis of which we could take action—for instance, like the act of judging de Man as either guilty or innocent. Reading suspends: it suspends knowledge and it suspends judgment, and it suspends, above all, the possibility of ever knowing whether we are doing one or the other. Reading suspends the decision between the thematic, referential meaning and the rhetorical, allegorical function that turns upon it. This is why reading is truly threatening and truly terrible—not because it suspends you between two meanings but because it suspends you between meaning and the material, linguistic conditions of meaning that always dis-articulate it radically as they make it possible)" (392).
10. Paul de Man, "The Resistance to Theory," *The Resistance to Theory* (Minneapolis: University of Minnesota Press, 1986), 11.
11. Paul de Man, "Phenomenality and Materiality in Kant," in *Hermeneutics: Questions and Prospects,* ed. Gary Shapiro and Alan Sica (Amherst: University of Massachusetts Press, 1984), 143.
12. Between earlier and later drafts of the essay that would be published as "Phenomenality and Materiality in Kant," de Man himself shifted from describing Kant's formalism as insufficiently formal to calling it material.
13. De Man's "Phenomenality and Materiality in Kant" moves through a discussion of the aesthetic appreciation of the body as a disarticulation that in turn produces a disarticulation of the language of Kant's text, "as meaning-producing tropes are replaced by the

fragmentation of sentences and propositions into discrete words, or the fragmentation of words into syllables or finally letters." It concludes with the assertion of the centrality of this linguistic fragmentation: "The bottom line, in Kant as well as in Hegel, is the prosaic materiality of the letter and no degree of obfuscation or ideology can transform this materiality into the phenomenal cognition of aesthetic judgment" (144).

14. *Responses,* 387.
15. Jacques Derrida, "Signature, Event, Context," *Dissemination,* trans. Barbara Johnson (Chicago: University of Chicago Press, 1981), 219–222.
16. Jean-Paul Sartre, *Imagination: A Psychological Critique,* trans. Forrest Williams (Ann Arbor: University of Michigan Press, 1972), 141.
17. Sartre in summary of Husserl, 141.
18. Rodolph Gasché frames his introduction to *The Tain of the Mirror: Derrida and the Philosophy of Reflection* (Cambridge, Mass.: Harvard University Press, 1986) as an argument against seeing Derrida's work as literary rather than philosophical (or as a serious challenge to a certain notion of the philosophical). This is an appropriate caution, given that Derrida's impact on literary criticism has been at least as considerable as his impact on philosophy. Yet Derrida's persistent interest not merely in literary (as well as philosophical) texts but also in painting connects very directly with a question of the special status of aesthetic images as articulated by Husserl and Sartre.
19. "Phenomenality and Materiality in Kant," 144.
20. See particularly Michel Foucault, *The Order of Things: An Archaeology of the Human Sciences* (New York: Random House, 1973), 303 ff., and most particularly his remarks on the distinction between eighteenth-century empiricism and the sciences of man, in which he formulates the central paradox that is framed by the modern episteme: "Man, in the analytic of finitude, is a strange empirico-transcendental doublet, since he is a being such that knowledge will be attained in him of what renders all knowledge possible" (318).
21. Paul de Man, *The Rhetoric of Romanticism* (New York: Columbia University Press, 1984), 280, quoted by Cynthia Chase, "Trappings of an Education" in *Responses,* 58.
22. See Chase's argument about totalization in *Responses* (esp. 49). She describes de Man's identification of the unimpeded operation of the performative function of language with the totalitarian state: "The sundering of that connection [between action and cognition] is also an exclusion of the other: of any other—including a signified or an intention—than the performing, functioning, structure itself. That the totalitarian state, with the limitless destructive power of its technical and technological function, is related to the performative power of language, of grammar, is the difficult thought being offered by this description of 'the machine.' "
23. Warminski, "Terrible Reading," *Responses,* 389.
24. See de Man, "Phenomenality and Materiality in Kant," and Jacques Derrida, "The Parergon" in *The Truth in Painting,* trans. Goeff Bennington and Ian MacLeod (Chicago: University of Chicago Press, 1987), 16–82.
25. Paul de Man, *The Resistance to Theory* (Minneapolis: University of Minnesota Press, 1986), 11, quoted in *Responses,* 392.
26. See particularly Steven Knapp, *Personification and the Sublime: Milton to Coleridge* (Cambridge, Mass.: Harvard University Press, 1985).
27. Thomas Weiskel, *The Romantic Sublime* (Baltimore: Johns Hopkins University Press, 1976).
28. Neil Hertz, *The End of the Line: Essays on Psychoanalysis and the Sublime* (New York: Columbia University Press, 1985), 230.
29. Jean-Luc Nancy, "L'offrande Sublime," *Po&sie* 30 (1984), 76.

30. Peter de Bolla, *The Discourse of the Sublime: History, Aesthetics and the Subject* (Oxford: Basil Blackwell, 1989), 6.

31. The notion of a structural unconscious may create the appearance of necessitating a qualification of my assertion here. I should, however, emphatically state that embracing the structural unconscious as "unconscious aim" rather than "conscious aim" seems to me no solution at all, because I take most accounts of the structural unconscious to lay claim to intention (whether conscious or unconscious) as an epiphenomenon of language rather than of human agency. As the main line of my argument indicates, the importance of the sublime lies less in the tragedy of observing human instrumentality in creating matter that one cannot be, cannot become identical with, than in the routine but nonetheless resonant movement between consciousness and unconsciousness, intention and intentionlessness, which occurs as the interchange between an idealist (or formal idealist or constructed) and an empiricist (or nonconstructed) account. In other words, the burden of Sartre's observation that "I am language" remains an issue: "In a universe of pure objects language could under no circumstances have been 'invented' since it presupposes an original relation to another subject. In the intersubjectivity of the for-others, it is not necessary to invent language because it is already given in the recognition of the Other." See *Being and Nothingness: An Essay on Phenomenological Ontology*, trans. Hazel E. Barnes (New York: Philosophical Library, 1956), 372.

32. See de Man, "Aesthetic Formalization in Kleist," *The Rhetoric of Romanticism* (New York: Columbia University Press, 1984), 277. In speaking of various forms of "resistance to intelligibility" in Kleist's *Über das Marionettentheater*, de Man cites, in illustration of Kleist's observation that "consciousness produces [disorders] in the natural gracefulness of man," a formal calculation of the mechanical operation of driving: "We can all remember personal versions of such a fall from grace, of such loss of innocence. (I for one remember trying to drive down a Swiss street after having just read, in a local newspaper, that for every 100 metres one drives one has at least thirty-six decisions to make. I have never been able to drive gracefully since.)"

33. Immanuel Kant, *Logic*, trans. Robert S. Hartman and Wolfgang Schwarz (New York: Dover Publications, 1974), 109–10. See in this regard an intriguing footnote, #10 in de Man's "Excuses (Confessions)," in which he deploys essentially the logic of the infinite judgment: "To deny authorship in a preface in the name of truth (as Rousseau did in the case of *Julie*) does not only mean that one's authorship of all texts can be put in question but also that all texts can be attributed to one. This is precisely what happens to Rousseau when a malevolent (or commercially enterprising) editor, in what reads like a transparent parody of the "Préface dialoguée," attributes to him a poor translation of Tasso's *Jerusalem Delivered* . . ." (*Allegories of Reading*, 297).

34. Warminski, "Terrible Reading," *Responses*, 387.

35. Derrida, *Truth in Painting*, 49.

36. This theme of Kant's Third Critique can be said to be crucial in the deconstructive interpretation of Kantian aesthetics. While Kant makes this claim in the service of an argument about the insufficiency of empiricism to explain aesthetic pleasure (since the pleasure is, for him, linked with ideas that cannot be presented in objects as objects), the deconstructive account chooses the object in contradistinction to the idea. For a particularly telling account of the role of the fanatic as the self-transcendentalizing empiricist, see Knapp's *Personification*, 79–82, 84.

37. See, in this connection, Alexander Welsh's suggestive account of the rise of circumstantial evidence, as opposed to the evidence of testimony from witnesses, in the English legal

tradition, *Strong Representations: Narrative and Circumstantial Evidence in England* (Baltimore: Johns Hopkins University Press, 1992).

38. Friedrich Schiller, *On the Aesthetic Education of Man,* trans. and intro. Reginald Snell (New York: Frederick Ungar, 1988), 129. In Schiller's circular definition, aesthetics cannot be immoral: "Aesthetic appearance can never become a danger to moral truth, and where we find it happening otherwise, it can be shewn without difficulty that the appearance was not aesthetic."

39. Kant, *Critique of Judgment,* 93.

40. G. W. F. Hegel, *Lectures on the History of Philosophy,* trans. E. S. Haldane and Frances H. Simson (New York: Humanities Press, 1974), 3: 443.

41. This lucid summary of Newton's discovery of infinite analysis appears in Carl B. Boyer, *A History of Mathematics* (Princeton: Princeton University Press, 1985), 432.

42. Kant's subtitle for section 28 of the Analytic of the Sublime, *Critique of Judgment,* 99.

43. See Kenneth Burke for one influential modern version of this observation: *The Rhetoric of Religion: Studies in Logology* (Berkeley: University of California Press, 1970), 19–21.

44. Ludwig Wittgenstein, *Philosophical Investigations,* trans. G. E. M. Anscombe (New York: Macmillan Co., 1968), 178.

45. Jean-François Lyotard, "The Sublime and the Avant-Garde," *Art Forum,* April 1984, 41.

46. Heidegger's understanding of the ways in which Kant revises traditional logic to assimilate imagination to logic is particularly important to my thinking, even though Heidegger's discussion centers on the First Critique. As part of his suggestion that imagination might be promoted to an equivalence with Kant's categories of understanding and reason, Heidegger observes: "That traditional logic does not treat of pure imagination is indisputable. But if logic wishes to understand itself, the question as to whether or not it need be concerned with the imagination must at least remain open. It is also undeniable that Kant always borrows from logic the point of departure for the problems which he formulates. And yet it is doubtful whether logic, merely because it has made pure thought, taken in a certain sense, its only theme, offers us a guarantee that it can delimit the complete essence of pure thought or even approach it." See Martin Heidegger, *Kant and the Problem of Metaphysics,* trans. and intro. James S. Churchill (Bloomington: Indiana University Press, 1972), 155.

47. Robert S. Zimmerman, "Kant: The Aesthetic Judgment," *Kant: A Collection of Critical Essays,* ed. Robert Paul Wolff (Garden City, New York: Anchor Books, 1967), 385–406.

2

The Sublime of Edmund Burke, or The Bathos of Experience

At the end of the *Prolegomena to Any Future Metaphysics*, Kant responded to a reviewer (for the *Göttingische gelehrte Anzeigen*) who had labeled the *Critique of Pure Reason* a work of higher idealism with the protestation, "By no means 'higher.' . . . My place is the fruitful bathos of experience."[1] Because the sublime has, like higher idealism, recurrently been conceived as a transcendence of experience, it may be useful to ask what the relationship might be between the sublime and the bathos of experience—and particularly in Burke's paradoxically urbane and pragmatic account of the sublime as the ne plus ultra of experience.

Although the notion of the sublime has received an increasing amount of attention during the last decade or so, its currency has not significantly enhanced its accessibility. For a number of critics, the sublime is so often merely a way of saying "O altitudo!" that any definition or explication of the notion is assumed to be as superfluous as a dictionary entry for "oh wow." The vagueness of our current use of the sublime is, moreover, especially curious against the backdrop of eighteenth- and nineteenth-century aesthetic treatises, which worry the limits of definition frequently enough for the very protestations against vagueness or popular misconception to appear as tropes— rhetorical conventions so well worn as to be "dead *definitios*." Not only does Wordsworth tell us that "poetry" is "a word of very disputed meaning,"[2] Coleridge informs us that the "term, pleasure, is unfortunately so comprehensive, as frequently to become equivocal." In addition, Coleridge despairingly recounts an anecdote from his experience to demonstrate the horrors of equivocation in matters of taste:

> Many years ago, the writer, in company with an accidental party of travellers, was gazing on a cataract of great height, breadth, and impetuosity, the summit of which appeared to blend with the sky and clouds, while the

> lower part was hidden by rocks and trees; and on his observing that it was, in the strictest sense of the word, a sublime object, a lady present assented with warmth to the remark, adding—'Yes! and it is not only sublime, but beautiful and absolutely pretty.'[3]

Although both the woman traveler and Coleridge perhaps come off rather badly in this anecdote—the first for gushing and the second for being something of a pedant of tourism, the moral of this brief story is that Coleridge, like his predecessors and contemporaries, was far more interested in constructing at least the illusion of referentiality for such ideas as the sublime, the beautiful, the imagination, poetry, and so on than modern critics have recently been.

My motive in citing the story is not to point to the ways in which "they" were better then than "we" are now, because not even they felt secure about the definitiveness of their attempts at definition; it is, rather, to suggest a major way in which "their" sublime differs from "ours." Definitions—or attempts at them—mattered more to a Coleridge than they do to a Harold Bloom in large measure because the notions of commonality and even universality were seen as an important, indeed necessary, validation of the individual. Thus, while for modern criticism, the sublime is the arena in which an isolated self can achieve a heroism of subjectivity, the sublime was important then less for rampant individualism and self-scrutiny than for the possibility of one's becoming representative. In this respect, Pope's celebrated pronouncement that Longinus's "own example strengthens all his laws," so that he "is himself the great sublime he draws," does not amount merely to an assertion that Longinus's writing coincides perfectly with his own maxims; it is, more significantly, a comment upon Longinus's achievement of a legislative and representative function, about the fact that he has, in Wordsworth's phrase, "created the taste by which he is to be enjoyed."[4] And while the truth functions or correctness of a particular representation were not seen as immutable, the sublime hero of the eighteenth and nineteenth centuries was strikingly different from our modern versions not only in that he quoted almost obsessively from epics but also in that he aspired to the condition of an epic hero, so that he, like Aeneas, might be taken as a metonymy of his culture.

Against the aim of representing one's culture properly, recent criticism has set the image of individual uniqueness, as Thomas Weiskel's description of Edmund Burke as sublime hero may indicate:

> *A Philosophical Enquiry into the Origin of Our Ideas of the Sublime and Beautiful*, published in 1757, was the book of a young man, informed but un-

inhibited by received speculation, who has a genuine idea. We delight in such books and forgive extravagance not only because it is usually interesting but also because it is often the price of originality.[5]

Now one effect of recent overindividualizing of the sublime is that the tradition is reduced to a series of aberrations that can be treated like interesting psychological case histories, so that the treatises on the sublime and the incredible number of graveyard poems, travel books, Gothic novels, and paintings of wild nature with which they were allied can be all too easily assimilated to the category of the "curious." Thus, the sublime can be treated merely as a symptom of a temporary peculiarity in taste that Weiskel characterizes as "an episode in melancholy"(97), but which might as easily be seen as a wholesale attack of nerves or intellectual hypochondria. Although such an account of the sublime serves the great purpose of interesting us in the notion (and proving, once again, the shrewdness of Burke's remark that "we have a degree of delight, and that no small one, in the real misfortunes and pains of others,")[6] it also tends to blind us to the ways in which the sublime tradition constitutes itself as a phenomenology of perception about aesthetics and psychology but not of them (in their usual extensions). In other words, the overwhelming mountains and bottomless abysses which we take to be the identifying marks of the sublime are beside the point even if we treat them symbolically, because the sublime tradition, like any other essentially phenomenological account of perception, cares less about what we see or that we see than about how we see. Thus, I can easily give you a modern example of the sublime by reminding you of the glare of the sun on the Arab's knife in Albert Camus's *L'étranger,* but, conversely, I haven't by that gesture told you anything about knives or Algerian sunlight in factual or symbolic terms.

Although what we call phenomenological criticism in the wake of Georges Poulet and others appointed the individual subject as the center of the universe, I ask you to think here in terms of a "redeemed" phenomenology which speaks of human interactions with the world without resorting to either one of two extremes—the notion that one can "pursue" idealism to the point of becoming solipsistic and thus casting out the world or the notion that the world can "impose" itself upon us though the sheer force of its completely nonsubjective being. Much recent criticism of the Romantics has been dominated by its choice of both extremes at once, so that individual poets are seen in an extraordinary battle with the world in which self and world alternate in their successes at doing one another in. The dangers would, I grant, be quite formidable could mind or world annihilate the other, even temporarily, but the account of such a struggle, while it makes a good story, merely images a desire for a definitive experiential housecleaning, one in which either mind or world would, finally, remain unsullied by the other. We are concerned here, however, with the impossibility of extricating mind and world from one another, or with the inevitability that dust will gather.

Edmund Burke's *A Philosophical Enquiry into the Origin of Our Ideas of the Sublime and Beautiful* provides an especially intriguing case for our understanding of the sublime and its phenomenology, largely because he has repeatedly been taken to espouse two logically exclusive positions. From Samuel Holt Monk's survey of the sublime to the present, Burke's "contribution" or "originality" has been located, first, in his empiricist account of the defiantly unempirical area of aesthetics and, second, in his emphasis upon the significance of the passions or, in other words, psychology. Obviously, Burke thus appears to be caught between a completely nonsubjective (nonidealist) scientism on the one hand and a completely subjective irrationalism on the other. And the criticism of Burke has repeatedly suggested that his achievement in the *Enquiry* was to have walked between empiricism and irrationalism, which he had set up like Scylla and Charybdis, proceeding along such a dangerous course only because he wasn't aware of the issues, and consequently failed to recognize that he was in danger. Burke, in this view, is interesting despite himself.

While I do not basically want to quarrel with the traditional identification of Burke's two fundamental positions, it seems important to redefine their relationship to one another, so that we can understand better what was at stake in his discussion of the sublime. Burke's scientific (or, as he would claim, neo-Newtonian) approach relies upon the absolute reality of objects and upon the immutable reality of differences among them. Thus, he presents himself as going "back to the basics" in the *Enquiry* by talking only about what there "really is." And one quite interesting result of this approach is that it quickly turns the old maxim "De gustibus non est disputandum" against itself, for the basic reality that Burke insists upon is that taste is common to all men and that "we do and must suppose, that as the conformation of their organs are nearly, or altogether the same in all men, so the manner of perceiving external objects is in all men the same, or with little difference"(20–21). Therefore, the man who prefers Don Bellianis to Virgil and the one who ranks Virgil above Don Bellianis operate according to the same principles of taste; the only difference between them is one not of kind but of the degree to which each has cultivated that basic faculty. Already, however, one begins to discern that Burke's deployment of scientific method has its peculiarities. If he were to find the Don Bellianis-lover and the Virgil-lover arguing about which had taste, Burke would, in line with all his other remarks, say, "There, there, fellow, you don't really disagree; you just have the same taste in different degrees." While we can easily imagine that neither of the disputants would be much swayed by this line of argument, the crucial point to be made here is that Burke is constructing a version of scientific empiricism which violates its own most basic tenets, because contradictory evidence, indeed all evidence, is taken always to point toward the existence of a common, universal faculty of taste. Thus, although Burke throughout the *Enquiry* speaks of the sublime and the beautiful as absolutely opposed principles that inhere in objects, various different testimonies about the sublime or beautiful perceptions of those objects count for nothing, and the notion of empirical reiterability becomes important as a theoretical rather than practical standard. On the one hand, this move shores Burke up against the charge that his ideas of the sublime and the beautiful are precisely that, his. On the other, it purchases universality of taste by invalidating empirical evidence and turning conflicts about taste into mere linguistic quibbles. Thus, in the preface to the second edition of the *Enquiry* we find Burke announcing:

> I am in little pain whether any body chuses to follow the names I give them (sublime or beautiful objects) or not, provided he allows that what I dispose under different heads are in reality different things in nature. The use I make of the words may be blamed as too confined or too extended; my meaning cannot well be misunderstood.[5]

This move to distinguish absolutely rather than relatively between objects recurs throughout the *Enquiry*, so that we find Burke making much of his assertion that pleasure and pain are *positive* terms rather than comparative ones based merely on the absence of the other. Yet Burke also rebuffs the possibility of evidence against that assertion so continually that we must grow suspicious of evidence in favor of it. In this case, Hume's point that "the contrary of every matter of fact is still possible" (e.g., the sun might not rise tomorrow)[7] gets completely overrun, and the impossibility of evidence contrary to Burke's basic assertions begins to erode the status of evidence in favor of them. Thus, we find ourselves in a rather peculiar bind when Burke continually appeals to linguistic practice to establish the objective standing of the objects and categories of perception. On the one hand, when Burke insists that "terror is in all cases, whatsoever, either more openly or latently the ruling principle of the sublime"(58), his main item of evidence is that "several languages bear a strong testimony to the affinity of these ideas. They frequently use the same word, to signify indifferently the modes of astonishment or admiration and those of terror. Θάμβος is in Greek either fear or wonder"(58). The argument to support the case that beautiful objects are small begins with the observation that "I am told that in most languages, the objects of love are spoken of under diminutive epithets. It is so in all the languages of which I have any knowledge"(113). And of course, the Introduction on Taste grounds the argument for the universality or commonality of taste in the following remark:

> All men are agreed to call vinegar sour, honey sweet and aloes bitter; and as they are all agreed in finding these qualities in those objects, they do not in the least differ concerning their effects with regard to pleasure and pain. They all concur in calling sweetness pleasant, and sourness and bitterness unpleasant.[14]

On the other hand, however, Burke presents himself in Part 1 of the *Enquiry* as merely clearing up an almost accidental confusion when he insists upon pain and pleasure as simple ideas and repudiates the opinion "that pain arises necessarily from the removal of some pleasure" and that pleasure results from "the ceasing or diminution of some pain." Also, he says, "people are not liable to be mistaken in their feelings, but they are very frequently wrong in their reasoning about them"(32). We find ourselves confronted with a strange version of the Cretan liar paradox here, for what has Burke told us in these passages except that language bears both true and false witness, that it sometimes makes the better appear the better cause and, sometimes, the worse?

It would be perfectly plausible in the face of this particular dilemma to resort to the kind of argument for omnipresent rhetoricity that Paul de Man offered in relation to Locke, Condillac, and Kant in his "Epistemology of Metaphor," which is most important for linking the notion of the shift from literal to metaphorical with the move from particular to general.[8] Along these lines, the distinction between the rhetorical sublime epitomized by Longinus and the natural sublime represented by eighteenth-century and Romantic writers would collapse, and we would recognize that rhetoric nullifies nature, in a manner of speaking. Burke's protestation that "even Longinus, in his incomparable discourse . . . has comprehended things extremely repugnant to each other, under one common name of the *Sublime*"(1) would turn out to be yet another example of protesting too much. The basic assertion that such an interpretative schema rests upon is that all evidence is rhetoric—and it is a virtually irrefutable position if one grants that all sign systems are language and that all language is rhetorical, that is, powerful precisely because of its incapacity or refusal to communicate itself either directly or completely.

Yet if all evidence is rhetoric, there remains an interesting fact about Burke's *Enquiry:* it quite explicitly uses the rhetoric of both ordinary language and literature as evidence. Thus, in the passages I cited earlier in which Burke invokes the universal testimony of languages, the claim for the force of the examples rests not upon any conception of language—or a portion of it— coinciding with its object and thus being truthful, as in the case of the heuristic arguments that language is God-given. Rather, the very efficacy of language for Burke resides in its obscurity, and poetry assumes the highest place in his ordering of the arts[9] because it is distanced from nature and defined precisely in terms of its not being an imitation of reality. It would, thus, be rather churlish to observe that Burke's empiricism is undone by its dependence upon language, which by virtue of its rhetoricity and hence its unreliability and subversiveness betrays the very claims to certainty that it desires, for the *Enquiry* has itself preceded us in this gesture. Yet it would be equally useless for us to applaud the text's canny (or uncanny) unraveling of itself or its own deconstructive gestures, because that move merely confirms the expectations we have engendered about the ways in which figurative language is, finally, always the "real story." Or, to apply the observation we made earlier about Burke, if we can imagine no evidence that does not confirm the power of rhetoricity, that fact inevitably taints any evidence in favor of it.

Thus, when Burke uses ordinary language as evidence, as in the examples from common usage I mentioned earlier, that move is part and parcel of the stress he lays upon words not as vehicles of metaphysical truth but as vehicles for the emotions: "The proper manner," he says, "of conveying the *affections* [his emphasis] of the mind from one to another, is by words"(60). And along these lines, it becomes rather unsurprising to see the ways in which Burke doesn't merely provide catalogues of objects that fall under the categories of the sublime and the beautiful but rather frames them with conventions of reading. If he asserts that "pleasure is only pleasure as it is felt"(33) he also laces his commentary on objects with the various types of seeing *as* (rather than "merely seeing") that push one beyond the mechanical operations of either the senses or their objects. Even as Burke insists "that there are pleasures and pains of a positive and independent nature" (which are, that is, not merely relative to their opposites), it is also clear that the objects that Burke cites do not function as examples of sublime or beautiful objects because their intrinsic natures are immediately apparent. Thus, instead of mere lists of names of objects, the *Enquiry* offers narratives about those objects, miniature fables that suggest the infinite differences between simply naming a horse and seeing him "in the two distinct lights in which we may consider him":

> The horse in the light of an useful beast, fit for the road, the draft, in every social useful light the horse has nothing of the sublime; but is it thus that we are affected with him, *whose neck is cloathed with thunder, the glory of whose nostrils is terrible, who swalloweth the ground with fierceness and rage, neither believeth that it is the sound of the trumpet?* In this description the useful character of the horse entirely disappears, and the terrible and sublime blaze out together.[66]

This brings us to an even more striking example of the way in which Burke uses language as evidence—by lacing the *Enquiry* with quotations that are explicitly rhetorical—from Homer, Virgil, Milton, Shakespeare, and the book of Job (which was something of a paradigm of sublimity for the time). In one sense, these quotations function analogously to the "ordinary language" examples, because they are all familiar enough to assert a commonality of literary experience between Burke and his readers; and quoting Milton's description of Death in arguing for the force of obscurity is not very far removed from the remark, "All men are agreed to call vinegar sour . . ." Yet of the forty-three passages explicitly quoted in the *Enquiry,* some twenty-four are misquotations, and familiarity increases inaccuracy, so that neither passage of the two from Shakespeare is correct as it stands and only two of the six passages from Milton are. This point is worth registering not to expose any scandal in Burke's infidelity to his texts; for although Christopher Ricks decries the willful individualism in Pater's misquotations, the *Enquiry* provides us with two alternative ways of comprehending these unscholarly lapses.[10] Because Burke's objectivity is an objectivity about the emotions, the iconicity and textual integrity of literary works have no force by comparison with the text's affective power. Thus, strangely, misquotation sometimes functions in the *Enquiry* as testimony to a passage's sublimity, in reflecting the reader's inability to imitate, as it were, exactly the movements of a text that is always "greater" than he. Yet, alternatively, misquotation can indicate the reader's excessive familiarity with the text, his diddling with it out of a "love" that approaches much nearer to contempt than we imagine.

Burke's basic alignment of the sublime with the "passions which concern self-preservation" and of the beautiful with the "passions of society" is well known. The sublime is the realm of estrangement, of power seen as greater than our own; the beautiful, the realm of familiarity, of power seen as lesser than our own. Yet recent discussions of the sublime, remarkably, all but delete the beautiful and present the sublime as functioning in supreme isolation from its companion and counterpoise, the beautiful. This indifference to the beautiful, of course, draws a certain authority from prominent eighteenth- and nineteenth-century accounts of the sublime and the beautiful. Burke, for example, has repeatedly been observed to droop in his discussion of the beautiful as if he could himself marshal little energy for its easy pleasures,[11] and Kant treats the beautiful as a more mixed and confused area of perception than the sublime. Yet it is still somewhat startling to find that critics influenced by structuralist and deconstructivist approaches ignore the neat binarism of "the sublime *and* the beautiful" in their rush to the "real" subject, the sublime. Strangely, we find that the beautiful all but disappears as Thomas Weiskel multiplies binary oppositions within the sublime, so that Kant's mathematical and dynamical sublimes are joined by metaphorical and metonymic sublimes (an adaptation of Roman Jakobson), positive and negative sublimes (of A. C. Bradley), rhetorical and natural sublimes (of Marjorie Hope Nicolson), and repressive and aggressive sublimes adapted from Freudian psychology.

Martin Price quite shrewdly observed (in 1964) that the doctrine of the sublime (like that of the picturesque) marked "a revolt against the tyranny of beauty,"[12] but he failed to elaborate on why one should revolt against beauty rather than war, pestilence, famine, and plague. And the question we must ask of Burke's *Enquiry* is what is tyrannical about the beautiful, or, why must it be resisted? For we cannot understand the force of the sublime unless we understand what it is an alternative to. Beauty, at first glance, is merely what both we and the sublime are superior to. Its fault is not excessive rationalism. The beautiful appeals to the emotions just as much as the sublime does, so that Burke can exempt the beautiful from rational judgment by showing the futility of arguing for it: "Who ever said, we *ought* to love a fine woman, or even any of those beautiful animals which please us? Here to be affected, there is no need of the concurrence of our will"(110). Yet the beautiful, in appealing to the domestic emotions, that is, love and its associated feelings, is consistently presented as operating on emotions much less intense than those of self-preservation on which the sublime works.

Thus we find that the sublime in its alliance with feelings of fear and pain produces the powerful passion of astonishment, in which the self is mastered:

> In this case the mind is so entirely filled with its object, that it cannot entertain any other, nor by consequence reason on that object which employs it. Hence arises the great power of the sublime, that far from being

produced by them, it anticipates our reasonings, and hurries us on by an irresistible force.[57]

The beautiful, however, contains all that the self masters. And the lines of the distinction become explicit when Burke asserts:

> There is a wide difference between admiration and love. The Sublime, which is the cause of the former, always dwells on large objects, and terrible; the latter on small ones, and pleasing; we submit to what we admire, but we love what submits to us.[113]

Although it is easy enough for us to understand the appeal of the sublime with its preference for intensity rather than the quotidian, we must, however, confront a difficulty concerning the availability of the sublime which plagues Burke and others. For if the sublime is on the side of novelty—that which surprises and astonishes, there are distribution problems here, because the demand quickly begins to exceed the supply. The force of such qualities as terror, obscurity, and vastness which Burke pronounces sublime depends upon primitive feelings of dread, and sublime qualities are associated throughout the *Enquiry* with the fear of death itself. Yet sublime delight only arises when danger and pain do not "press too nearly"(40); one, in other words, enjoys danger only from a position of safety.

On the one hand, Burke connects the sublime with death in order to attest to the genuineness of sublime emotions; for if we remember that time-honored belief that a dying man (if he isn't Voltaire) is the epitome of truthfulness, we can understand the sublime's approach to death as prompting a similar authority or authenticity. On the other hand, the safety net—the condition that danger and pain must not "press too nearly"—threatens to render the sublime something of a shell game. Without the distancing of death, there wouldn't, of course, be much to talk about, but the problem that haunts Burke's *Enquiry* is the possibility that repeated exposure to the sublime may annihilate it altogether. The sublimity of Mont Blanc becomes in some sense factitious once Mont Blanc becomes an obligatory stop on every gentleman's grand tour, and it obviously suffers even more greatly from daily exposure.

The sublime, then, dwindles as soon as familiarity converts the necessary distance of danger and death into an absolute banishment of those dreads. And the very fashionableness of the notion of the sublime represents a self-destructive combination. To speak of an habitual or fashionable sublime, though such a thing certainly finds ample documentation in late eighteenth-century and Romantic texts, is to suggest a certain logical difficulty. A major dilemma of the sublime is that of preserving its *difference* from the custom, habit, and fashion which are continually launching insidious assimilative forays upon it. As Burke says, "custom reconciles us to everything."[13]

Now Longinus, Kant, and Wordsworth (among others) snatch the sublime from within the habitual in their adherence to what I call (for want of a better name) the "educated sublime." For all these writers, the sublime involves the recognition of the habitual and the familiar as especially remarkable not in spite of their familiarity but *because of* it: the familiar is, thus, always being defamiliarized and rehabilitated. By comparison with such accounts as these, Burke's denunciations of custom, habit, and the familiar are particularly striking, and we can see that the antiintellectualism with which Burke is frequently charged operates in the *Enquiry* in opposition to the habitual. "It is our ignorance of things that causes all our admiration, and chiefly excites our passions. Knowledge and acquaintance make the most striking causes affect but little"(61). While judgment (as the employment of reason) receives due acknowledgement as necessary for distinguishing truth from falsity, it figures as both a derived and necessary evil:

> for almost the only pleasure that men have in judging better than others, consists in a sort of conscious pride and superiority, which arises from thinking rightly; but then, this is an indirect pleasure, a pleasure which does not immediately result from the object which is under contemplation.(25)

We thus arrive at a critical impasse for the notion of sublimity in the *Enquiry:* on the one hand, the very possibility for validating perceptions of the sublime rests upon the assertion that taste is universal, a proposition that of necessity can be validated only by custom ("all men are accustomed to . . ."); on the other, communal assent to any account of sublime experiences robs the sublime of its singularity, its difference, and threatens to shift the sublime into the beautiful, the arena of custom. In fact, the sublime at moments resembles a null set, or a category of experience that can be spoken of only elegiacally:

> In the morning of our days, when the senses are unworn and tender, when the whole man is awake in every part, and the gloss of novelty fresh upon all the objects that surround us, how lively at that time are our sensations, but how false and inaccurate the judgments we form of things? I despair of ever receiving the same degree of pleasure from the most excellent performances of genius which I felt at that age, from pieces which my present judgment regards as trifling and contemptible.(25)

Knowledge is purchased only by the loss of power and the loss of sublimity. Yet the power relations of the *Enquiry*, we may recall, operate along quite different equations than this alignment of power and sublimity suggests; for the beautiful has been defined as what we love because it submits to us and the sublime as what we admire for its power over us. Unless we take the step of asserting an identification between the perceiver and sublime objects (a step which itself erodes the notion of the sublime as the different by definition), we wonder at this nostalgia for what appears as almost purely masochistic experience.

Burke has already presented an account of perception that rehearses the common eighteenth-century praise of Longinus for linking things usually seen as opposites:

> When two remote objects are unlike to each other, it is only what we expect; things are in their common way; and therefore they make no distinct impression on the imagination: but when two distinct objects have a resemblance, we are struck, we attend to them, and we are pleased.[17–18]

The perception of "similitude in dissimilitude" (as we have come to call this movement) wins Burke's applause because by it "we enlarge our stock" and "produce *new images*" (18; emphasis his). Yet his discussion of the whole question of resemblance takes a rather surprising turn when he offers a specific example:

> A piece of news is told me in the morning; this, merely as a piece of news, as a fact added to my stock, gives me some pleasure. In the evening I find that there was nothing in it. What do I gain by this, but the dissatisfaction that I have been imposed upon? Hence it is, that men are much more naturally inclined to belief than to incredulity.[18]

Although this example may appear to provide scant justification for Burke's assertion of the primacy of belief, its real issue is that of falsifiability. And it becomes the basis for an enthusiastic account of the inevitability that primitive writers should have excelled in similitude without "taking care to have them exact" (18). The inexactness of literary comparisons renders them unassailable, whereas the piece of news has all in it or nothing in it according to its likeness to its object. It may sound as though Burke here provides a version of familiar defenses of literature—that its truth or falsity doesn't matter, or that such questions matter differently in literature than they do in real life. Yet the most remarkable feature of the passage is that it, like all of Burke's claims for the power of obscurity over clarity, locates the sublime in literature (and in all its forms) as precisely *that which can never be taken*

away from you by someone else. Further, even though the sublime object is such because it is more powerful than the perceiving individual, any humiliation or abasement that may be involved in one's submission to a sublime object is preferable to humiliation by another person. For the story of the piece of news relies not just upon the resemblance of the news to its real object in the world, but, more important, upon the likeness between the source and the recipient of the news; when a man like oneself relates news as truth and another man like oneself contradicts the truthfulness of the news, the dissatisfaction of being imposed upon merely registers the awareness that the inexactness of resemblances is particularly distressing in relations between people.

Burke pursues his account of the pleasures of impotence in the face of the sublime in his section "Power," when he avers that he knows "of nothing sublime which is not some modification of power," which inspires terror(64), because power is defined as the ability to hurt. To aid us in comprehending this sublimity of power, Burke offers a series of examples: dogs are strong but not sublime; wolves, having no more strength than some species of dogs, are sublime; powerful men such as Job are sublime; and God is sublime. The distinction between dogs and the other three terms echoes Burke's frequent expressions of scorn for the tame, the domesticated.

> Dogs are indeed the most social, affectionate, and amiable animals of the whole brute creation; but love approaches much nearer to contempt than is commonly imagined; and accordingly, though we caress dogs, we borrow from them an appellation of the most despicable kind, when we employ terms of reproach; and this appellation is the common mark of the last vileness and contempt in every language.[67]

Now at first glance the assertion that "love approaches much nearer to contempt than is commonly imagined" appears to be an example of virtuosity in perceiving similarities between extraordinarily different things; but the chain of examples suggests a giddy reversibility in these power relationships. We understand perfectly well that dogs as dogs are social and affectionate toward men but that when we call men "dogs" we conjure up images of servility, fawning, and flattery. While wolves are like dogs in that they are undomesticated relatives to dogs, they are different in representing power without constraint. Yet the use of Job as the example of a powerful man challenges our certainty about the firmness of the dividing lines. For Job in the passage that Burke cites ("When I prepared my seat in the street . . . the young men saw me, and hid themselves" [29:7]) only memorializes his *past* power in the same speech in which he continually expresses astonish-

ment that he is reviled by young men "whose fathers I would have disdained to have set with the dogs of my flock" (30:1). Although Job chose his friends because they were men like him, only his fall from power is necessary for them to present themselves as absolutely different. While Job's friends are "flatterers" (dogs) to their friend, the difficulty that Job recognizes is that men change their appearances with appalling ease. Wolves, over time, can become dogs; but men move from being men and friends like oneself to being dogs to being wolves. For flattery never appears as merely annoying in the book of Job, because the doglike behavior of Job's friends repeatedly reveals the ways in which "man is a wolf to man." Thus, a series that began by locating stable power relationships evolves into an account of mutability, of which the case of God is the culmination. While the story of Job might suffice to inspire us with terror at God's power, Burke provides additional testimony, beginning with David's exclamation, "fearfully and wonderfully am I made" (Psalm 34:14), which affirms God's omnipotence while at the same time recalling that man is made in the image of God. The shift from dog to God in this passage may be, as we say, purely accidental, but the appalling message of the series is that one may be able to trust dogs to be dogs and wolves to be wolves but that there is real danger in resting secure in relations that assume stable similarities between one man and another or between God and the man made in his image. If the perception of resemblance between distinct and different objects is exalting, the perception of difference between likes is appalling.

Recent criticism of the sublime has treated the "natural sublime," as if being inspired by fear of a mountain when one wasn't really in danger were the whole story. And this attachment to the question of whether Nature does or doesn't betray the heart that loves her is of a piece with critical neglect of the beautiful. For the beautiful, as it turns out, figures in the *Enquiry* not just as the domestic and social or as that which submits to us, it is also the deceptive par excellence. In the case of the sublime, Burke says, "we are forced," while with the beautiful, "we are flattered into compliance"(113). Moreover, the beautiful, far from representing perfection, "almost always carries with it an idea of weakness and imperfection," an assertion for which Burke provides the following evidence:

> Women are very sensible of this; for which reason, they learn to lisp, to totter in their walk, to counterfeit weakness, and even sickness. In all this, they are guided by nature. Beauty in distress is much the most affecting beauty. Blushing has no little power; and modesty in general, which is a tacit allowance of imperfection, is itself considered as an amiable quality, and certainly heightens every other that is so.[110]

Beauty, like the sublime, demands no assent from our reason—which is a good thing, because it recurs throughout the *Enquiry* in the form of a seductive and indirect assault on the reason, so that the general notion that "gradual variation" is a component of beauty finds justification in an example like this:

> Observe the part of a beautiful woman where she is perhaps the most beautiful, about the neck and breasts; the smoothness; the softness; the easy and insensible swell; the variety of the surface, which is never for the smallest space the same; the deceitful maze, through which the unsteady eye slides giddily, without knowing where to fix, or whither it is carried.[115]

If we find a beheaded woman as the epitome of beauty, her deceit is not less powerful for having no rational or volitional origins, and the *effects* of such a "deceitful maze" as this become more than indifferent and less than amiable when Burke outlines the physical concomitant of the emotions that beauty inspires.

> When we have before us such objects as excite love and complacency, the body is affected, so far as I could observe, much in the following manner. The head reclines something on one side; the eyelids are more closed than usual, and the eyes roll gently with an inclination to the object, the mouth is a little opened, and the breath drawn slowly, with now and then a low sigh: the whole body is composed, and the hands fall idly to the sides. All this is accompanied with an inward sense of melting and languor.[149]

Should we mistake this languor in the face of the beautiful for healthy relaxation, Burke later aligns bodily entropy with the beautiful quality of sweetness, which appeals to the sense of taste yet finally "very much enfeebles the tone of the stomach"(154). And the Trojan War itself appears in illustration of beauty's disastrous consequences not only for the body but for the body politic as well.

> It may be observed, that Homer has given the Trojans, whose fate he has designed to excite our compassion, infinitely more of the amiable social virtues than he has distributed among his Greeks. With regard to the Trojans, the passion he chooses to raise is pity; pity is a passion founded on love; and these *lesser*, and if I may say, domestic virtues are certainly the most amiable.[158]

Both death and defeat—loss of collective liberty—accompany the amiable virtues. Although we love (and pity) that which we see as weaker than we are, the danger in beauty is that its appearance of weakness does not prevent its having an effect, which is always that of robbing us of our vigilance and recreating us in its own image.

After the beautiful has been joined with physical and political entropy issuing in death, the importance of the sublime in exciting the passions of self-preservation becomes apparent. For although the sublime inspires us with fear of our death, the beautiful leads us toward death without our awareness; and along these lines, later commentators who see the sublime as authorizing suicide appropriately extend the Burkean desire to gain control over one's life, one's death, for it is precisely the function of the sublime to elaborate its own paradoxical explicitness: one will die, one is less powerful than sublime objects and forces; but for all the obscurity of sublimity, there is a peculiar clarity as well—you know the danger you're in.

In one sense, Burke's account of the sublime repudiates the premium that the rhetorical sublime (that is, Longinus and his descendants) places upon the concealment of one's art, one's power; his sublime would surprise and astonish but always reveal its power.[14] Yet, in another sense, the notion of concealment remains as crucial as it was for Longinus, though with Burke it is negatively valued and defined as the beautiful. But if the beautiful insidiously induces a dangerous relaxation (that can "take away the vigorous tone of fibre which is requisite for carrying on the natural and necessary secretions,"135), the sublime acts as the antidote to the dissolution produced by the beautiful. All its strainings follow the dictates of the work ethic: "The best remedy for all these evils (produced by the beautiful) is exercise or *labour*; and labour is a surmounting of *difficulties*, an exertion of the contracting power of the muscles . . ."(135).

If the sublime becomes linked with labor while the beautiful associates itself with a slow and almost imperceptible movement toward death, we may recall when it was that labor and death entered the human world—with the Fall of Man. And while the Romantic poets often portray Satanic energy as sublime, the labor of Burke's sublime is explicitly labeled as a providentially ordered capacity for mitigating the force of the beautiful that brought about both the Fall and the very possibility of the Fall (see 134). For the fatal flaw that Burke's category of the beautiful uncovers in man is his need for "social communication," as Milton's Adam puts it in his request that God supplement his individual self with a likeness.[15] Moreover, while the implicit Burkean account of the Fall echoes Eve's decision to tempt Adam and Adam's decision to chuck his beatific state because neither one can do without the other, to Burke it must have seemed no accident that Satan's initial sublime overstatement aroused Eve's suspicions as his later chivalrous politesse did not. For in the terms of Burke's account, a paradigmatic instance of the beautiful must certainly be Genesis 3:4—"And the serpent said unto the woman, Ye shall not surely die,"[16] in which the mere ordonnance of the words converts an outright lie into the kind of polite deceit upon which Burke's version of social discourse sustains itself.

Early in the *Enquiry* (in the Introduction on Taste) Burke described "the pleasure of resemblance" as "that which principally flatters the imagination" (18), and the axiom that likeness is flattery reaches its apogee in the beautiful when we recognize the costs of the preservation of likeness. For while tyrants are sublime in the *Enquiry,* only the beautiful, with its commitment to companionable resemblance between humans, disguises the disequilibrium of power so effectively that we all, like Adam, become accomplices in our own deaths. Although the sublime masters us while we are superior to the power of the beautiful, the *Enquiry* suggests that we invariably misconstrue those power relationships by failing to recognize that what we term the weaker has greater sway over us than the sublime with its palpably awesome force. And if the beautiful has no warning label announcing that it "may be hazardous to your health," it turns out that "the only thing we have to fear is fearlessness itself."

Notes

1. Immanuel Kant, *Prolegomena to Any Future Metaphysics,* rev. of Carus trans., ed. Lewis White Beck (Indianapolis: Bobbs-Merrill Educational Publishing, 1950), n. 2, 122–23.
2. William Wordsworth, Advertisement to *Lyrical Ballads,* in *The Prose Works of William Wordsworth,* ed. W. J. B. Owen and Jane Worthington Smyser, 3 vols. (Oxford: Clarendon Press, 1974), 1:116.
3. Samuel Taylor Coleridge, "On the Principles of Genial Criticism," in *Biographia Literaria with His Aesthetical Essays,* ed. J. Shawcross (Oxford: Oxford University Press, 1907), 2:224.
4. Wordsworth, Essay, Supplementary to the Preface of 1815, *Works,* 3:80.
5. Thomas Weiskel, *The Romantic Sublime* (Baltimore: Johns Hopkins University Press, 1976), 85–86.
6. Edmund Burke, *A Philosophical Enquiry into the Origin of Our Ideas of the Sublime and Beautiful,* ed. J. T. Boulton (Notre Dame, Ind.: University of Notre Dame Press, 1958), 45.
7. David Hume, *An Inquiry concerning Human Understanding,* ed. Charles W. Hendel (Indianapolis: Bobbs-Merrill Co., 1955), 40.
8. Paul de Man, "The Epistemology of Metaphor," *Critical Inquiry* 5, no. 1 (Autumn, 1978): 13–30. De Man's concluding remarks on how rhetoric is not reducible to a series of codes are surely right, but it is also possible to see how the primacy of rhetoric in his critical system verges on establishing a metaphysics of rhetoricity.
9. See Burke, 60–62.
10. Christopher Ricks, "Pater, Arnold and Misquotation," *Times Literary Supplement,* no. 3, 948 (Nov. 25, 1970): 1383–85. For Ricks misquotation is a moral issue; misquotation

involves an unseemly assertion of self, while proper quotation of texts implies decorous self-effacement.

11. See Samuel H. Monk, *The Sublime: A Study of Critical Theories in XVIII-Century England* (Ann Arbor: University of Michigan Press, 1960), 84–100, which is heavily weighted toward the sublime and its more sensational and terrifying aspects. See also J. T. Boulton's introduction to his edition of the *Enquiry*, xl, and passim. His remark that "Burke is consistently interested in strong emotional responses and clearly prefers, on grounds of intensity, the sublime to the beautiful" (xl) is typical of his view of the relative importance of the sublime and the beautiful.

12. Martin Price, *To the Palace of Wisdom* (Garden City, New York: Doubleday and Co., 1965), 362.

13. Burke is here (148) discussing the phenomenon of becoming accustomed even to the terrifying effects of darkness and blackness.

14. For an exceptionally acute examination of Longinus, see Neil Hertz, "Lecture de Longin," *Poétique: Revue de théorie et d'analyse littéraires* 15 (1969): 194–213. That essay appears in English in Hertz, *The End of the Line*, 1–20.

15. *Paradise Lost*, 8.429.

16. I follow the King James version here.

3

Burke to Kant: A Judgment Outside Comparison

In Burke's *Enquiry* the uncertain placement of experience, now as testimony to the similarities between persons that continually reconfirm the notion of society, now as testimony to the distinctness of the individual, becomes problematic not merely because it pits the individual against society but also because it ultimately sets any individual at odds with his or her own experience. That is, the mere repetition of experience, in establishing the familiarity that causes objects once seen as sublime to come to seem merely beautiful, makes individual experience its own worst enemy. And this is the case because Burke's account continually identifies aesthetic experience with the physical sensations of pleasure and pain. The emotions of love and fear that bespeak the perceptions of beauty and sublimity may seem to separate them from ordinary (that is, nonaesthetic) experience, but only because they introduce the notion of comparison into the self that might seem to function as a unit.

The operation of the senses would, in the terms of the Burkean account, be self-annihilating if it operated efficiently. One would continually be experiencing and acting out (producing the physical symptoms of one's experiences) in a series of sensations that would themselves be overtaken by whatever sensation came next. The inefficiency of sensation, however, emerges as a confusion of experiences with images that makes response participate in its own misfiring, its inability to separate an experience from an image of an experience. For although increasingly strong sensation seems required to produce an effect on the inertia of individual experience, Burke also depicts inertial force operating in exactly the opposite direction—as effects outliving their immediate causes in sensation. And even as he is affirming the difference between the removal of pain on the one hand and positive pleasure on the other,[1] he gives an example that suggests a different problem altogether:

> As when a wretch, who conscious of his crime,
> Pursued for murder from his native clime,
> Just gains some frontier, breathless, pale, amaz'd;
> All gaze, all wonder![2]

For Burke, the point of the example is that the man who has "just escaped an imminent danger" does not feel pleasure because he has escaped the immediate causes of his terror; rather, the reaction of the spectators bears witness that he continues in a version of the terror he was in before he made his escape. Burke concludes that "when we have suffered from any violent emotion, the mind naturally continues in something like the same condition, after the cause which first produced it has ceased to operate"(35). To that extent, the example and the inertial account of the emotions to which he ties it do serve to establish the point that positive pleasure and the absence (or removal) of pain are not identical. But in suggesting that one continues in a state of residual terror even as one is distancing oneself from it, he is distinguishing pleasure from pain while at the same time introducing a fundamental equivocation about the communication of emotional experience. The spectators' apprehension of the fugitive's countenance testifies to the continuation of his terror (rather than to his pleasure at escaping the occasion for feeling that terror); their gazing in wonderment itself replicates his expression of amazement. Yet the communication of emotions between persons occurs, in this example, precisely at the point at which those emotions have lost a clear connection with their causes. The spectators see—and thus stand to confirm—the emotional impact of a terror that the fugitive has lost any external reason to feel.

The example of the Homeric fugitive forms an interesting companion piece to an example I cited earlier—that of the piece of news that was later discovered to have "nothing in it." In that earlier example, Burke discovered an argument for credulity in our love of resemblance. We love stories that we take to be truthful, his discussion suggested, because we like thinking that there are correspondences between things and our stories about them. Moreover, we love stories that we take to be truthful because we love being able to enlarge our "stock" of such pieces of news, being able to see the bits themselves not merely as bits but as analogues to one another, all alike in being parts of one's "stock." The same thing may be said about both of these accounts of resemblance—that neither one of them rests upon a question of accuracy or truthfulness. Insofar as the kinds of resemblance that Burke describes are formal, the pleasures one takes in them could be entirely unaffected by the discovery that they were false. When the piece of news told you in the morning turns out to be false, it is always open to you (on

Burke's account) to discover a pleasure in the resemblance between the false story you heard and a true one. You can, that is, override the lack of resemblance between the false story and the truth with an awareness of the resemblance between stories that are false and stories that are true.

Earlier I argued that in Burke's handling of the example of the piece of news one could see a desire to coordinate two different kinds of resemblance—that between things and their representations and that between one person and another. In the state that appears most nearly ideal to Burke, seeing someone else registering terror is to assume that bodily expression and thus to take on that terror oneself. The proliferation and transfer of the emotions from one person to another sustain sensations and keep them distinct from the associations and reasonings we have about them.[3] In that sense, experience can remain honest in the process of being communicated. One can relate one's feelings to another with entire accuracy, but without any guarantee that those feelings remain reliable indexes to current sensation. (As with Richardsonian letters that may be "written to the moment" but continually arrive as relics of emotions no longer being felt by the characters who penned them, the recipient may participate in a sensation that the letter writer no longer feels.) The communication of feelings thus always occurs, in spite of the faithful replication of one person's feelings by another, as an acceptance of resemblance with "nothing in it." Burke continually tries to patch up this difficulty by describing anticipation and memory as being much like physical sensation, and thus casting the state of expectation created by a series of sounds or objects as tension, or the cause of tension:

> And it must be observed, that expectation itself causes a tension. This is apparent in many animals, who, when they prepare for hearing any sounds, rouse themselves, and prick up their ears; so that here the effect of the sounds is considerably augmented by a new auxiliary, the expectation. But though after a number of strokes, we expect still more, not being able to ascertain the exact time of their arrival, when they arrive, they produce a sort of surprise, which increases this tension yet further.[140]

Burke develops the description in terms of the mutual opposition between expectation, being poised by a pattern to anticipate hearing another sound, and the surprise that results from not knowing exactly when the expectation will be fulfilled. Moreover, he specifically credits this oscillation between expectation and surprise with heightening the tension "to such a pitch" that the sense—hearing—"is brought just to the verge of pain." And this tension results in a peculiar reversal of the customary Burkean pattern for describing objects of sense and their operation on the mind: the organs of hearing, under the pressure of the tension of expectation and surprise, refuse to be surprised and continue to produce the effects of sensation in the absence of external objects: "Even when the cause has ceased; the organs of hearing being often successively struck in a similar manner, continue to vibrate in that manner for some time longer; this is an additional help to the greatness of the effect"(140).

Anticipation, in looking forward to sensation, ends up making the memory of sensation equivalent to sensation itself. And as sensation and its inertial force in memory become virtually indistinguishable, sensation becomes a conspicuously unreliable basis for establishing communication both between persons and within the experience of one individual. The very process of extending sensory experience over time so that it can be documentable and communicable rather than merely transitory and private comes to mean that the report of sensation—and this involves, of course, the perception of sensation for the Homeric fugitive and his observers, as well as for the dog or human expecting to continue a particular line of sensation—will be a piece of news with "nothing in it." The terms for judging veracity shift dramatically here. Burke's concern with the accuracy of the news report initially registered an anxiety about a potentially manipulatable discrepancy between one person's knowledge and another's; the examples I have just pointed to, however, indicate a more serious problem, for they are examples of an individual's inability to have sensory experience that can claim the kind of truthful connections to objects that Burke had earlier seemed to found the *Enquiry* on.

The representation of sensation, then, seems to threaten sensation as a reliable index to the existence of objects. Yet it is important to stress exactly how deep that equivocal representation is shown to run. If one could simply avoid the representations of others, then Burke's celebrated and naggingly incomplete argument for the human preference for a real execution over a staged tragedy would stand as an axiom for determining the relative weights and values of "real sympathy" (47) and its staged representation.

> But be its [the tragedy's] power of what kind it will, it never approaches to what it represents. Chuse a day on which to represent the most sublime and affecting tragedy we have; appoint the most favourite actors; spare no cost upon the scenes and decorations; unite the greatest efforts of poetry, painting and music; and when you have collected your audience, just at the moment when their mind are erect with expectation, let it be reported that a state criminal of high rank is on the point of being executed in the adjoining square; in a moment the emptiness of the theatre would demonstrate the comparative weakness of the imitative arts, and proclaim the triumph of the real sympathy.[47]

In glossing the example, Burke makes a vigorous argument against the view that "in either real or fictitious distresses," it is "our immunity from them which produces our delight"(48). Our immunity is, for him, a necessary but not a sufficient condition of our having any "delight" in the sufferings of others; the sympathy we feel toward a man being executed would be unavailable to us were we ourselves dead. But Burke's eagerness to dispel the hold of an argument that we might take to revolve around *Schadenfreude,* a pleasure in other people's pains, highlights the degree of tension that exists between his account of a sensory event and his account of a narrative of such sensory events. It is not merely that Burke makes an invidious comparison between the real and the represented as he ascribes to the public execution a greater drawing power and greater hold on its audience than the theater with its illusory representations of suffering. Rather, it is that questions of illusion and reality have been redefined so that the only vehicle of testimony about the world that Burke admits, sensory experience, has been shown to become duplicitous as soon as it develops narrative extension of any kind. Whether remembering or anticipating (extending remembrance into the future), sensation loses its standing in the process of becoming a representation. Initially having served as an effect that betokens a cause, representation duplicitously serves sensation by producing it. The representation of sensible experience desubstantializes sensation by extending it as its own self-haunting phantom, interlarding the perception of things that are with the perception of things that aren't. Memories and anticipations of sensations do not so much record sensations as duplicate them.

The difficulties of remedying the problem of sensory self-ventriloquism become apparent as Burke describes public enthusiasm for an execution as opposed to a staged drama. For it is not nearly so much that Burke is rejecting theatricality per se for the greater reality of the "real" execution as that he is choosing an example that will itself represent extremity. An actor in a tragedy is something like the working definition of what it means for someone to lose track of the difference between one sensation and another—between the experience of the tragic character and that of the actor, as well as between the experience of saying the same words on one night and on another. In that sense, he combines the threat of mistaken reference between persons with the threat of mistaken reference within one's own experience. The public execution is, thus, not merely real by comparison with a theatrical representation. By virtue of its approach to death as the limit to the proliferation of experiential images, it is real by comparison with any notion of representation at all. You can avoid the theater, but the possibility of there being such a thing as a piece of news—or anything that can be reported by one person to another—and the possibility of there being memory and anticipation in one's own experience make it difficult, at the very least, to imagine representations that would not be, in the ultimate opposition that Burke projects between experience and all the constructions of it, disastrously in conflict with the sensation on which he would found them.

When Burke in his later discussion of the effects of succession claims that the supplanting of sensation with its phantom proxy becomes "apparent in many animals"(140), it becomes clear that this is not merely a conflict produced by consciousness as opposed to sensation. Even the minimal representations available to an *animal non capax rationis* interfere with the accurate transmission of sensation and make an animal say "the thing that is not." The repetition that creates a pattern for a dog preparing to hear "any sound" allows for the violation of the pattern—the surprise of a different interval, but it also extends the pattern in the absence of the stimulus that had once seemed necessary for it.

If an animal is incapable of "telling the truth" to itself about the nature of its sensory stimuli, the public execution becomes emblematic of sensation that is incapable of either deception or self-deception. The public execution, that is, functions as the definitional moment of sensation; the man about to die represents someone who is conventionally supposed to tell the truth (having nothing more to lose than the life that he is imminently to lose) and, more important perhaps, someone who doesn't have the time to become untrue to his own sensation. The execution itself is the emblem for the resistlessness of sensation that Burke continually posits. In its inevitability and its absolute opposition to the concerns and wishes of the condemned man, it establishes sensation on the ground of a contradiction. The moment of unequivocal sensation can be imagined only as a by-product of the total loss of sensation, an anticipatory sensation of the impossibility of continuing the various series of sensations that have, in their reiteration, made sensation imperceptible.

The execution reinvents the sensations, as if imminent death were an antidote to the intrusion of intermediate and mutually contradictory sensations that had occurred since "the morning of our days." And it not only reinvents them for the condemned man but for his spectators as well. He knows what he feels, and they know what he feels, as the imminence of death makes experience contract into a point; the imminence of having no sensation at all produces the sensation of having sensation. The prospect of immediate death provides experience that cannot, by definition, become habitual.

If the anticipation of death thus clarifies the experience of the condemned, what is the spectacle's attraction for an audience? Burke imports a providential argument to explain that people flock to a public execution because "our Creator has designed we should be united by the bond of sympathy" and should thus be attracted to situations "where our sympathy is most wanted, in the distresses of others"(46). This providential utilitarianism constitutes a particularly strange explanation for the delight that spectators experience in witnessing executions, one that is peculiar on two counts. First, it suggests a direct conflict between society and sympathy: the legal system through which society punishes a failure of social sympathy becomes the occasion for individuals to experience a bond with a person who is being executed in the name of the social bond. Thus, while providence has arranged human emotions so that one's presence seems required in any situation in which one might help, the execution calls forth those emotions on behalf of someone who is, presumably, being executed for having acted with some indifference to such sympathetic response.

Second, it establishes a parallel contradiction between emotion and action, between the immediate response of sympathy, which enjoins action to remedy or alleviate the distresses of others, and the reason, which interrupts that response. And while the opposition between emotion or instinct and reason might seem to be a settled and predictable one by this point in Burke's discussion, here the tension between the affective and the rational elements is more than a mere repetition of categorically opposed faculties. The emotions and the reason compete, not merely in the sense of trying to overcome their opposite numbers. Rather, they present themselves as mutually exclusive explanations of the same phenomenon: while the passion of sympathy requires our presence at the sufferings of others so that we may remedy them, the rational account of the execution is that it is itself a remedy. The passion of sympathy, that is, enjoins the spectators of an execution, "Do something," while the interpretation on behalf of reason claims, "This is what has been done." If crime is a cause of punishment, sympathy and the sensations it promotes become their own causes.

The contradiction between the emotions of the spectator at an execution and the social injunction to redress crime is instructive here. Just as Kant will later argue that aesthetic experience gives an indication of the state of one's soul (because one must have soul to participate in an experience from which one stands nothing to gain, since one cannot identify the gain to be had from an object that has purposiveness without purpose), so Burke is suggesting that the "delight we have" in witnessing calamities is significant not so much in spite of the contradictions between our interests (in sustaining an orderly society or redressing crimes) and our sympathies as because of those contradictions. Whereas he initially identified reason and habit as obscuring the real causes of our responses, this example culminates a series in which sensation is clearly put into conflict with the notion of a cause outside the frame of a mimeticism that takes the individual body, human or animal, as its appropriate unit. The sublime occasions that Burke identifies in the example of the fugitive who has succeeded in escaping, in that of the dog that continues to hear sounds when they are no longer made, and in that of the spectator at the execution importantly separate sensation from content. They are instances of sensation becoming adept at imitating itself.

Habit and deception appear to present threats to the possibility of communication between persons for the same reason that they imperil the possibility of one's own internal communings with oneself: the repetition of the same forms can make them so readily perceptible as to render them virtually imperceptible. These examples, however, secure sensation by linking it not to external objects or even to intentional states but by making it recur as its own effect. Thus, Burke on the one hand argues that habit interferes with the senses, and at the same time describes sublime and resistless experience in terms of habitualized sensation, sensation so self-repeating that it needs no external cause or correlate.

The most important feature of Burkean empiricism—of the "physiological" account with which Kant contrasted his own transcendental exposition of aesthetical judgments—is, for our purposes, its progress from an apparently straightforward set of causal relations between objects and sensations to an account in which sensations end by becoming their own causes. Kant rightly identifies "these analyses of the phenomena of our mind" as "psychological observations." They are psychological not because they are eccentric, or even because they are, as Kant puts it, "exceedingly beautiful."[4] They are, instead, psychological by virtue of their making the subjective connection between representations and "gratification or grief" appear primary, so that the judgment of an object is subjectivized by the process of becoming less and less perceptibly distinct from a judgment on oneself. Burke's two mutually contradictory accounts of habit—one as the annihilation of the possibility of attesting to the force of an object, one as the institution of the necessity of sensation becoming self-proliferating—provide support for this observation. Burke's line of argument can "afford rich material for the favorite investigations of empirical anthropology"[5] because its observations can be generalized—because it has secured generalization on the basis of social enumeration. Having flirted with questions of the relationship between one's experiences and the objects that prompt them and with concerns about the changes that communication between persons effects in the relationship between persons and objects, that is, Burke appeals to linguistic testimony and category-making as if he were a sociologist *avant la lettre.*

Another way of putting this point is to observe that Burke's Introduction on Taste ultimately amounts to a conclusion on taste. Even if it is a "scientific" account of taste, an analysis of the kinds of social testimony that people give in expressing what looks like individual preference, it describes taste not by explaining individual tastes as relationships toward aesthetic objects but rather by redefining what it might mean to give an explanation of taste. Explaining taste turns out to be pointing to other tastes like this one, admitting, that is, that one cannot give a very good explanation of individual taste but can show that there is more (i.e., collective taste, in the form of the social, the class, the local, etc.) where it came from.

Burke begins from a position that argues the naturalness of taste, or the ways in which aesthetic experience provides evidence of the reality of things in the world, and ends by making it look as though the feeling of the naturalness of anything is always a kind of overestimation or misreading of the force of social agreement. Although Burke writes what is, from one standpoint, a key text in the emergence of aesthetics in the eighteenth century, his *Enquiry* finally resolves aesthetic experience into more and less explicitly social formations—beauty being the conspicuously functional social form, the sublime being the apparently dysfunctional social form that enables society to continue by providing illusions of individuality for its component parts.

Aesthetics can never, that is, emerge from a sociological account of art, can never come into being as a separate and separable realm of inquiry because Burke's account makes the imaginative aspects of perception look as if they could no more distinguish between the individual and society than between an experience of an object and an experience of an imagined object. Individual taste appears merely a mystification of the social. This is a position worth rehearsing, moreover, not merely because it is one of Kant's principal antagonists in the *Critique of Judgment* but also because it has been so actively revived in the work of such writers as Adorno and Bourdieu.[6] In Adorno's view, Kant enabled art to pass through a moment of disinterestedness, but that moment only provided the occasion for a new assertion of interest as the inevitable produce of life in society:

> The trajectory leading to aesthetic autonomy passes through the stage of disinterestedness; and well it should, for it was during this stage that art emancipated itself from cuisine and pornography, an emancipation that has become irrevocable. However, art does not come to rest in disinterested-

ness. It moves on. And in so doing it reproduces, in different form, the interest inherent in disinterestedness.[7]

That is, the (Kantian) notion of the disinterestedness of aesthetic experience points toward a separation of aesthetic pleasure from pleasurable sensation, dividing literature from pornography and aesthetic taste from the taste for good food. But Art "moves on." And thus Adorno produces an account of art's importance in setting individuals in opposition to society's desire for conformity that ultimately testifies to the impossibility of resisting that desire. For his history of the progress of art is socialized by the very aesthetic theory that would seem to save it, to make it look less like a massive confusion of sensory perception or an effort to create a social propaganda for the moral sense in all its abstract self-identity. Thus, the progress of art continually bespeaks what counts for Adorno as the death of art because art dies, for him, a little every time it becomes the vehicle of communal symbolic understanding. The social, for all its arbitrariness, is continually trying to pass itself off as an orderly arrangement—or at least insisting upon creating order in the individuals that compose it; art, insofar as it would be art, must operate outside such an order-inducing framework. Yet this particular opposition means that Adorno can both enumerate the topics that identify art in terms of its opposition to social conformity and express a desperate longing to stand apart from his own thematic identifications. He thus can speak of the importance of music in modernism, can implicitly praise Karl Kraus for having "in line with his critique of capitalism" "aimed at . . . the redemption of repressed phenomena, particularly animals, landscapes and women," and can object to Hegel's aesthetics, and to "his theory of language too," on the grounds of Hegel's "general lack of understanding for non-significative elements of communication"(111).

Adorno's understanding of the "non-significative elements of communication" establishes a conundrum at the center of his account of aesthetics. Inasmuch as it relies on the social to create it by giving it something to be against, it must simultaneously be communication directed and communication resistant. Failing of communication, it might cease to be a social act but it would also cease to be an aesthetic object. Achieving communication, it effects a collapse of the nonsignificative into communication, as it becomes perfectly clear that the representation of "repressed phenomena" such as "landscapes, animals, and women" is no solution at all. It is, instead, a way of definitionally enlisting the repressed to be the representatives of art as art itself is defined against the very notion of social hierarchies that involve the authoritarian determination of some people by others. Moreover, it risks reformulating class determinations in purely aesthetic terms, so that the interest that can attach to the repressed on account of their being repressed—therefore beneath certain kinds of notice, therefore as indeterminate as imperceptible—merely echoes Adorno's handling of thematics as if it were always a matter of determining an idea of indeterminacy that was then contaminated by the very moment of its determination. Adorno, for all his appreciation of the "non-significative," thus presents an essentially utilitarian account—that art's function is to remind society of the importance of the socially underrepresented (as if art were the second house in a parliamentary system whose first house represented social power quite directly).

In defining art against society and then redefining a portion of society against society (as social hegemony), Adorno's description of aesthetic history as a loss of the notion of disinterestedness fulfills its own prophecy. That is, he combines the important insight that Kant's account of disinterested enjoyment "makes enjoyment unrecognizable"(18) with a commitment to coming clean about one's enjoyment. Combining two mutually exclusive positions, he continually oscillates between a contempt for a society that "has no use for art" and a contempt for an art that has no use for society:

> Society today has no use for art and its responses to it are pathological. In this society, art survives as reified cultural heritage and as a source of pleasure for the box-office customer, but ceases to have relevance as an object. . . . Happiness is an accidental moment of art, less important even than the happiness that attends the knowledge of art. In short, the very idea that enjoyment is of the essence of art deserves to be thrown overboard. As Hegel noticed, every emotional response to an aesthetic object is tainted by contingency, mostly in the form of psychological projection. What works of art really demand from us is knowledge or, better, a cognitive faculty of judging justly: they want us to become aware of what is true and what is false in them.[22]

The demand from art releases the individual from seeing himself or herself as merely the answer to a demand from society. Yet in eschewing both the (Burkean) equivalence between aesthetic pleasure and more directly sensational pleasures and the emotively, psychologically contingent response, Adorno repudiates not merely society as a public demand for individuals but also the sensationist and psychological versions of individuality that would count as the fullest possible versions of privacy. In doing so, however, he defines the work of art as the demand for just judgment, leaving unspecified why the notions of justice and those of judgment should be best served by works of art.

What art wants of us, for us, is, on Adorno's account, an individualized and purified version of epistemology and justice, individualized in that it is to be a knowledge never compared with or confirmed by that of others, purified in that it is to be a judgment uncompromised by situation. Art, in other words, materializes a demand for subjectivity, and reformulates the question of the utility of art as a question of the motivelessness of subjectivity itself. Art, inspiring emotion, is contingent, in these terms, less because of any temporal or logical limitations than because of its being tied to a psychology that is merely an individual judgment on sensation—so that affect is continually subjectivized. And just as Adorno approvingly notes the separation of pornography and cuisine from the aesthetic, so the moment in which he depicts art speaking to us is one in which art enables us not to express individual motivation but rather to escape it.

Adorno's argument has, with breathtaking speed, finished off his accounts of art and its justifications by imagining works of art as, themselves, embodiments of disinterestedness. Unlike pornography and cuisine, they do not appeal merely to the senses. Unlike political justice, they do not continually struggle with a perpetual conflict between means and ends. Works of art do not merely, and with apologies, use falsehood in the service of truth but also ask, in true self-abnegation, for "us to become aware of what is true and what is false in them." At just this moment, it would appear that Adorno would lay the groundwork for an argument similar to that of Hannah Arendt, who essentially claims in "The Crisis in Culture" that art provides the basis for society, in continually testifying to an "enlarged mentality" in excess of the senses that gives the categorical imperative its imaginative force, that harnesses the senses to the work of the legislation of morality.[8] What he does instead is instructive, in that it involves setting aside his own rehearsal of contradictory positions in something like discursive quotation:

> Kant shall have the last word on aesthetic hedonism. In his analysis of the sublime, which is set apart from art, Kant wrote that happiness in relation to works of art is the feeling they instill of holding one's own, of resisting—a notion that is more nearly true for the aesthetic realm as a whole than of individual works.[22]

If art works had, from the late eighteenth century, repeatedly been identified as wholes greater than the sum of their parts, Adorno is not simply applying that organicist account on a more massive scale. Rather, his continual oscillation between a sociological and an ontological account rehearses the problem that we encountered most conspicuously in Burke's *Enquiry*—that anything available for communication has a hard time distinguishing itself from social practice, and anything that seems like social practice continually enters as the contingent. (Bourdieu would eliminate this quarrel between the sociological and the ontological considerations of art by eliminating the philosophical altogether, in his assertion that even Derrida's deconstructive examinations of the erosions of truth from within itself recapitulate the fundamental error of philosophy, which is always to imagine that there is something beyond the force of greater and lesser numbers of contingent individual opinions inflected by class organization and so forth.) Even at the moment at which Adorno portrays society and art as mutually disappointed in one another, even as he describes a split between a cultural heritage that gives no pleasure and a pleasure that presumably passes out of mind as art "ceases to have relevance as an object," he re-creates an ideal of subjective aesthetic pleasure in his description of art as not escapist—"not a chunk of reality from which art itself ran away"—but escaping.

In his commentary on Kant, the identification between aesthetic satisfaction and resistance proceeds on two fronts—the relationship between the individual and society and the relationship between one work of art and art in general. Schopenhauer's account of escape has been countered by Hegel's critique of the merely psychological and therefore contingent, and has emerged as Kant's account of aesthetic experience as resistance. Works of art, instilling the feeling of "holding one's own, or resisting"[9] provide an occasion for consciousness of individuation, of one's distinctness from and resistance to an aesthetic object, as if that distinctness from the object were itself not merely an analogy for but a version of resistance to society.

Adorno, however, is here inserting a key emendation of Kant in claiming for works of art the same kind of response that Kant restricts quite explicitly to natural objects. Where Kant describes the dynamical sublime in terms of a pleasure in the feeling of resistance which the individual experiences in relation to natural objects that have physical power in excess of individual human physical power, Adorno generalizes to see resistance as the central aesthetic response. One can track the force of that generalization in the way in which Adorno must qualify Kant's supposed "last word." The notion of the work of art instilling a sense of resistance is, he says, "a notion that is more nearly true of the aesthetic realm as a whole than of individual works"(22). Now, since Kant quite specifically did not apply the notion of resistance to works of art, which he saw as continually importing empirical questions of the "interest that indirectly attaches to the beautiful through our inclination to society,"[10] Adorno's emendation has all the interest of the textually unmotivated. He is, it would seem, suggesting that Kant was right to describe aesthetic pleasure as distinct from the kind of pleasure one might take in an action well performed or a knowledge well communicated. Aesthetic pleasure is, to provide a rationale for Adorno's use of Kant, a pleasure that one can very incompletely ground in utility. For there are two difficulties with the view that art produces pleasure in order to instruct—that it remains unclear why indirection is better than direction and that it is unclear what, other than pleasure, is communicated. Thus, Kant's account of aesthetic objects as having the look of purposiveness without having purpose recasts an empirical observation in formal terms. It speaks to the inadequacy of justifications of aesthetic pleasure by making the inadequacy of those justifications part of the definition of an aesthetic object.

Moreover, Kant's insistence upon the aesthetic judgment as revolving around one's own feeling of pleasure, rather than a report of someone else's, introduces an emphasis on individual judgment that Adorno seems implicitly to be relying on here. Aesthetic judgment is individual, produces individuals, that is, inasmuch as it imagines the possibility of a judgment that can operate independently of others. Yet while for Kant the confirmation of independent judgment in no way undercuts one's aesthetic pleasure, Adorno's coda suggests that "the aesthetic realm as a whole" exists by establishing the impossibility of its having any instances of the aesthetic. For Adorno seems here to be postulating the aesthetic as an antagonist to the social, and hinting that an individual work ceases to count as properly aesthetic if it does not produce a resistance to society, which it obviously cannot sustain in acquiring an audience of more than one.

Adorno's opposition between the aesthetic realm as a whole and the individual work, then, uses a collection that is composed out of the contradiction between it and the various elements that would constitute it. It establishes an implicit analogy with Adorno's conception of the aesthetic individual, who constitutes society in opposing it rather than in instantiating it. The individual develops the feeling of resistance to society through aesthetic experience; the particular aesthetic object exists as a resistance to—or a blot on—what Adorno describes as the aesthetic realm as a whole. For all the psychological acuteness of this scheme, it suffers from two related difficulties. First, it creates the category of the aesthetic realm as a whole as a purely theoretical one that, in being at odds with particular aesthetic objects, runs into opposition with the particularity of aesthetic experience that would seem to ground the opposition, the opening for the resistance, between the individual and society. Just as society in Adorno's description "has no use" for art and art "ceases to have relevance as an object," so the aesthetic as a whole does not merely differ from its particular parts but completely opposes them, so the individual work, failing to instill resistance (to it? to society?), comes to resist the whole of which it might be a part. Second, Adorno has here converted the problem of providing a direct account of aesthetic utility into what verges on a pure opposition to utility: the aesthetic comes to look as if it were aesthetic out of a determined dysfunctionality. That is, Adorno moves toward a position that is an inverted analogue to the Benthamite assertion that "poetry is as good as pushpin" as soon as he begins to make it sound as though the simple resistance to work and a direct antagonism toward society's demands were centrally at stake in aesthetic experience. Sports, carnivals, games, and, in general, the notion of leisure as time off from work begin to look as aesthetic as a work of art. Even fireworks come to seem a new aesthetic medium, the logical successor to an aesthetic that sees the increasingly evanescent as the most nearly satisfactory aesthetic expression of the desire to escape from what can be socially and publicly possessed.[11]

The restless search for an art that cannot become assimilable to social purpose locks Adorno into a series of laments for escapes that failed. The evanescent cannot be fleeting enough for the idea of evanescence not to survive the spent fireworks. And Adorno increasingly worries that the desire for the aesthetic, out of its determined resistance to society, is and produces behavior that is not merely asocial but antisocial.

The position that Adorno takes thus becomes remarkably similar to that of Burke in the *Enquiry,* with its suggestion that the aesthetic is a continual masking of social motivation. Although the sublime scenario may precipitate a consciousness of individuality, the feeling of difficulty overcome in sublime experience comes, for Adorno as for Burke, to look more like a socially determined notion of individuality than it does an individualism free of society. It becomes a matter of genre or fashion, a taste for individualism and distinction that is no less socially determined, no less socially oriented for taking itself to be individualistic. What is presented as resistance, or nature, rather than society, looks like an effort to represent opinion as neutral. And, as Barbara Herrnstein Smith puts the argument about nature and culture in her recent *Contingencies of Value,* "We have come to recognize that invocations of the "natural" are always ideologically loaded."[12]

If this generalization seems astute enough, it also is of a piece with a certain now current way of reading Kant. For what counts as ideological loading in this scheme is precisely Kant's interest in describing the "nature" of aesthetic experience and in emphasizing the importance of natural beauty in validating the beauty of art. From the standpoint of this account of Kant, the justification of art duplicitously relies upon an essentializing and universalizing gesture that imposes the particular views of some upon all, and art comes to be a version of political might in that it illegitimately extends the particular and contingent while contending that it does no harm, has no interest. This line of argument seems to me infinitely stronger in regard to Burke, where the empirical project is one of deriving sensory rules that have probability rather than of imagining the grounds of legitimacy for the rules (and thus converting them into laws of thought, as in the Kantian scheme). For Burke, that is, the senses work not only to conflate image-objects with thing-objects but also to naturalize society, by making equivalent sensory effects count equivalently, whether they are prompted by nature or art. Where Burke's *Enquiry* includes both artifacts and natural objects in its catalogue of experience both the beautiful and the sublime, however, Kant's Third Critique mingles the two sets of aesthetic objects only in the discussion of the beautiful and restricts the experience of sublimity exclusively to natural objects. (The nearest thing to an exception to this generalization is that Kant speaks of the possibility of beautiful paintings of sublime nature, establishing the possibility of sublime representations as a form of quotation from the experience of sublimity in nature.)

This division, moreover, does more than establish a distinction between nature and culture that stubbornly, and against all odds, refuses to collapse. For the division itself is made in the service of an argument about what it would mean for there to be an aesthetic judgment that might be free. If it is to be independent, it should not represent a merely empirical response, as a "judgment of sense," or "material aesthetical judgment" does (in, say, arguments about every individual's having a right to his or her "own" pleasures, however incomprehensible they might be to other people). The entire discussion of the nonprogressive character of art (and thus the unpredictability of genius) emphasizes this aspect of the "freedom" of aesthetic experience and its objects. Art's freedom, translated as the inability to predict in advance what one will be struck by and what one might strike other people with, distinguishes it from a social norm, a standard of human taste that might be empirically derived by consulting a wide variety of people.

To recall these aspects of the Kantian argument, the terms and conditions it sets for itself, is to see the importance of the formal argument for defeating the comparative judgments that are always operative in the social norm. The comparison between the testimony of one's own senses and the testimony of others', the comparison between one's own present experience and one's memory of the past, tend to make the representation of experience look like a hollowing out of that experience; the multiplication of experiences that would allow a process of mutual confirmation to occur produces representations that come increasingly to approximate the experiences and substitute for them (as in the case of the dog responding to sounds that exist only in anticipation). The Burkean project, moreover, suffered from another sort of problem of representation. In establishing his *Enquiry* as an ongoing comparative project in which all experience could be sorted into the category of the beautiful or of the sublime, Burke made categorization involve constructing identity as a form of alienated dependency, making a thing's empirical existence seem to rely on another thing with which it can be contrasted. The beautiful is beautiful only from not being sublime, and vice versa.

Now this recourse to the comparative judgment is both a recurrent and a plausible way of speaking in relation to aesthetic experience. Because aesthetic experiences do not occupy themselves exclusively with ontology, because they are not principally concerned with what Kant called the "existence of the object," the comparative provides a certain solution—or at least a serviceable substitute. As a matter of quantitative judgment (the more beautiful than *x,* the less sublime than *y*) and as judgments of likeness and difference (in the terms of the analogical reasoning that Derrida takes Kant to ground the Third Critique in or in the terms of the differential, antianalogical perspective that he himself proposes in *La vérité en peinture*), comparison shifts the issue from that of aesthetic *objects* to that of aesthetic *relationships* (and nonrelationships). Thus, instead of needing to argue that aesthetic objects exist in themselves in a transportable form, one can argue that they are by virtue of being environment-dependent. The field of comparison catalyzes the ur-object of aesthetic experience into an object. (Whether as a simple structuralist opposition between paired terms, or as the deconstructive refinement on them that knows how to oppose the material features of a text—its spacings between words, the spatial relationship it establishes between text and note—to such terms, the comparative argument has prevailed in aesthetic discussions.)

Given the prominence of the comparative argument, it should not be surprising that the aspect of the Kantian sublime that has received the most extensive treatment is the dynamical sublime (the portion of the sublime in which Kant employs the notion of resistance which Adorno later adapts). The dynamical sublime, that is, features an interlocking pair of comparisons with alternate outcomes, the first being an acknowledgment of natural might as greater than human might.

> Bold, overhanging, and as it were threatening rocks; clouds piled up in the sky, moving with lightning flashes and thunder peals; volcanoes in all their violence of destruction; hurricanes with their track of devastation; the boundless ocean in a state of tumult; the lofty waterfall of a mighty river, and such like—these exhibit our faculty of resistance as insignificantly small in comparison with their might.[13]

The second phase reverses the hierarchy:

> And so also the irresistibility of its might, while making us recognize our
> own [physical] impotence, considered as beings of nature, discloses to us
> a faculty of judging independently of and a superiority over nature, on
> which is based a kind of self-preservation entirely different from that which
> can be attacked and brought into danger by external nature.[101]

This latter phase, the one that enables the experience of the sublime to be
aesthetic rather than simply life threatening, recognizes the comparison between natural might and human might as inapplicable. "Bold, overhanging
and as it were threatening rocks" could, were they to fall on a human frame,
easily overcome its might, but the representation of the dire consequence
of the actual comparison between the human and the natural is treated as
an accomplishment. While the actual comparison between human and natural might involves a catastrophe from the human standpoint, the registration of potential force as just that, merely potential, shifts the terms of the
comparison to include the imagination of a potential state.

Kant's demurral "as it were" in describing the rocks as "threatening" is
less academic than pointed here. For his bracketing serves both to qualify
the personification and to underscore it. In so doing, it adumbrates the
underlying relationship between this discussion and that of the pleasures of
tragedy. Burke's argument—that a providential design arranges human beings
in such a way that sympathy continually supplies volunteer rescue workers
to deal with catastrophes—clearly becomes more than a little irrelevant when
one compares oneself, in strength and in vulnerability, to a rock rather than
to another person. The central issue becomes one less of voluntary or involuntary sympathy than of the recognition that no rock, however "bold,
overhanging, and as it were threatening" ever has potential power. The projection that enables Kant to speak of the rock's future or potential ability
to harm establishes an image of natural might in abeyance, or in other words,
a physicality in reserve.

If the question of mental reserve (or, mental reservation) underlies the
problematics of human theatrical representation (so that the truthfulness or
deceptiveness has nothing to do with what words get uttered), that is, the
Kantian sublime redirects aesthetic discussion by creating a natural theatrics
in which deceptiveness can scarcely be a relevant notion. For the possibility
of deceptiveness, presenting images of what one does not feel or believe,
here resolves itself to the mere notion of potentiality. A rock may not ever
tell the truth or a lie, may kill but never threaten persons. The potential
power of nature—all that one thinks of when one thinks of force that might
be released when existing elements were reconfigured—indeed becomes the
most important aspect of the personifying projection, not because a threat-

ening rock is seen to be acting like a threatening person but because the imagination of connection between actual and potential, present and future, is human rather than natural.

Natural objects figure prominently in the *Critique of Judgment,* first, because they introduce the question of what one is being pleased by in an act of aesthetic judgment. For Kant utility or inutility provide inappropriate lines of distinction, as do communicability and incommunicability—which is why Kant can verge on collapsing the pleasure in scientific concepts with the pleasure in aesthetic contemplation. The study of natural elements may provide knowledge that may be put to use, and this study must once have produced, incidentally, the kind of pleasure that Kant associates with "the discovery that two or more empirical heterogeneous laws of nature may be combined under one principle comprehending them both."

> We no longer find, it is true, any marked pleasure in the comprehensibility of nature and in the unity of its divisions into genera and species, by which all empirical concepts are possible, through which we cognize it according to its particular laws. But this pleasure has certainly been present at one time, and it is only because the commonest experience would be impossible without it that it is gradually confounded with mere cognition and no longer arrests particular attention.[24]

Aesthetic objects are not in and of themselves different from objects of cognition; the aesthetic domain contains no object that cannot be shared, as material, with the understanding or the reason. Rather, aesthetic objects are constituted not merely by a shift from seeing them in terms of properties to seeing them in terms of formal functions. It is that this formality can appear as an imitation of empirical objects, the empty or superfluous imitation of the look of function. If the pleasure of discovering connection between "two or more heterogeneous laws of nature" can initially be pleasurable because its function is not immediately apparent, the loss of aesthetic pleasure occurs as soon as this functionality looks so immediately apparent as to make empirical determination sufficient. (Thus, pure science, to the extent that it involves the notion of making discoveries that will be of later use, is itself for Kant as unaesthetic as the tool of some past civilization that has lost its identifiable function for its archaeologists. The aesthetic is not, thus, a system for storing or delaying use.)

The natural, as Kant deploys it in the Third Critique, is thus not a mechanism for borrowing the authority of reality. Instead, if human art involves a quotation or imitation of natural objects, natural beauty presents itself as a quotation from art, as speaking as if it knew prose. If the purposiveness of human art makes it appear open to manipulation, the appeal of natural beauty lies in its aping purpose, or in its reality being the reality of ven- triloquized purposiveness, a borrowed finality attributed to objects without memory and anticipation, without ends of their own. Now straightfor- wardly empiricist accounts of aesthetic pleasure analogize aesthetic judg- ments to cognitions, in that they imagine that recognizing an aesthetic ob- ject as an aesthetic object is largely a matter of understanding it as we would any object, with the conventions of fictionality added on or built in. And readings of Kant that accommodate his aesthetic argument to an essentially empirical one thus tend to speak of the notion of "purposiveness without purpose" as something like an identifiable trait that we could, with the aid of our conventions, locate in an aesthetic object. And, from that standpoint, it begins to seem possible to imagine works of art as the outrunning or mere avoidance of purpose, as Adorno continually suggests.

The account of reciprocal quotation that I am giving here involves the argument that aesthetic pleasure, in Kant's account, is neither purely social nor a direct escape from society. For Kant describes aesthetic pleasure in a way that links human art with natural beauty only by way of understanding natural beauty as if it were itself a human product. There can be art because there is nature, and there can be nature only because there is art.

Art's quotation of nature may make it look as though human beings, the makers of aesthetic objects, are engaged in the project of demonstrating that nature speaks to humans. Nature's quotation of art, its look of purposive- ness, may make it look as though humans speak to nature. Thus, Kant's examples of the aesthetic pleasures that were once available in biological classification[14] and in ancient astronomy[15] overlap with scientific cognition in a crucial deviation from Burkean empiricism. The "particular attention" of the aesthetic pleasure differs from "mere cognition" not by virtue of being a confused cognition, or a refusal of thought, or an insistence upon novelty per se. Rather, while habit, custom, and scientific progress make the inter- change between humans and nature look like a routine matter of translation (in which this tree can be assimilated to a humanly produced taxonomy), the aesthetic contemplation of nature produces itself as a consciousness of the fact of translation itself, the collision between the empirical and the for- mal accounts that makes aesthetic objects look almost like the objective equivalents of mental images.

The account I am giving of reciprocal quotation here demands to be dis- tinguished from a similar but, I think, crucially different, formulation. That is, it may seem equivalent to Ruskin's description of the "pathetic fallacy," which it clearly resembles in imagining communication between nature and persons. Where Ruskin describes, and debunks, the pathetic fallacy for casting natural objects as personae in dramas of feeling, however, the reciprocal quotation that I am identifying in Kant's account is singularly uninterested in empirical psychology. For it is singularly uninterested in emotions and in fantasizing that natural objects can feel an individual's feelings more thoroughly than any human can. It is, in other words, subjective but not psychological. Subjective, in that it "is conceived independently of any concept of the object," and so "can be nothing else than the state of mind, which is to be met with in the relation of our representative powers to each other, so far as they refer a given representation to *cognition in general*"(52). Not psychological, in that psychology from Kant's standpoint would reimport the more or less generalizable form of the personal and normative into aesthetic experience. (The entire Freudian and Lacanian projects thus take up a crucial Kantian challenge in arguing that the emotions can be made in a certain sense scientific, and that the unconscious is structured like a language, i.e., that even the psychological is not particular but generalizable and formalizable.)

The implicit psychologism of Ruskin's pathetic fallacy illuminates the difficulties that Kant was trying, I would argue, to resolve by segregating the beautiful from the sublime. The question of human beauty enters the Analytic of the Beautiful, in section 17, toward the end of Kant's discussion of beauty, but its complexity is apparent only from the retrospective position of the sublime's exclusion of human experience. For if natural beauty is free in escaping any definite concept or purpose, that humans can and do look beautiful to one another complicates the beautiful immeasurably. The beautiful continually labors under the fact that humans cannot help looking purposeful rather than purposive to one another. Moreover, from Kant's standpoint, they cannot help looking purposive to one another because they are. "The only being which has the purpose of its existence in itself is *man*, who can determine his purposes by reason; or, where he must receive them from external perception, yet can compare them with essential and universal purposes and can judge this their accordance aesthetically"(69–70). That is, the beautiful may be an arena of experience in which one can appreciate art that looks like nature because nature looks like art, but that reciprocal movement between purpose and purposiveness (what has human purpose and what merely looks, to our eyes, as if it did) founders upon a conflict that arises from the very similarity between persons. Persons, that is, not only appear purposive, but are; and the aesthetic judgment that attributes purposiveness thus establishes a new contradiction between the purposes that persons actually have and the ones that they come to possess by the process of ascription. Human beauty vitiates the aesthetic judgment because human beings have purpose rather than the mere illusion of purpose.

With the introduction of the human figure as an object of aesthetic pleasure, then, Kant suggests the problems that human beauty poses for the aesthetic judgment. If nature can only look beautiful by looking as purposely and deliberately produced as if it were art, human beauty, looking natural to look beautiful, continually invites not sympathetic identification but an identity by attribution, an ascription of purposiveness in excess of the actual purposes that the human continually sets. For human beauty continually threatens to collapse beauty and sociability, the power to and desire for communicating one's state of mind that Kant had earlier identified as insufficient for grounding the aesthetic judgment. The beauty of the human figure is always, in Kant's terms, adherent, because people cannot stop having purposes. Thus, it is not enough to explain the aesthetic experience as a particular way of looking at an object, because human beauty can never be made free, can never be detached from the imperative that it remain bound to human purposes:

> We could adorn a figure with all kinds of spirals and light but regular lines, as the New Zealanders do with their tattooing, if only it were not the figure of a human being. And again this could have much finer features and a more pleasing and gentle cast of countenance provided it were not intended to represent a man, much less a warrior.[66]

This is more than an ethnocentric remark. Kant here employs the example of the human figure tattooed, that is, used as a ground for abstract design to acknowledge that it occurs, to suggest that it is wrong, and to suggest why. It is wrong, he would say, in that it produces an impersonation of purposelessness in the human figure—in ways that correspond to Bourdieu's and Smith's claims that Kantian aesthetics are always the empirical masquerading as the ideal and disinterested. To tattoo the body is to make the body impersonate purposelessness in much the way that the actor so conspicuous in Burke's account and so conspicuously absent in Kant's impersonates fictitious motivation—not merely as if it were his or her own but as if a fictitious motivation could actually overcome his or her own.

Where Kant will later speak of the sublime as an occasion in which "humanity" can act "in our person" (and remain unhumiliated in the face of the might of nature in the dynamical sublime), in section 17 of the Analytic of the Beautiful he presents two distinct accounts of the way the form of a person might be taken to represent humanity—in terms of the physical presentation of an idea of what humans in general look like, and in terms of an allegorical use of the physical presentation of human form to suggest a moral ideal. The aesthetic *normal idea* of the human might make the human figure become representative, in that the shape of individual humans might be averaged into a collective idea of what humans look like. The normal idea of the beautiful can be arrived at for humans as a version of concrete generalization; one can come at an aesthetic norm for humans, as for other "animals of a particular race," on the basis of experience.

> We must remark that, in a way quite incomprehensible by us, the imagination cannot only recall on occasion the signs for concepts long past, but can also reproduce the image of the figure of the object out of an unspeakable number of objects of different kinds or even of the same kind. Further, if the mind is concerned with comparisons, the imagination can, in all probability, actually, though unconsciously, let one image glide into another; and thus, by the concurrence of several of the same kind, come by an average, which serves as the common measure of all.[70]

Kant's effort, in essence, appears to be to imagine a norm for human beauty that will be a standard for the objects of human beauty just as Hume had searched for an empirical standard of taste in the judgments of beauty. We are interested here, however, not merely in his hypothesis that one might arrive at an empirically derived norm for pleasurable objects but also his account of the procedure for producing it.

> Everyone has seen a thousand full-grown men. Now if you wish to judge of their normal size, estimating it by means of comparison, the imagination (as I think) allows a great number of images (perhaps the whole thousand) to fall on one another. If I am allowed to apply here the analogy of optical presentation, it is in the space where most of them are combined and inside the contour, where the place is illuminated with the most vivid colors, that the *average size* is cognizable, which, both in height and breadth, is equally far removed from the extreme bounds of the greatest and smallest stature. And this is the stature of a beautiful man.[70–71]

The process of averaging involves differences of color, on the most rudimentary level, in allowing for different empirical conditions: "Thus necessarily under these empirical conditions a Negro must have a different normal idea of the beauty of the [human figure] from a white man, a Chinaman a different normal idea from a European, etc."(71). Differences in the colors of the human figure as an object of sight become, however, less important than differences in the colors produced by the imagination, which acts in this account as an optical averager, stacking individual figures as if "to fall on one another" to produce contour by way of color. The average size of a beautiful man becomes, that is, the concentration of color (with the elimination of the afterimages or halo effect of the extreme bounds of individual deviation, or the individually characteristic).

The "contour, where the place is illuminated with the most vivid colors"(71) is the imagination's version of abstraction, producing normality out of individuality, and producing it, moreover, not as the attenuation of color but as the intensification of color achieved by overlapping images. The color is the form. In that sense, the aesthetical *normal idea* seems to distinguish itself from the notion of color that Kant has introduced earlier—as being, with tone, an appendage that lends charm but is itself too thoroughly bound to the immediately sensory to lend itself to aesthetic representation. Color has, that is, entered as a potential enhancement of line and figure, to make the form "more clearly, definitely, and completely intuitable"[61].

Now the depreciation of color (and tone) in Kant's discussion has seemed to Jacques Derrida, in his influential reading of Kant in *The Truth in Painting*, to attempt a suppression of the heterogeneity of aesthetic experience. This heterogeneity, through which the aesthetic object or the signifier can please or signify not by escaping its materiality but by mobilizing it, seems from Derrida's perspective ultimately to be the target of Kant's attack on heteronomous taste. The autonomy of taste would correspond to an autonomous object which would be like a sign that did not recognize its complete implication in the materiality of the signifier, which continually reimports other, and alien, contexts because the "same" word can, with the same material, move along tracks and into contexts that are radically different from one another.

The subordination of color to line, in this reading, becomes isomorphous with the Kantian tendency to define works of art in ways that privilege the essential over the accidental, the work "itself" over what is a parergon— decoration, stuff around the real work of art, like a frame around a painting and gilding on that frame.[16] The hierarchy of line and color thus reinforces Kant's maintenance of a traditional hierarchy between form and matter. And in determined quotation of Kant to preserve the form of Kant's statements as a resolute challenge to such a notion of hierarchy, Derrida seeks to elide that difference much as he elsewhere elides the use-mention distinction of analytic philosophy, which identifies the difference between an utterance made to indicate one's views and a quotation of that kind of utterance. Citationality, or iterability, for Derrida reaffirms the material claim as an assertion of the persistence of signifiers that continually leave themselves open to redeployment. The notion of color here is a crucial target for this argument in that it has seemed just barely material. Like the text that seems more central by virtue of having blank margins and bands of footnotes surrounding it and underlining it, color seems to count only as an adjunct of something else.

More traditional philosophical commentators have seen Kant's discussion of color as linked—in a rather cryptic way—to the Lockean doctrine of primary and secondary properties of objects, or have linked it with Kant's First Critique and his attempt there to ground perception in uniform representational structures rather than those that, like color perception and tonal sensitivity, are haunted by continual reminders of their fallibility, in the form of color blindness and tone deafness. With Kant's discussion of the imagination's attempt to come at an aesthetic norm, however, neither an account of the properties essential to the object nor an account of the fit or lack of fit between objects and the human senses seems to be at stake. For Kant's description of the aesthetical norm is one that is not committed to empirical accuracy. That is, while begun empirically—"everyone has seen a thousand full-grown men"—it has produced a standard that, despite its empirical origins, is counterfactual, in that it corresponds to no individual.

> It contains nothing specifically characteristic, for otherwise it would not be the *normal idea* for the race. Its presentation pleases, not by its beauty, but merely because it contradicts no condition, under which alone a thing of this kind can be beautiful.[72]

This way of understanding the operation of the imagination in producing an aesthetical norm, in fact, would seem to satisfy precisely the claims about the parergonal, the auxiliary and ancillary, that Derrida is making. While it has begun with a cognition, an understanding of what counts as a man, it has moved to a noncognitive image that is formed by color. It is an ideal produced, not by a repudiation of sense, but by sense.

On the one hand, Kant raises the possibility of imaginative averaging to suggest the way in which aesthetic agreement might occur. The kind of coincidence among the thousand images within one person's imagination might be the basis for an argument about a similar coincidence between one individual's norm and those of another thousand persons. On the other hand, he opposes this *normal idea* to the *ideal,* "which latter, on grounds [of human purpose] already alleged, we can only expect in the *human* figure." This ideal "consists in the expression of the *moral,* without which the object would not please universally and thus positively," and although we derive from experience the "visible expression of moral ideas that rule men inwardly"(72), the moral ideal overwhelms the sensible.

The Analytic of the Beautiful thus moves toward the apparent impossi-

bility of grounding aesthetic judgments. For the entrance of the human figure has, while appearing to represent multiple solutions, exhausted three
potential arguments about the way human products may elicit human pleasure that is more than merely sensory. First, the idea of the beauty of human
form might have, in Burkean fashion, shored up an argument from Providence: God, wanting us to want society, created beauty as a principle of
motivation that would draw humans toward one another when all other
motives ceased to suffice. Moreover, the beauty of the human form potentially suggests two different forms of resemblance—the resemblance that can
be seen between one human and another (that is emphasized in the notion
of the aesthetical *normal idea*) and the resemblance between the inward and
the outward in giving "visible expression of moral ideas that rule men inwardly," in making the connection "with all which our reason unites with
the morally good . . . visible as it were in bodily manifestation"(72). Having
laid out what would seem to be the constitutive elements of aesthetic judgment, however, Kant registers extreme dissatisfaction. The presentation of
the *normal idea* "pleases, not by its beauty, but merely because it contradicts
no condition, under which alone a thing of this kind can be beautiful. *The
presentation is merely correct*"(72). However empirical its origins, the normal
image has created an unavailable model (like that of a family with 2.3 children), unable to correspond with the particular shape of anyone's experience, much less pleasurable experience. The average fails to represent, because it can represent only negatively, by not interfering with anyone's
individual representation. It is "merely correct," not beautiful. And it is correct in that it can replicate only what has already been imaged and produce
images within the bounded range of earlier images. (At this point one sees
the importance of the materialist argument to Derrida's insistence upon what
is "*toujours déjà*" and how a difference in the approach to materialism leads
Kant and Derrida to very different accounts of the place of novelty, which
looks to Kant like a by-product of construction that is beyond the boundaries of previously empirically available images and which looks to Derrida
like an effort to establish a notion of originariness.)

The presentation of moral ideals in beauty is, likewise, no help. For it
also represents only negatively, because it cannot be a "mere judgment of
taste." More than "merely correct," it represents a notion of averaging from
a different perspective, in that it hypothesizes that in an aesthetic image one
can simply combine in an average the respective claims of the material and
the ideal. The demands of "such an ideal of beauty" (72) ultimately even-
tuate in its failure ever to "be purely aesthetical," moreover, because its exclusion of sensible charm pushes it toward a pure iconography, the stipulation of patterns of association between specific virtues and specific images.

The Analytic of the Beautiful, I am suggesting, founders as soon as Kant takes up human beauty in an attempt to understand how the human body might be, in Wittgenstein's phrase, the best picture of the human soul. And this is the case because Kant is granting rather than summarily dismissing Burke's claim about the importance of the body as both perceiving pleasurable sensation and representing purposes:

> It is also not to be denied that all representations in us, whether, objectively viewed, they are merely sensible or are quite intellectual, may yet subjectively be united to gratification or grief, however imperceptible either may be, because they all affect the feeling of life, and none of them, so far as it is a modification of the subject, can be indifferent. And so, as Epicurus maintained, all *gratification* or *grief* may ultimately be corporeal. . . .[119]

The ultimate objection to Burkean empirical psychology, from Kant's standpoint, is that it continually uses the body to make motion and motive look equivalent, to make it appear that all corporeal modifications of the subject are, by virtue of being motion, equivalent evidence of purposive action. The body is the location in which causes and effects look alike, so that a purposive action and a response to someone else's action look alike.

This conflation between cause and effect that the Burkean account registers means that the kind of collapse between individuals and society that we earlier described in the *Enquiry* continually arises. The sublime, in this account, may provide the sensation of individuality, the sensation of labor, without being able to distinguish itself from someone else's individuality, someone else's action. Moreover, bodily modification in the Burkean account leaves all social interaction seeming like an act of assault (that only boredom can protect one from), since response is less an act of exchange than a matter of one's being acted upon.

This is to say that Kant finds particular problems when he addresses the human body, not because it has too little meaning but because it has too much. It cannot, from the aesthetic standpoint, be the best picture of the human soul, not because it yields no picture of the human soul, but because it cannot stop producing pictures that are hopelessly mixed. The body, always representing intentions as actions, would appear always to commit aesthetic representation of bodies to the dilemmas of theatricality—where the production of drama continually relies on the way in which equivalent representations can absorb differing intentions and conflate intentions and effects.

It is in the light of Kant's dissatisfaction with all empiricist efforts to base aesthetics on the human body that we must understand the restriction of the Analytic of the Sublime to natural objects. Although Burke's model of aesthetic experience as formal contagion or transfer is one that he, and we, can distinguish from mere deception or bad contract, it continually makes the ability to communicate aesthetic pleasure look identical with aesthetic pleasure. The communication of aesthetic pleasure is thus converted from evidence of pleasure into its origin and end point, so that it seems as if there could be no pleasure if it were not communicated. For what is essentially wrong with the empiricist account from Kant's standpoint is that it continually makes aesthetics based on the human body a matter of avoiding the potential privacy of sensation by falling into a different trap, that of inferring my pleasure from your response. In separating his own arguments from empiricist aesthetics, thus, Kant is employing natural objects in much the same way that Rousseau uses objects in general in *Emile,* for their immobility, for their not coming when one calls and adjusting themselves in relation to an individual. Their unavailability recommends them.

Thus, while the Analytic of the Beautiful revolves around both natural beauty and artifacts, the restriction of the Analytic of the Sublime exclusively to natural objects underwrites even the beauty of the beautiful, first by making it seem that beauty can be distinguished from ingratiation (someone's— or something's—presenting itself, like one of Burke's dogs, for attention and favor), and second by making it seem that aesthetic pleasure can operate without society, without, that is, itself being the instrument by which people ingratiate themselves to one another. The solitude that Kant constructs in his account of the sublime is, then, not just incidentally or embarrassingly escapist. Instead, it supplies a moment in which the conversation or communication between persons and objects can take place as a respite from the din of excessive purposiveness that occurs with the beautiful and especially with the beautiful human form. (The Derridean critique of Jacques Lacan as illegitimately appropriating a claim to truth suggests the relevance of this aesthetic conflict between the formal and the empirical for psychoanalysis. The analyst's formal mobilization of the language of the unconscious to produce a story that patients are incapable of producing in the form of testimony about their own situations replicates the problematic of the beautiful human form. A paradigmatic example here would be Freud's "A Child Is Being Beaten," with its pattern of memory by ascription; whereas having a memory of something has in many accounts seemed to identify the boundaries of the self, psychological formalization both supplements and undermines the testimony of the actual remembering subjects by producing memory equivalents.)

Nature becomes the model for art, then, not to naturalize art or make it look like nature, but rather to insist that aesthetic pleasure does not properly revolve around a manipulatable skill—being good at taking the averages of sizes of beautiful men or being well schooled in the socially stipulated connections between certain virtues and certain physical expressions. And in the service of this point, Kant offers an example of the same form having two very distinct effects:

> The song of birds proclaims gladsomeness and contentment with existence. At least so we interpret nature, whether it have this design or not. But the interest which we here take in beauty has only to do with the beauty of nature; it vanishes altogether as soon as we notice that we are deceived and that it is only art—vanishes so completely that taste can no longer find the thing beautiful or sight find it charming. What is more highly praised by poets than the bewitching and beautiful note of the nightingale in a lonely copse on a still summer evening by the soft light of the moon? And yet we have instances of a merry host, where no such songster is to be found, deceiving to their great contentment the guests who were staying with him to enjoy the country air by hiding in a bush a mischievous boy who knew how to produce this sound exactly like nature (by means of a reed or a tube in his mouth). But as soon as we are aware that it is a cheat, no one will remain long listening to the song which before was counted so charming. . . . It must be nature or be regarded as nature if we are to take an immediate interest in the beautiful as such . . .[144–45]

If all the material elements of the song remain the same, what difference does the deception make? The song remains the same; the sole thing changing is the ambivalent understanding of the status of its material identity. The birdsong can yield pleasure in the intentionlessness of its production because it cannot, by definition, involve questions of agreement. Thus, Kant relaunches his aesthetic attack on the notion of agreement. The agreement between an imitation and its original clearly has no place in this account. The boy's imitation loses its charm when it is perceived to be an imitation, and the bird's song is pleasurable only when there is no indication of what it might be an imitation of. Similarly, and as a corollary to this former suspension of imitative agreement, agreement between persons is suspended as an aesthetic claim. Agreement becomes an irrelevant or empty notion as soon as it becomes impossible to establish a correlation between an originary intentionality and the song. However great a consensus persons may achieve about their common pleasure in the same objects, the quantity and intensity of their responses cannot translate into any meaningful agreement about what they are agreeing about.

From one standpoint, it may seem that Kant's emphasis on natural beauty converts aesthetic experience into pure narcissism, as subjectivity that does not brook contradiction and therefore contents itself with experiences that take themselves to be unfalsifiable merely because they happen to be un-falsified (as Kant's qualification of "it must be nature" with "or regarded as nature" suggests). And on this account the aesthetic is identical with a fear of deception, a fear of mistakenness, which accompanies a principled mis-anthropy, the conviction that all empirical persons are themselves funda-mentally mistaken. Thus, although "empirically the beautiful interests only in society"(139), the aesthetic trajectory toward sublimity seems to start sub-stituting abstract persons for empirical ones.

> There is indeed a misanthropy (very improperly so called), the tendency to which frequently appears with old age in many right-thinking men, which is philanthropic enough as far as *good will* to men is concerned, but which, through long and sad experience, is far removed from *satisfaction* with men. Evidence of this is afforded by the propensity to solitude, the fantastic wish for a secluded country seat, or (in the case of young persons) by the dream of the happiness of passing one's life with a little family upon some island unknown to the rest of the world, a dream of which storytellers or writers of Robinsonades know how to make good use.[117]

Robinsonades, in this passage, provide empirical evidence of a psychological tendency that is exactly congruent with a host of eighteenth-century attacks on the romance as both unreal and antisocial. Yet, far from merely rejecting these "fantastic" wishes for being fantastic, Kant suggests ways in which the story of the deficiencies of humans can itself be both accurate and fatally deficient. For it takes an imagination of solitude as a cure for society and converts that into the means by which storytellers and writers can contin-ually work on their readers, exploiting the "beautiful observations" of "em-pirical psychology."

But, to rotate the example of the "mischievous boy" somewhat, why isn't it possible to take the song as especially charming because the boy who intended to deceive produced something more appealing than he knew? In such a hypothetical account, the image of the trickster who is himself de-ceived would serve as the distributive justice of the system of artistic de-ception. The material identity of the sounds that the auditors had greeted with alternate pleasure and displeasure would be no more help to him than to them. Just as their pleasure in terms of a formal account disappeared in the face of the pressure of an empirical account, so his pleasure in having pulled off a trick would be nullified by its subsumption in their formal ac-count.

The boy's deception, in other words, would turn out to be the auditors' irony. In that reading, the example would be absolutely of a piece with the terms of distinguished identities that we have come to associate with Romantic formalism. For irony, ambiguity, and allegory, all versions of having said more than one thing with one and the same material, emphasize material identities that are continually distinguished. Burke's theater-based account of aesthetic imitation suggested that a lie could only appear as a low-intensity truth (in a version of the Hobbesian description of memory as decaying sense), because the performance even of an action that one did not mean carried a bodily commitment with it that made it tell some version of the truth. One must mean what one says because the lie can only succeed by its material resemblance to the truth it would compete with and supplant, and for Burke the material resemblance begins producing its own content. Kantian constructionism is less material not merely on account of its idealism but on account of its attempt to understand the claims of artistic novelty as a way of displacing the question of artistic deception. For if the point of Kant's discussion of the aesthetic norm is to demonstrate the inadequacy of the optical averaging that material impressions can generate, an additional point to be made is that the sublime provides the model for pleasure that cannot be lied about—not because one can't lie about natural objects but because it becomes hard to apply the language of truthfulness and deception to pleasurable sensations that are only indirectly tied to empirical experience. (Explorers may come home with Othello-like stories that testify to strange creatures elsewhere, but the Kantian sublime emphasizes not such improbable possibilities but rather the altogether nonempirical.)

The two versions of the sublime, the mathematical and the dynamical, then, operate in ways that look strikingly formal and formalized, because nature can speak only in such an uncolloquial idiom. The mathematical enters in the first place as a particularly clear-cut example of the application of a human schema to the natural sphere, and of the way in which the schema comes to extend beyond the application. The link between objects in nature and number thus produces the notion of connection between number (which is, in itself, without reference) and intuition, and the conflict between reason and understanding that Kant sees the mathematical sublime producing is one that emerges from the persistent attempt to keep intuition coordinated with number. "Nature is . . . sublime in those of its phenomena whose intuition brings with it the idea of its infinity," not because it is infinite but because "it makes us judge as *sublime*, not so much the object, as our own state of mind in the estimation of it"(94).

The mathematical sublime, that is, uses the coordination of number with intuitable objects to project the numerical scheme past intuition, so that the representation clearly exceeds its object. Although the "logical estimation of magnitude goes on without hindrance to infinity," the movement from intuition to the unintuitable becomes a self-reflexive conflict when Kant introduces reason's demand for "comprehension in *one* intuition, and so that [joint] *presentation* of all these members of a progressively increasing series"(93). (This is form demanding empirical representation.)

The imagination that had, with, say, the beautiful superimposition of images to achieve an average where the colors were most intense, here operates to produce an extension of images past the point of intuitive comprehension. Yet because the reason's effort at comprehension in *one* intuition "renders it unavoidable to think the infinite . . . as *entirely given*"(93), the mathematical sublime presents itself as a conflict between infinite multiplicity and absolute unity. The mathematical, that is, while it could conceivably be deployed for the purposes of illustrating regularity of intervals or some notion of progression, serves to illustrate a conflict within the faculties in the capacity to represent things at all. For the mathematical continues the production of similarity, going on from one unit to another larger unit, until the expansion of units becomes, not measure, but measurelessness.

Whether as counting (in the sense of taking an inventory) or as measuring, the mathematical could make the sublime appear to be an extension of the empirical (as it is in Neil Hertz's), and the production of the infinite out of the finite series would be a version of empirical psychology analogous to Burke's. In answer to the question, how does the finite turn into the infinite, one can testify to individual affect, the empirical testimony of subjective response. In either Thomas Weiskel's casting of the mathematical sublime as an Oedipal drama designed to make the reason struggle to subdue the imagination so as to produce a sense of an empowered self or in Hertz's critique of it, the self is a by-product of a desire for control. And from this perspective, the sublime seems designed to stage the illusion of control and thus the illusion that one can have a self, if only temporarily. The self, always wanting to be a self, gets to remedy its own sense of deficiency in setting a limit between the finite and the infinite.

These very powerful psychological accounts claim the priority of apprehension over comprehension, so that the notion of continuing the series has standing, while the idea of comprehension, apprehending its elements as a unity, does not. That is, what for Hertz and Weiskel looks like a moment of forcing, of imposing a pattern. And one would be willing to grant the justice as well as the appeal of their accounts were it not that they essentially recast Kant in empiricist terms, so that the infinite seems like the next stage up from the size or number that one can comfortably comprehend.

Where Weiskel and Hertz present a continuum that is only interrupted and given shape by analogizing the experience of objects—conceived as including even such an abstract system as mathematics—to the psychological experience of other persons, however, Kant's description almost determinedly excludes such an analogy as it proceeds from an objective account of the representation and the subjective movement:

> The measurement of a space (regarded as apprehension) is at the same time a description of it, and thus an objective movement in the act of imagination and a progress. On the other hand, the comprehension of the manifold in the unity—not of thought but of intuition—and consequently the comprehension of the successively apprehended [elements] in one glance is a regress which annihilates the condition of time in this progress of the imagination and makes *coexistence* intuitible.[98]

In such a description Kant has shifted the notion of representation from one that centers on likeness (in terms of continuing in a series) to one that insists upon the convergence of that onward movement with its opposite (the series as a unity). That is, he has shifted the aesthetic discussion from the question of mimesis in claiming that aesthetic representation does not involve a process of making persons look like other persons or, indeed, of making objects look like persons. Instead, he has established aesthetic representation as an impossible identity that makes the finite and the infinite impersonate one another, as the more empirical and more formal versions of each other. (A series pursued becomes its own contradiction; material reissued becomes its own irony.) Moreover, this account of sublime representation indicates how thoroughly Kant is here repudiating the hypothetical arguments for standards of beauty derived from empirical grounds. If he earlier rejected the aesthetical norm for the beautiful human figure, as producing an empirical average that will never coincide with any actual beautiful human, the point of the mathematical formalization is to project the infinite as the opposite to an aesthetic norm, which makes the perception of novelty look like a mere process of recombining already perceived and imaged objects.

Now there is little in Kantian aesthetics particularly and in Romantic aesthetics generally that has been more violently embraced and rejected than the insistence upon unity that Kant invokes with the mathematical sublime. On the one hand, such an account of unity has seemed to call for a specific artistic practice, one committed to substituting an organic, and thus self-motivating and self-completing, object for the dramatic notion of motive in the imitation of an action. In the artistic practice that we call Romantic, this notion of organic unity has seemed to call for a series of self-delusions that involved a mystification of making, as if by calling oneself a genius one could achieve a blissful schizophrenia in which one could imagine that one's own production was one's own accident.

The deconstructive critique of the application of Kant has taken as its central terms the impossibility of establishing either such a unified work of art or a unitary self, of which the Romantic genius, always made rather than making, is the exemplary instance. Were the Kantian description of the unity involved in the mathematical sublime a unity ever discernible in empirical terms, either in actual artistic products or in actual persons, this critique would be absolutely disabling for the claims of aesthetics to be anything other than a version of psychology, conceived of as the greater exercise or greater quiescence of the individual will. Thus, even though Paul de Man conspicuously distanced himself from psychoanalytic accounts and Jacques Derrida has criticized psychoanalysis in general and Lacanian psychoanalysis in particular for continually supplying a systematic unity, their analyses are likewise haunted by the notion of motivation that seems never quite to be expunged. In Derrida's splendid opening to *"Parergon,"* for instance, the elements of the systematic unity of everyday academic and nonacademic life find rearrangement, as if the separation of elements enabled one to see their true contingency. The constructedness of every construction that appears systematic seems continually, like Nietzsche's account of grammar, to reintroduce metaphysics.

From this standpoint, Kant's resorting to the sublime looks like a movement in precisely the wrong direction. The sublime can seem like an attenuation of all that attracts the eye and a subordination of the claims of the imagination to those of abstract reason. Yet one extremely peculiar thing about Kant's handling of the sublime deserves mention here. The Analytic of the Sublime, despite its exploration of the representation of formlessness, is, by explicit contrast to the Analytic of the Beautiful, virtually teeming with specific examples. Moreover, the examples frequently appear as successful versions of precisely the thing that was found deficient in the Analytic of the Beautiful. The Analytic of the Sublime, for instance, can give an aesthetical ideal of a man:

> . . . For what is that which is, even to the savage, an object of the greatest admiration? It is a man who shrinks from nothing, who fears nothing, and therefore does not yield to danger, but rather goes to face it vigorously with the most complete deliberation. Even in the most highly civilized state this peculiar veneration for the soldier remains, though under the condition

that he exhibit all the virtues of peace, gentleness, compassion, and even a
becoming care for his own person. . . .[102]

Indeed, even the kinds of stipulated connection that Kant had rejected in
the Analytic of the Beautiful as going beyond the aesthetical and merely
grafting ideas to images reemerge as valid in the Analytic of the Sublime.

> The charms in beautiful nature, which are so often found, as it were, fused
> with beautiful forms, may be referred to modifications either of light (colors)
> or of sound (tones). For these are the only sensations that imply, not merely
> a sensible feeling, but also reflection upon the form of these modifications
> of sense; and thus they involve in themselves as it were a language by which
> nature speaks to us, which thus seems to have a higher sense. Thus the
> white color of lilies seems to determine the mind to ideas of innocence;
> and the seven colors, in order from the red to the violet, seem to suggest
> the ideas of (1) sublimity, (2) intrepidity, (3) candor, (4) friendliness, (5)
> modesty, (6) constancy, (7) tenderness.[144]

The set of associations between specific colors and specific virtues could be
seen as one as personal as that of Vladimir Nabokov's set of associations
between specific colors and specific letters of the alphabet. Or, it might,
instead, be seen as a mark of the extraordinary incursions of cultural agreement—that accommodates even the most material aspects of experience to
representative ideas. In Kant's handling, however, it immediately precedes
the discussion of the manufactured birdsong, the sound of which is pleasing
until one discovers that it "is only art," an art which cannot please for the
sole reason that it meant to please.

Nature and art here similarly have colors. They may even have the same
colors, in that the eye might never be able to discern the difference between
a naturally and an artificially produced color. Kant's earlier remarks about
the ways in which colors appeal to the sensory and therefore the private are
here revised into an argument about the meaningfulness of seeing colors as
significant if one imagines them in terms of a prism splitting the whiteness
of light. But, as the example from the same paragraph suggests, this reading
depends upon distinguishing a color from a color—green, for instance—on
the basis of its production.

> A mere color, e.g. the green of a grass plot, a mere tone (as distinguished
> from sound and noise), like that of a violin, are by most people described
> as beautiful in themselves, although both seem to have at their basis merely
> the matter of representations, viz. simply sensation, and therefore only de-
> serve to be called pleasant. But we must at the same time remark that the

> sensations of colors and of tone have a right to be regarded as beautiful
> only in so far as they are *pure*.[59]

Kant's gloss on this notion of pure color involves rehearsing Leonhard Euler's hypothesis that "colors are isochronous vibrations (*pulsus*) of the ether, as sounds are of the air in a state of disturbance"(60) and raising the possibility that the mind perceives not only the sensation of color and tone but also the regularity of the pulses. Yet he lays out this account only to doubt that sensation builds such order into itself and to offer a definition of purity that is distinctly tautological. "But 'pure' in a simple mode of sensation means that its uniformity is troubled and interrupted by no foreign sensation, and it belongs merely to the form"(60). Yet if it seems only like an unpacking of the definition of "pure" to say that it is "unmixed," or that "its uniformity is troubled and interrupted by no foreign sensation," Kant's distinction between pure and composite color is crucial. It is crucial, moreover, for enabling him to insist upon an identity between form and sensation, and to suggest that such an identity is the basis for aesthetic pleasure.

For Kant has argued from the claim that "pure" color produces a "mode of sensation" that "belongs merely to the form" to a claim about the way the judgment operates on "pure" and "mixed" colors. "Hence all simple colors, so far as they are pure, are regarded as beautiful; composite colors have not this advantage because, as they are not simple, we have no standard for judging whether they should be called pure or not"(60). The distinction seems to be this: pure color is a color that one may derive by analysis; mixed color is a color that is composed, created by a process of adding color to color.

Color suffers, that is, as soon as it is thought of as if one could make an induction from one's experience of color. For, on Kant's account, the attempt to imagine a standard for beautiful color as an induction from the experience of color is as inadequate as the attempt to imagine a standard, an aesthetical norm, for a beautiful human body. The beauty that can be produced is not any less beautiful on account of its being produced; pure color can be produced by dividing white light with a prism. Color is, however, less beautiful as soon as the color becomes inductive, as soon, that is, as it becomes subject to the descriptions of empirical induction, that can provide a social history of taste but not a justification of aesthetic judgment.

We may see in Kant's discussion of color, then, a culmination of his attack on the adequacy of empiricist accounts of aesthetics in the peculiar notion of pitting two versions of the same color against one another. For the notion of a composite color here does not involve its looking different from a simple color. Rather, it looks exactly the same, or else there would be no occasion for worrying "whether they should be called pure or not." Thus, a color produced by a prism could be matched by a color produced by mixing paints so that the two colors looked identical to the naked eye. Color can be made to resemble color, just as a human being (by means of a reed or a tube) can make a song that resembles birdsong.

On the level of color, however, the argument from deception begins to look more than a little strained. The example of the boy fabricating birdsongs involves his passing himself off as an object that can be intentional by virtue of being itself intentionless, but the distinction between pure color and its counterfeit is harder to draw. For the very tendency of empiricism to relegate color to a secondary property, something one could not rely on to establish any cognition of an object, registers the sense that color may represent a mismatch between the organs of perception and their objects. The etymological connection between *color* and *celare*, to hide, conflates manifestation and concealment, as if to emphasize a fundamental tension between the ways in which physical bodies exert an action on white light to have their color and the ways in which color is an effect on the eye. Indeed, such a tension about whether color was in light or in objects or in the eye reached its apogee in Goethe's *Theory of Colours* of 1810, which insisted that color was continually produced not as transmission but as opposition. (Thus, he could claim both that "every decided colour does a certain violence to the eye, and forces the organ to opposition" and also that one's present sense of color is an oppositional response to the eye's memory of an earlier color. Similarly, color finds description as a mark of the opposition between things and their backgrounds.)[17]

On the matter of color Kant makes a minor but, I think, important adjustment. Between the First Critique and the Third, he shifts his example of choice for color. Where it was cinnabar or red in the First Critique, it becomes green for the Third. One could hypothesize many justifications for the change. This shift might merely be in consonance with the insistence upon natural beauty as the centerpiece in an argument for the freedom of aesthetic judgment. One could hazard the allegorical observation that green may be nature's color in a treatise devoted to naturalizing judgment. Moreover, in Kant's association of the spectral colors, green is friendliness; and the notion of nature's seeming to speak to us could, thus, seem to be bound up in the friendliness of that green.

On the other hand, the shift from red to green might merely register a way of defining the aesthetic as a recuperation of the errancy of perception. Thus, the red that red-green color blindness might convert to green would be less a mistake than an indication of a noncommunicable perception that had its justification in pleasure. Green might then make pleasure the sensory version of opposition to society; to take pleasure in a green that is a red would make sensation itself a version of individuality that imagined its privacy as an opposition to communication.

There is, however, another account of green that seems to me to explain its place in Kant's aesthetics. The primary colors for painting are red, yellow, and blue, so that green always appears as a mixed color. The primary colors for optics are red, green, and blue, so that green appears as an unmixed or pure color. Green, thus, emerges as the only primary color that is mixed on one account and pure on the other. The significance of this pivotal position lies in this—that, precisely by differing from one descriptive system to another, this self-resembling point of color becomes the means for moving between one system and another. The incommensurability of the two systems becomes apparent in green—not, however, to underscore the empiricist claim for the nontransmissibility of color but to insist that there is a version of green that justifies the mixed green of painters and works of art. Green, as a mixed color, is no more satisfactory than the birdsong that could be real but is feigned, not merely because it raises questions of deception and the inequality between one person's skill and another's but also because it imitates the wrong thing. Continually taking the greens of experience, it comes up with the notion of mixed color as an equivalent to the mixed form of the stereotype (that was discoverable by color) in Kant's discussion of the norm of the beautiful human figure.

This account of Kant's treatment of color confirms one central aspect of Derrida's account of Kant in *La vérité en peinture*—that Kant's epistemology and his aesthetics are continually interrelated. Yet Derrida would stress that Kant's "fundamental humanism" ties him to a replication of his own culture (a pragmatic reinstatement of empiricism rather than an escape from it):[18]

> . . . this moral semiotics which ties *presentation* to the expression of an inside, and the beauty of man to his morality, thus forms a system with a fundamental humanism. This humanism justifies, at least surreptitiously, the intervention of pragmatic culture and anthropology in the deduction of judgments of taste. There we have the wherewithal to make sense of a sort of incoherence-effect, of an embarrassment or a suspended indecision in the functioning of the discourse.[19]

In the first place, Derrida argues that Kant's suspension of the question of the domain of the aesthetic makes the aesthetic hostage to the purposes of the practical reason. Thus, while the inability to enunciate the rule of the exemplary judgment attracting universal adhesion might from one vantage avoid the pitfalls of an empiricist aesthetics, Derrida sees Kant as escaping from a mimetic account of aesthetics only to substitute an analogical account. The aesthetic judgment, by analogy with the practical judgment, seems to import "an idea of the unanimous universal community which orients its idealizing process." And in so doing, "moral law allies itself with empirical culturalism to dominate the field"(116). Similarly the aesthetic judgment continually deploys an analogy between art and human language to establish an analogy between human purposes and natural finality: "natural finality, as a priori concept deriving from a reflexive judgment, is conceived by analogy with human art which gives itself a goal before operating"(117). The movement toward collapse thus "reconstitutes the economy of mimesis. This latter is the same (economimesis), the law of the same and of the proper which always re-forms itself.

Against imitation but by analogy so as to reestablish the 'economimesis,' the economy of mimesis that Kant displaces."[20]

Essentially, Derrida's argument revolves around the presumption that Kant's idealist account of aesthetics duplicates, from a different perspective, the empiricist impasse of the aesthetic norm. Whereas the Humean argument about a standard of taste collapses because it can produce only a correctness that it must supplement with the pragmatic argument that one encounters models of good taste, the Kantian argument collapses, Derrida suggests, because the claim to universality, with its rule left unenunciated, requires a similar pragmatic supplement. Pragmatism, in Derrida's account, would enunciate the universal in the aesthetic object by means of an ethnocentrism that imagines an identity between reason and the individual who takes him- or herself to reason, even of pleasure. Thinking globally is always, from this perspective, acting locally.

Derrida's version of Kant, then, recapitulates certain aspects of the social formation critique of Kant that we identified earlier with Adorno and Bourdieu, but it does so in the name of a desire to set aside the conceptual "framing" that makes aesthetic pleasure look unitary and universal. Indeed, one of the strongest rhetorical gestures of *La vérité en peinture* is its recurrent use of fractured frames, graphic "illustrations" (quotations are Derrida's) of the claim that the material aspect of language is too continuously shifting to be brought under the control of any universalizing argument. The series of fractured boundaries, with Derrida's puns, would themselves mount an argument to the effect that examples, like individual words, make more points than any system can accommodate. The perception of unitariness, as glosses on examples or as determination of individual words, thus operates as a pragmatic assertion of local agency and intention in the absence of any justification; it creates a work as an essential unity and purity only by using a frame, an addition external to the representation.

Yet Derrida's argument that the materiality of the signifier erodes efforts at conceptual unity and his repeated illustration of that argument in the pun is, perhaps, less a challenge to Kant than might appear. For Kant's remarks on color suggest that there can be a color, green, that is itself a pun at least as material as any word can provide. Moreover, the point of this color punning in Kant—to put a series of visual colors into contact with a series of physical colors—is to indicate that, even in the relatively formed arena of the beautiful, the issue is not one of the difference between matter and form. It is, rather, one of the relationship between stereotype and sequence, the one which arrives at a notion of the ideal or norm from superposition and mixture of color, the other which arrives at an individual color through analysis.

Even in the beautiful, that is, Kant's emphasis on the formlessness of the sublime is at stake in this account of color, which takes the sole interest of aesthetic pleasure to lie in the impossibility of making the empirical norm and the analytic form identical. In this it replicates the related if distinct patterns of the mathematical and dynamical sublimes, which are the aesthetics of science. They are the aesthetics of science, moreover, not because they confuse determinate cognitions or unsettle claims to knowledge but rather because they use the incommensurability of competing systems to argue for the impossibility of making the empirical representation and the formal representation coincide, and for the continual possibility of this non-coincidence appearing as momentary likeness. Thus, while Kant claims mathematical judgments as synthetic a priori judgments rather than empirical judgments in the *Prolegomena*[21] and congratulates himself rather extensively for this recognition, the mathematical sublime involves more than merely the recognition that the numerical estimation of space (measure) is not an empirical operation. For as in the dynamical sublime with its account of natural might and human perception as opposed principles of causation, alternately conceived as motives and effects, the notion of materiality comes to be important because it continually relies on and produces the notion of formality. Thus, the material, far from being set free from the frame, gets to be material because of the formal, and the formal, far from being a moment or act of framing, gets to be formal only by its momentary coincidence with the material. The Kantian account, that is, insists not just upon likeness, the ability of painters' green to imitate spectral green, but also upon the absolute differences that are entailed in their emerging from different representative sequences. For it ultimately concerns itself so little with properties or qualities or objects in themselves that, as Paul Guyer has argued, "Kant's search for justificatory criteria oriented toward the objects rather than the subjects of taste is a failure."[22] It instead deploys the momentary likeness of similar elements that are different because of their different functions in dissimilar sequences to make the aesthetic a continuing commentary not on deception, the production of false likeness, but on the ways in which even mixtures can have a temporary resemblance to the pure, and even the formal and the empirical can ape one another. Modifying both correspondence and coherence accounts, the competition between production and reception localizes itself in the fleeting correspondences of antithetical coherences.

Notes

1. See Section 3, *A Philosophical Enquiry*, ed. J. T. Boulton (Notre Dame, Ind.: University of Notre Dame Press, 1968), 33–35, for Burke's discussion of the proposition "that pain and pleasure are not only, not necessarily dependent for their existence on their mutual diminution or removal, but that, in reality, the diminution or ceasing of pleasure does not operate like positive pain; and that the removal or diminution of pain, in its effect has very little resemblance to positive pleasure."
2. Burke, as Boulton points out in his annotations to the *Enquiry*, here misquotes Pope's *Iliad* 24. 590–93. See *Enquiry*, 34.
3. "For besides such things as affect us in various manners according to their natural powers, there are associations made at that early season, which we find it very hard afterwards to distinguish from natural effects. Not to mention the unaccountable antipathies which we find in many person, we all find it impossible to remember when a steep became more terrible than a plain; or fire or water more dreadful than a clod of earth; though all these are very probably either conclusions from experience, or arising from the premonitions of others; and some of them impressed, in all likelihood, pretty late. But as it must be allowed that many things affect us after a certain manner, not by any natural powers they have for that purpose, but by association; so it would be absurd on the other hand, to say that all things affect us by association only . . . (130–31).
4. Immanuel Kant, *Critique of Judgment*, trans. J. H. Bernard (New York: Hafner Publishing Co., 1966, 119.
5. Ibid.
6. See particularly Theodor Adorno, *Aesthetic Theory*, trans. C. Lenhardt (New York: Routledge & Kegan Paul, 1984); and Pierre Bourdieu, *Distinction: A Social Critique of the Judgment of Taste*, trans. Richard Nice (Cambridge, Mass.: Harvard University Press, 1984).
7. Adorno, *Aesthetic Theory*, 18.
8. Hannah Arendt, *Between Past and Future: Eight Exercises in Political Thought* (New York: Viking Press, 1968), 220.
9. Adorno, *Aesthetic Theory*, 22.
10. Kant, *Critique of Judgment*, 140.
11. I am indebted to Paul Bialek for pointing out to me Adorno's repeated use of the image of fireworks in *Aesthetic Theory*.
12. Her argument, focusing on evaluation, continually produces evidence from the history of taste to argue for the contingency of judgments of individual literary and artifactual objects. By eliding the discussion of aesthetic experience with the history of taste, Smith essentially replicates the tendency to discover social psychology in art objects, and to see

the existence of such tendencies as disabling claims for the merits of those objects. See Barbara Herrnstein Smith, *Contingencies of Value* (Cambridge, Mass.: Harvard University Press, 1988).

13. Kant, *Critique of Judgment*, 100.

14. "We no longer find, it is true, any marked pleasure in the comprehensibility of nature and in the unity of its divisions into genera and species, by which all empirical concepts are possible, through which we cognize it according to its particular laws" (Kant, *Critique of Judgment*, 24).

15. "It is a true joy to see the zeal with which the old geometers investigated the properties of lines of this class, without allowing themselves to be led astray by the questions of narrow-minded persons as to what use this knowledge would be. Thus they worked out the properties of the parabola without knowing the law of gravitation, which would have suggested to them its application to the trajectory of heavy bodies . . ." (Kant, *Critique of Judgment*, 209).

16. "The deterioration of the *parergon*, the perversion of the adornment, is the attraction of sensory matter. As design, organization of lines, forming of angles, the frame is not at all an adornment, and one cannot do without it" (Jacques Derrida, *The Truth in Painting*, trans. Geoff Bennington and Ian MacLeod [Chicago: University of Chicago Press, 1987], 64).

17. Johann Wolfgang von Goethe, *Theory of Colours*, trans. Charles Lock Eastlake (Cambridge, Mass: M.I.T. Press, 1970), 25.

18. See J. Hillis Miller, *The Ethics of Reading* (New York: Columbia University Press, 1986), 13–39.

19. Derrida, *Truth in Painting*, 115.

20. Derrida, "Economimesis," *Mimesis: Des articulations* (Paris: Flammarion, 1975), p. 118.

21. See Kant's elaboration of his claim that "*Synthetic Judgments Require a Different Principle from that of Contradiction*" in his statement that "*Mathematical Judgments* are all synthetic. This fact seems hitherto to have altogether escaped the observation of those who have analyzed human reason; it even seems directly opposed to all their conjectures, though it is incontestably certain and most important in its consequences. For as it was found that the conclusions of mathematicians all proceed according to the principle of contradiction (as is demanded by all apodeictic certainty), men persuaded themselves that the fundamental propositions were known from the principle of contradiction. . . . First of all, we must observe that properly mathematical propositions are always judgments *a priori*, and not empirical, because they carry with them necessity, which cannot be obtained from experience (*Philosophy of Material Nature: The Complete Texts of Prolegomena to Any Future Metaphysics That Will Be Able to Come Forward as Science and Metaphysical Foundations of Natural Science*, trans. James W. Ellington [Indianapolis: Hackett Publishing Co., 1985], 13).

22. See "Abstraction and the Freedom of the Imagination" in Guyer's *Kant and the Claims of Taste* (Cambridge, Mass.: Harvard University Press, 1979), 255, where Guyer advances the thesis that "Kant's aesthetics cannot lead to the introduction of any specific restrictions on the kinds of objects that might turn out to be beautiful, or place *a priori* limitations on our search for natural or artistic beauty" without being "supplemented with particular theories of art and perceptual and cognitive psychology."

4

The Gothicism of the Gothic Novel

The problem of the relation between self and society, as it has been efficiently if inelegantly termed, has been with us for some time. The human tendency to collect into societies, despite the apparent separability of the individual human body from that collection, did not begin with the rise of the early modern state with its increasing rationalization of the roles of the people that were its elemental parts.[1] Yet with the notion of system emerged an antitype to the notion of society as a collection of individuals. Whereas empirical induction might (as Kant's discussion of the aesthetical normal idea of a beautiful man suggested) create a norm as an average different from all—and, indeed, any—individual cases of beauty, the rise of systematization in the eighteenth century (from Adam Smith's economic theory to biological classification) amounted to a claim for unexperiential existence. If past experience from an empirical standpoint can serve only as an indicator of the probability rather than the necessity that future experience will continue the same, predictability can be obtained from a systematic standpoint precisely by severing it from any grounding in experience.

The incongruity—even more, the nearly absolute incompatibility—between a systematic account and the inductive account appeared to reach one kind of resolution (or, one kind of impasse) in the Kantian description of the aesthetic particular about which one can make a universal claim. In the work of Jeremy Bentham, it found another. For Bentham's famous effort to rationalize the English law essayed to resolve just such an incompatibility between the inevitably empiricist individual perspective and the systematic perspective. The "legal fiction," the attempt to establish meaning by stipulation, is the result. Thus, although legal fictions had done extensive duty in the law for many centuries (in the form of such notions as that of legal infancy that could be established arbitrarily and uniformly without any actual determination of the relative maturity or immaturity of the legal infant), one could argue that Bentham first recognized its full significance. His contribution was, that is, not merely to classify the law so that individual moral agents might know "where they stood"; it was also (and infinitely more importantly) to insist upon the legal fiction as a bridge between the individual and the systematic. The law was, simultaneously, clarified by a rationalization of the common law that emphasized the intentional nature of genuinely moral and legal choices and supplemented by a collection of legal fictions that made individual epistemology and intention supremely irrelevant.

I have discussed the legal fiction or statutory stipulation in conjunction with Richardson's *Clarissa* and the psychological novel elsewhere.[2] There I argued that Richardson identifies Clarissa's heroism not merely as a function of her being personally unusual, a paragon for her sex, an object of worship for humankind. Instead, her standing as a paragon works itself out as a novelistic contest between a notion of empirical evidence, what is available to sensation, and what can be, from the perspective of system, asserted in spite of its opposition to all sensory evidence. *Clarissa's* continuing importance for the novel (and the Gothic novel in particular) thus lies less in its having established the setting and props of the psychologically harrowing than for having established the novelistic interest in an account of experience as self-haunting, by forcing the issue of the relationship—the conflict—between experience and the formal construction of it which such ideas as statutory stipulation entail.

In *Caleb Williams* and *Frankenstein*, the Gothic novels we are concerned with here, that haunting takes the form of doublings or character echoes. Caleb, the young man of modest means and immodest curiosity or ambition, seeks to know, to love, to be Falkland, the older man whom he serves as secretary. Victor Frankenstein creates his artificial offspring, his monster, only to be pursued ceaselessly by him. These are the gross facts of the way character figures as doubling in the plots of the novels. Yet the implicit argument of the novels makes these doublings less a matter of characters' relationships and attractions than a precipitate of the conflict between the individual perspective on society (which stresses individual agency and experience) and the societal perspective on the individual (the formal claim that an external categorization of an individual can be definitional regardless of the individual's actual experience and action). Lovelace's desire to possess Clarissa, Caleb's desire to be Falkland, and the monster's desire to be loved by Victor may thus bring on stories of love and death, but the heterosexual and homosocial bonds are here epiphenomena of the conflict between individually occupied and socially occupied identity.[3]

Near the end of *Caleb Williams,* Caleb, portraying himself as totally cut off from all human friendship and sympathy, finds a figure for the twinned character: the individual and his species are not the one and the many. They are one twin and another. Or, rather, they are one twin but not really another—Siamese twins joined from birth so that separation can be only disastrous but continued combination remains at best cumbersome.

> I had never experienced the purest refinements of friendship, but in two instances, that of Collins [Falkland's steward, who first confided to Caleb the story of Falkland's repeated clashes with Tyrrel, the man for whose murder the tenant-farmers, the Hawkinses, were executed] and this of the family of Laura [with whom Caleb lived in Wales during his flight from Falkland's agents]. Solitude, separation, banishment! These are words often in the mouths of human beings, but few men, except myself, have felt the full latitude of their meaning. The pride of philosophy has taught us to treat man as an individual. He is no such thing. He holds, necessarily, indispensably, to his species. He is like those twin-births, that have two heads indeed, and four hands; but, if you attempt to detach them from each other, they are inevitably subjected to miserable and lingering destruction.[4]

As Godwin put it in the appendix to *Political Justice* entitled "Of Cooperation, Cohabitation and Marriage," "It is a curious subject, to enquire into the due medium between individuality and concert."[5]

Godwin's conclusion in that appendix to *Political Justice* is, "We ought to be able to do without one another"(3: 505). This statement can, in one aspect, be seen as a version of the claim of the sublime aesthetic. More than a mere advocacy of rustication, Kant's interest in the sublime had represented the most serious version of that heuristic conclusion. It meant, in the first place, that one could hear without the benefit of individual testimony, without benefit of the guises in which persons present themselves. It meant, in the second place, that the formalization of perception that was possible in the absence of persons could, in the presence of persons, create a competitive speech that counterpointed their testimony.

Godwin's account of "the due medium between individuality and concert" in *Political Justice* projects a world in which individuals in concert will merely be one another's siblings, freed of the monstrosity that results when one twin is an individual and the other, continuous with it, is not equal but the composite rendering of the species. He thus envisions the withering away of government as men "are perpetually coming nearer to each other" as "mind is in a state of progressive improvement"(2: 501). The individual reading of circumstance, that is, will enable persons to unite more efficiently than the reading of persons can ever do. The coercions of government and its legal institutions will become irrelevant as soon as local agreements between persons are abandoned in favor of universal agreement arrived at through different routes of individual error and self-correction. Disagreement, rightly understood, is uniformity: "The proper method for hastening the decline of error, and producing uniformity of judgment, is not, by brute force, by laws, or by imitation; but, on the contrary, by exciting every man to think for himself"(2: 501). On this model, universal individuality produces the closest possible approximation to uniformity of judgment. Thus, the peculiar virtue of individuality for Godwin is that it is conducive to the cause of society, in that a society in which everyone thinks for himself is a society in which all individuals will agree without needing to understand one another.

Yet that version of the absolute convergence between individualism and society is as remote from the Gothic novel generally and from *Caleb Williams* particularly as individual agency and fate are from one another. Thus, critics have repeatedly seen the novel as repudiating the political philosophy, and have seen the opposition between them as supporting the view that Godwin was an extraordinarily inconstant thinker, as changeable in his beliefs about individuals as in his religious views. From William Hazlitt's early comment on the differences between Godwin's two modes ("it was a new and startling event in literary history for a metaphysician to write a popular romance") to Angus Wilson's discussion of a "schizophrenic tendency" in Godwin, critics have found the novel to identify society, not with the collection of freely choosing individuals that Godwin projected in *Political Justice,* but instead with something much closer to fate. If A. D. Harvey has claimed that "in the last resort, it is not society but fate which hounds Caleb," the project of *Caleb Williams* is to collapse the difference in that distinction, to make the Siamese twin of individual volition be fate rather than collectivized action.[6]

Now the Gothic novel in general features the plight of young persons—particularly and notoriously young women in distress, as if to lay stress on the importance of circumstances in forming and enforcing character. The extreme account of character—that it is always being determined by external agency—appears most clearly perhaps in a novel like *The Monk,* where Ambrosio's virtue is instantly convertible into vice, and the circumstances make the man. Indeed, even where virtue persists in spite of its distress, it becomes conspicuous less as moral choice than as frustration. From this perspective, Godwin's choice of the Gothic mode appears less schizophrenic and more consistent with his interest in the politics of romance. For the Gothic both echoes and intensifies his remark in *Political Justice* that "every man that receives an impression from any external object, has the current of his own thoughts modified by force; and yet, without external impressions, we should be nothing"(2: 505). Concert, in the form of similar circumstances, may be compulsion; the alternative to being "nothing" may be the haunting of the unsealed border between the Siamese self and Siamese other.

Moreover, because Godwin conceives of the individual as requiring external impressions to be an individual at all, more than "nothing," the achievement of equality among men, can result only from what Godwin calls "equality of conditions." And this equality is not to be effected solely through redistribution of wealth, so that equal circumstances will produce equal individuals. Rather, the yielding of one's own benefits must arise from the inability of the individual ever to have been an individual: inherited knowledge and the possibility of one's actions being inherited by another become the explanation and motivation for altruism, "rendering the cession, by him that has, to him that wants, an unrestrained and voluntary action." "There remain," he says, "but two instruments for producing this volition, the illumination of the understanding and the love of distinction"(2: 469). "The illumination of the understanding" is, in his view, inevitable, for two related but distinct reasons: first, that anyone who sees "the merits of a case in all their clearness cannot in that instance be the dupe either of prejudice or superstition" because "truth and falsehood cannot subsist together"(1: 307); and second, that the invention of the printing press has given virtually all men an acquaintance with the advances that human thought has already made, thus making it possible for individuals to avoid wasting their time trying to do such things as discover the laws of gravitation on their own and also making it possible for there to be many who were more competent judges of truth than there had been before the widespread dissemination of books. The ability to relate to other humans, then, does not rest on sympathetic identification or a Kantian imperative to accord other persons a respect that will not involve disrespect for one's own contractual obligations with oneself. Rather, it ratifies both rationalism and altruism on the grounds of heritability, the persistence of the consequences of individual actions on the level of society. "The love of distinction," then, in part represents a characteristic English turn on what was perceived as French misanthropy; following Adam Smith's account of benevolence toward others as a primary source of individual satisfaction, Godwin insists that an individual's account of his own worth is always to be perceived in terms of his estimation of his worth to other people. Morality without consequence would, that is, be no morality at all: "no being can be either virtuous, or vicious, who has no opportunity of influencing the happiness of others"(1: 50).

Human beings, in other words, are, like the printing press, tools. Both self-improving and causes of improvement for others, humans would lose not merely an audience were they alone but would cease to have distinction by ceasing to have effect. Godwin's account of the importance of benevolence, distinction, and virtue represents, that is, what we might think of as a reversal of Berkeleyan philosophy: if a man commits a crime or a virtuous act in a forest and no one hears him, neither the crime nor the virtuous act has any real existence.

In *Caleb Williams,* by contrast with *Political Justice,* this very issue of consequentialism produces its own self-doubling. For it is not only that Falkland, the man of rank and reputation, possesses a love of esteem which both makes his character and breaks it, rendering him equally capable of exceptional valor (risking his own life, for example, to save persons trapped in a fire) and excessively inclined to obey the "laws of honour" which "are in the utmost degree rigid" and which can lead him to speak of his own actions as dictated. Thus he can say to Count Malvesi, with whom he almost duels in Italy, "there was reason to fear that, however anxious I were to be your friend, I might be obliged to be your murderer."[7] This discrepancy between volition and necessity, between the consequences one would choose and the consequences that choose one, becomes the interference of the notion of character with individuality, who one must continue to be by virtue of one's self-inheritance rather than by virtue of one's action.

Falkland's virtuous acts, that is, produce his reputation, but his reputation serves to nullify his vicious acts, to render invisible his murder of Tyrrel and to make it visible only as the action of another (Hawkins, the innocent man who, it appears, played Good Samaritan to his former oppressor Tyrrel). In short, Falkland has so much "character," in the sense of reputation, that his actions cease to have consequences. Or rather, they come to have only private consequences, the melancholy that attends the man with every apparent reason (wealth, station, learning) for happiness.

The Gothic character of *Caleb Williams* thus looks like character itself, the extension of individual action through narrative until it has become romance, the impossibility of action. And from this perspective, the initial ending that Godwin sketched for the novel looks inevitable. In that ending, Caleb accuses Falkland of having murdered Tyrrel and having allowed suspicion to fall on the Hawkinses, who were, *père et fils,* executed for a murder that they did not commit. Falkland in turn accuses Caleb of false accusation, of having maliciously accused him of murder in retaliation for Falkland's having brought theft charges against Caleb. Rank, on this account, enables one character to trump another when they make equal and opposite charges. Rank is not only inherited but also serves as the character of character, the persistence of its claims in the absence of corroboration. Thus, the tenant Hawkins can have a "record" of extreme probity and indeed forbearance in dealing with the bullying landholder Tyrrel, but character unsupported by rank looks as though it could do anything—which, in this case, means that he suddenly seems capable of committing a murder merely on account of having a motive. (Tyrrel's rank, conversely, mitigates the consequences of his reputation.) And if the desire for distinction is the desire for consequence, for having a real effect on other humans, reputation combined with rank is the inability to stop being seen to continue "in character," to produce any consequential actions that are anything other than more of the same.

The Gothicism of this Gothic, then, is not merely injustice, the inequities and inequalities of "things as they are," the leading portion of Godwin's title in the first edition of 1794. It is, instead, that the perception of the way things are can convert itself into an insistence upon seeing things as they are not, to making character less the consequence of action than the impossibility of avoiding one's character as one's inheritance, so that character becomes less a predictor of action than an emblem of the irrelevance of action.

Godwin's initial conclusion, in other words, first staged a contest of characters—Falkland against Caleb (echoing Falkland against Tyrrel, Falkland against Hawkins)—that made character look like character only when it was "supported by witnesses," in the form of the public opinion that sees character as producing all the circumstances of evidence.[8] It also, however, made character its own contest, a competition between a character based on consequential action and a character as the invisibility of consequential action. The version with which Godwin finally concluded the novel, however, disclosed Falkland's direct and indirect crimes (his murder, his complicity in having allowed the Hawkinses to be framed and executed, his active contrivance to trump up charges of theft against Caleb). The "truth" comes out; Falkland acknowledges that Caleb has been right about him, and the fact that "the perpetrator [Falkland] knew that I [Caleb] was in possession of the truth upon the subject"(317) ceases to be a liability to Caleb and becomes his asset.

The sunniness of such an outing of the truth might seem to compromise the novel's standing as a Gothic, were it not for one thing. The courtroom drama in which Falkland praises Caleb's nobility of mind and Caleb explains Falkland to himself ("But thou imbibedst the poison of chivalry with thy earliest youth,"326) may resolve the contradiction within character, may make character look again like the consequence of action. It does so, however, by insisting upon punishment without consequence as the inevitable companion piece to action without consequence. Godwin had, in *Political Justice*, crucially disagreed with such prominent contemporary writers on crime and punishment as Cesare Beccaria by insisting upon the centrality of individual intention in determining the criminality of an action—to which Beccaria's riposte was, "If the intention is to be taken into account, we need a fresh law for every crime."[9] Unintended consequences, he maintained, should go unpunished. And he had similarly asserted that crimes incapable of amendment ought to be forgotten and go forever unpunished.

In *Caleb Williams*, however, the novel finally, revisedly, ends with truth emerging only as punishment that can have no consequences. Falkland, aged, broken, and only days away from his death, discovers in himself a character of consequence only at the point at which the consequence can only be annihilated, or preserved merely in the register of character. "Getting Falkland," that is, involves connecting his actions with consequences only when he is past both punishment and reformation, so that the legal record anneals the crimes as the forever unrealized legend on his character (as if a coat of arms and its motto were competing with one another). Indeed, the trial scene's resemblance to a deathbed scene can only insist upon the alternative claims of a truth that can be told simply because it can have no consequences and a truth that need not be told because it can have no consequences.

Or, because it can have no consequences for Falkland. For if the projected ending envisioned a contest between characters in which the problem with justice looked as if it were reducible to an opposition between the truth and the appearance of truth, Caleb's being right and Falkland's always looking right, the revised ending makes Caleb himself count as the consequence of Falkland's character. Falkland, having murdered to preserve his honor, can have his honor impugned, but only by Caleb's having claimed to have murdered him: "He survived this dreadful scene but three days. I have been his murderer"(325). The connection—or lack of it—between character (or honor, or reputation) and action maintains itself, in that the conviction of the identity between character and action makes Caleb a murderer when he has struck no blow—in exactly the same ways that it had kept Falkland from being one when he had. Caleb, in amending Falkland's public character, cannot come into his own:

> I thought that, if Falkland were dead, I should return once again to all that makes life worth possessing. I thought that, if the guilt of Falkland were established, fortune and the world would smile upon my efforts. Both these events are accomplished; and it is only now that I am truly miserable.[325]

He who "began these memoirs with the idea of vindicating my character" has "now no character" to "vindicate"(326). For character looks like the Siamese twin that keeps the individual from being alone and whose detachment subjects the so-called survivor to "miserable and lingering destruction."

In Mary Shelley's *Frankenstein,* the tradition of monstrosity continues. As if in producing her novel in commentary on her father's work, Shelley worded her dedication this way: "To William Godwin, Author of *Political Justice, Caleb Williams,* &c. These Volumes Are respectfully inscribed By the Author."[10] Given the scope of Godwin's literary work, which ranged from political journalism like that of *The Enquirer* to school books for children by the time Shelley published *Frankenstein,* one might speculate that not merely did Shelley want to double her father in the process of writing a story of the doubling of creator and creature but that she also conceived that doubling to involve the questions of social monstrosity raised in *Political Justice* and *Caleb Williams.* Yet if those works suggested that the "due medium between individuality and concert" was difficult to attain, *Frankenstein* virtually burlesques the question in portraying its impossibility.

In a novel that celebrates both solitude and friendship, that is, solitude itself is both friendship and a recommendation for friendship. Even Victor's apparently solitary appreciation of nature (as a respite from care, as a departure from society) tends to look less like the kind of pathetic fallacy that Ruskin so loathed in Romanticism than like the species identification of the individual.[11] While in *Caleb Williams,* character as the public version of one's probability held one hostage to society, in *Frankenstein,* individuality (in the person of Victor) continually projects its extension in the formalization of nature.

It is thus not simply comic that Victor has abandoned his family so as to make a creature to keep him company, and that he has abandoned (and fled) his creature so as to be alone to search for friends. Rather, this amiable isolation, like Victor's persistent inclination to think that his creature murderously stalks him (even as one after another of the members of his extended family fall to the monster), makes creatures and friends in Quixotic fashion, by never attending to experience and its inductions.

The landscape that is presented as a companionable form commends Victor to companions is sociability without society, a love that rests always on the way people might be (were they artificially and formally generated) rather than the way they are. (In this Victor's amiability exactly corresponds to Kant's description of sublime misanthropy.) Thus, the capacity to respond to the sublime aspects of nature is a trait for which the framing narrator Walton esteems Victor in his letters home to his sister Mrs. Savile in England: "Even broken in spirit as he is, no one can feel more deeply than he does the beauties of nature. The starry sky, the sea, and every sight afforded by these wonderful regions, seems [sic] still to have the power of elevating his soul from earth"(23). A love of nature, a love of no consequence, recommends one more than any social guise. Indeed, it may console one for living in a world of disguise and reputation, the one that Victor needs consolation for because the servant girl Justine has been falsely tried and executed for his brother William's murder. "Sublime and magnificent scenes afforded me the greatest consolation that I was capable of receiving. They elevated me from all littleness of feeling; and although they did not remove my grief, they subdued and tranquillized it"(91). In his account of the same Alpine excursion, moreover, Victor elaborates on the virtue of sublime scenes to intervene between a man and his pettier cares:

> The sight of the awful and majestic in nature had indeed always the effect of solemnizing my mind, and causing me to forget the passing cares of life. I determined to go alone [to the summit of Montanvert], for I was well acquainted with the path, and the presence of another would destroy the solitary grandeur of the scene.[92]

Of all the situations described in *Frankenstein*, the ascent to the summit of Montanvert may well be the most perilous, as Victor suggests when he says that one of the paths "is particularly dangerous, as the slightest sound, such as even speaking in a loud voice, produces a concussion of air sufficient to draw destruction upon the head of the speaker." In the face of the kind of danger that Victor had earlier been praising for its solemnizing influence, however, he begins to lament, " 'Alas! why does man boast of sensibilities superior to those apparent in the brute; it only renders them more necessary beings. If our impulses were confined to hunger, thirst, and desire, we might be nearly free; but now we are moved by every wind that blows . . .' "(92–93). Victor, having acted to produce a creature whose existence seems beyond empirical bounds, has, in a strange twist on Falkland's situation, produced a murder by proxy for which he can never be blamed. The formal extension of one person (Victor) into another (his creature) has collided with the necessity of humans being sociable creatures, which in the case of *Frankenstein* means that Victor's defense of Justine looks ever more generously specious the more he advances it. And the landscape that becomes dangerous only as it acquires speakers is, from this standpoint, merely emblematic of the dangers of a world in which people speak at all, in which the telling of the truth may be not merely ineffectual but also murderous.

This point, moreover, begins to seem particularly obvious when a figure appears to disrupt the awful calm of the landscape. The figure is that of the monster, who has come to reproach Victor for his misery, and who provides an implicit gloss on the nature of the necessity that Victor has earlier been lamenting. Describing his observations of various forms of community that appear especially idyllic to him because he has been excluded from them, the monster begs entrance into society as necessity, the very necessity and probability that has made Victor's testimony go unheard and indeed count as proof of Justine's guilt rather than exoneration. For "necessity" in *Frankenstein* translates into something like "community," "love," and "friendship"—and particularly the costs attendant on the human need for them.

Victor, that is, has dreamed of a generation that would proceed ideally and formally, without being founded on the social induction for which "character" counted in *Caleb Williams* and for which language, society, and the family count in *Frankenstein*. The monster, like a living impersonation of Victor's testimony in Justine's trial, dreams of entering that world and coming to have visibility in it. Victor, having created an individual detachable from society, thus, discovers that individual to be monstrous—monstrous, however, not on account of being an artificial creature but on account of insisting that his individual birth requires Siamese twinning. Whereas the monster continually personified landscapes as hecklers, as if his every effort to make nature a companionable presence for him were yet another mark of the insufficiency of ideal form, Victor repeatedly tries to make nature an alien form precisely because he seems doomed to community, that is, to the impossibility of his ever being alone. Throughout the novel, Victor announces his desire to be alone—so that he can work in his laboratory, so that he can avoid the gazes of his family after he recognizes the devastation wrought by the monster he has created, and so forth. The novel frustrates Victor's desire for solitude by having the monster appear at Montanvert. But it does so as well by providing a would-be friend in the form of Walton even when Victor goes to such an extreme and deserted place as the North Pole and by, in a stroke of genius, having the monster strew graffiti through the landscape, when "sometimes, indeed, he left marks in writing on the barks of trees, or cut in stone, that guided me, and instigated my fury"(202).

Victor's desire for solitude of course manifests itself most strongly as a desire not to pass any time in the company of the monster he has made. He thus initially responds to the monster's request for companionship by expressing his willingness to create a monster-mate (who would provide the company he is so unwilling to provide) and heeds the argument that the monster has advanced about the ways in which affection will give him a stake in justice and humanity: " 'If I have no ties and no affections, hatred and vice must be my portion; the love of another will destroy the cause of my crimes, and I shall become a thing of whose existence everyone will be ignorant.' "(143). The monster, always a good deal cleverer than his creator, has of course presented the case for the creation of another monster by suggesting that a proliferation of monsters will render him—and the two of them—invisible. Already invisible to most of the world, the monster would, he promises, become invisible even to Victor were he given a species identity. Because Victor wants to get the monster out of his life, he responds to the request and sets about manufacturing a female monster. He destroys his half-finished product, however, when he thinks of a future society of monsters:

> "Even if they were to leave Europe, and inhabit the deserts of the new world, yet one of the first results of those sympathies for which the daemon thirsted would be propagated upon the earth, who might make the very existence of man a condition precarious and full of terror. Had I a right, for my own benefit, to inflict this curse upon everlasting generations?"[163]

Whereas the monster has argued that the union of two monsters into a community will produce a harmony that will distract him from his desire to have revenge on Victor for denying him his society, Victor sees the union of monsters as multiply monstrous. And in doing so, he recurs to his earliest image of the monster in his initial moments of life. For the individual monster has, it appears, never been individual at all, but has always incorporated the disjecta membra of society. As Victor inquired of his journal on the event of the creature's "birth,"

> "How can I . . . delineate the wretch whom with such infinite pains and care I had endeavoured to form? His limbs were in proportion and I had selected his features as beautiful. Beautiful!—Great God! His yellow skin scarcely covered the work of muscles and arteries beneath; his hair was of a lustrous black, and flowing; his teeth of a pearly whiteness; but these luxuriances only formed a more horrid contrast with his watery eyes."[52]

One might argue (as Victor nearly does) that Victor is a poor technician or that his inexperience at creation makes him incapable of coming up with anything but the roughest kind of prototype for a creature. What gives significance, however, to Victor's perception of the monster as beautiful parts and hideous whole is that it recapitulates his view of society more generally and the novel's depiction of domesticity.

For even though Victor's own family appears to represent bourgeois domesticity in its most thoroughly accomplished form, it was from the start monstrous, as Victor's nearly obsessive desire to be away from home registers. Yet the nature of that monstrosity is anything but apparent. Why would anyone want to leave such an idyllic domestic circle as that of the

Frankensteins? The answer to that question lies, I would suggest, in the way in which the Frankenstein family itself is presented as an analogue to Victor's monster in being composed of beautiful parts that are rendered hideous when unity is imposed upon its various members. The family assembled is almost as much an experiment in social engineering as the monster is an experiment in physical engineering. Frankenstein *père* (who is named only as *père* in the novel) arrives at Caroline Beaufort's hovel as she is weeping over the coffin of her impoverished and humiliated father, his friend; he conducts her to Geneva after her father's burial, and two years later, makes her his wife (28). Not only do they produce Victor, Ernest, and William, "bestowing on the state sons who might carry [M. Frankenstein's] virtues and his name down to posterity"(27) as intended, but they also expand their family circle by including Elizabeth, who is either the only child of M. Frankenstein's deceased sister (as in the 1818 text) or an Italian foundling (as in the 1831 text), the servant girl Justine, who is taken into the Frankenstein family when Mme Frankenstein perceives the girl's mother's aversion to her, and Victor's dear friend Henry Clerval, who is recurrently described as very nearly a brother to him.

Although the monster initially attacks and kills William, Victor's youngest natural brother, it is striking that Elizabeth, Justine, and Clerval—that is, all three of the children assimilated to the Frankenstein family—perish because of the monster. On the one hand, the monster may be seen to attack the four most recent additions to the family because they are the ones whom Victor loves most dearly. But, on the other, it is almost as if the monster attacked these figures in particular because he imagined Victor's repudiation of him as an argument that the family unity could only be stretched among so many persons—and because he imagined, further, that the existence of those persons made it impossible for Victor to expand his notion of the family enough to include him, the monster.

If the monster might seem to be naïve to imagine the substitution of one person for another in the domestic affections (and the substitution of an unnatural connection for a natural one), he is not alone in such imaginings. For marriage in the novel appears to be founded on the substitution of the father for the husband in a very literal way: the death of Caroline Beaufort's father leads quite directly to her marriage to M. Frankenstein, and monster's tale of the DeLaceys involves Safie's fleeing her father, "the treacherous Turk," and seeking out her lover Felix instead. A woman's going forth from her father's house and cleaving to her husband is, of course, the standard means through which a new family is created and continued. Yet while this process may look fairly normal much of the time, in *Frankenstein* it comes to seem strangely monstrous. The skin of the family appears in the very process of seeming to be stretched too tight to cover the various parts. Family unity comes to entail division as this skin of inclusiveness turns out not to incorporate new elements but to require the complete annihilation of certain family members.

Victor's horror at the prospect of any such kind of overextension is very consistent. Whereas he delights in the transport that sublime scenery affords him, he complains of any situation that demands any kind of adulteration of the self. Thus, he thinks of generations of monsters with particular loathing because he imagines them all under his own skin; just as he had earlier fantasized that "a new species would bless me as its creator and source"(49), so he later thinks of future generations of monsters as only partially separable from himself—what they might do will be his responsibility. Although Victor represents the most extreme version of the belief that responsibility can never be delimited and restricted to the individual who lives in society, enough other characters in the novel share a version of this belief for there to be a substantial collection of people confessing to murder. When William's dead body is discovered, for instance, Elizabeth, Justine, Victor, and the monster all take the blame for his murder. The monster obviously bears some responsibility, as the one who directly committed the murder, and Victor can be said to bear some, as the one who created the monster, but Elizabeth accuses herself of murder only because she had allowed William to wear a miniature of the late Mme Frankenstein, and Justine, because she thought she might have prevented the murder had she not gone to her aunt's house for the night. Being treated like members of the family strangely implicates both Elizabeth and Justine in the role of mother to William, and motherhood here is merely the domestic version of the infinite responsibility that the monster tries to inspire in Victor.

Yet while the sheer extension in time of family ties appears as a terrible burden for the Frankenstein family, the monster's account of the DeLacey family might seem to offer an alternative vision of idyllic family life. Whereas the Frankensteins write to one another, they don't seem to talk much among themselves (as Victor's autodidacticism in his medical studies would suggest), but the monster describes the DeLaceys' language as a model of communicative transparency: " 'I found that these people possessed a method of communicating their experience and feelings to one another by articulate sounds. . . . This was indeed a godlike science, and I ardently desired to become acquainted with it' "(107). This "godlike science" enables the transfer of information, which Victor's creature begins to rehearse. As the monster becomes more familiar with the cottagers' language, he discovers the " 'names of the cottagers themselves. The youth and his companion had each of them several names, but the old man had only one, which was *father*.

The girl was called *sister,* or *Agatha;* and the youth, *Felix, brother,* or *son* "(107–8). Although the monster merely recounts the existence of an increasing number of names or roles for the members of the family, one might well imagine that Victor Frankenstein would have seen in Felix's "several names" a cause for the fact that Felix "was always," in direct contradiction of the message of his name, "the saddest of the groupe"(108). For just as the effort to unify the monster's disjecta membra under one skin renders hideous what was beautiful in its parts, so Felix's effort to unite in one person the several roles of brother, son, and—later—husband recapitulates the awkward diffusion of the self that marks the Frankenstein family. It is, moreover, a diffusion made especially painful by the fact that it is continually being reconnected. The definitional assertion of what family is incessantly reinstitutes the union no matter what distances in space and what differences in blood separate its various units.

From the perspective of the horror of domestic overextension, Victor's particular delight at the prospect of the path to Montanvert appears inextricably linked with the fact that "the slightest sound, such as even speaking in a loud voice, produces a concussion of air sufficient to draw destruction upon the head of the speaker." For if language from one standpoint facilitates the kind of communication between persons which enables families and civilized societies to exist, it also makes the expression of reproach possible. And what attracts Victor Frankenstein to the sublime dangers of landscape is precisely the way in which the landscape continually threatens to silence any who should direct reproaches at him. While the sublime continually raises the specter of the annihilation of the self, even such annihilation looks like a consolidation beside the constant stretching necessary to any self that attempts to honor the various claims on its attention and affection. Thus, although there is more than a little self-delusion in Victor Frankenstein's argument that his actions are constrained by society—that he can't tell the true story of William's murder because no one would believe him, that he can't create a monster-woman because generations of monsters might destroy human society, there is also some truth to his apologies for himself. In *Frankenstein* the sublime willingness to entertain the prospect of the annihilation of the self turns out to reflect a desire for purity of selfhood which is only imperfectly satisfied by the schadenfreude of observing the annihilation of others. One might well maintain that this is the knowledge from which Victor Frankenstein protects his creature in refusing to make a monster-mate for him. For the monster thus retains a mystified understanding of the operations of the human affections and never experiences any of the further stretching of his skin that would have resulted from his having become not just son or creature but also husband, father, and so on. The monster may not have enough skin to cover his tissues with complete ease, but the true *peau de chagrin* is that of the domestic world in which the consciousness that humans are "necessary beings" makes it seem impossible for any one person to fulfill the responsibilities imposed by his multiple ties. If the monster longs for companionship, Victor Frankenstein does bequeath him one rare—and sublime—privilege: being alone means never having to say you're sorry.

Notes

1. Michael Foucault's account of the disciplinary state in *Discipline and Punish: The Birth of the Prison*, trans. Alan Sheridan (New York: Pantheon Books, 1977) produces the most recent masterful account of this process, with its attention to the spatialization of power and its interest in suggesting the power of architecture as organized space to organize consciousness. From my perspective, however, *The Order of Things*, with its account of the movement from empiricism to idealism, is particularly important for understanding the structures of the Gothic novel, in which the fear is continually that one person's experience merely figures as an element in the system of another.

2. See "Rape and the Rise of the Novel," *Representations* 20 (Fall 1987), 88–112.

3. See Eve Kosofsky Sedgwick, *The Coherence of Gothic Conventions*, with a new preface (New York: Methuen and Co., 1986), for an account of the relationship between the Gothic and what Sedgwick terms the "homosocial." From my perspective, Sedgwick's interest in the Gothic is particularly useful for suggesting the Gothic's collision between empirical and formal accounts of identity. If the Gothic locates horror in the simultaneous existence of competitive accounts of gender (one based on the empirical evidence of biology, another based on the formal reading of action), it also (in Sedgwick's view) establishes the homosocial bond as if empirical accumulation of enough instances of this conundrum of identity could be the normality of society.

4. William Godwin, *Caleb Williams*, ed. David McCracken (London: Oxford University Press, 1970), 303.

5. William Godwin, *Enquiry concerning Political Justice and Its Influence on Morals and Happiness*, facsimile 3d ed., ed. F. E. L. Priestley, 3 vols. (Toronto: University of Toronto Press, 1969), 3: 499.

6. For a representative sampling of intelligent critical response, see William Hazlitt, "Review of *Cloudesley* and Estimate of Other Works," *Edinburgh Review* 51 (April 1830), 144–59; Leslie Stephen, "Godwin and Shelley," *Cornhill Magazine* 39 (1879), 281–302; Angus Wilson, "The Novels of William Godwin," *World Review* 28 (June 1952), 37–41; and A.D. Harvey, "The Nightmare of *Caleb Williams*," *Essays in Criticism* 26 (1976), 236–49.

7. Godwin, *Caleb Williams*, 15.

8. Godwin, *Caleb Williams*, 101–2. This is the phrase Falkland uses in court when he is describing himself as incapable of having murdered Tyrrel: "what sort of a character is that which must be supported by witnesses?"

9. Beccaria, *On Crimes and Punishments*, tr. David Young (Indianapolis: Hackett Publishing Company, 1986), 16.

10. Mary Shelley, *Frankenstein; or, The Modern Prometheus* (1818 text), ed. James Rieger (Indianapolis: Bobbs-Merrill Co., 1974), 5.

11. I claim no originality for the view that *Frankenstein* concerns the relationship between individuals and society in concerning the relationship between Victor Frankenstein and his monster. The long-standing interest in the novel's doubling raises this issue from several different perspectives, the most influential being those that see the existence of the monster as a version of fractured identification. For a review and reconsideration of psychological accounts, see Paul Sherwin, *"Frankenstein:* Creation as Catastrophe," *PMLA* 96 (1981): 883–903. For readings of psychological doubling in terms of gender, see such accounts as those of Ellen Moers, *Literary Women* (Garden City, N.Y.: Doubleday & Co., 1976) and Barbara Johnson, "My Monster, My Self," *Diacritics* 12 (1982) 2–10.

5

Malthus, Godwin, Wordsworth, and the Spirit of Solitude

At the end of the eighteenth century in England, the population debate that had been in progress for more than fifty years took a curious turn.[1] The debate in its early stages had proceeded as part of eighteenth-century England's efforts to assess itself in relation to the ancients. Populousness was taken for a sign of national success and good government. The received wisdom was that modern states produced smaller populations than ancient ones had, and that this population decrease betokened a larger pattern of decline.[2] Thus, when Malthus, in his *On the Principle of Population* of 1798,[3] predicted that populations could well increase faster than food supplies, he was considerably revaluing a topic that had long been invested with a sense of crisis. This perspective appeared compelling, however, not because there were in 1798 too many people in the world—not even Malthus claimed that the world was overpopulated at the time he wrote. Rather, as I will argue, Malthus' *Essay,* instead of being a response to the pressure of too many bodies, registers the felt pressure of too many consciousnesses, and his specter of overpopulation represents what might be called a Romantic political economy, much as the sense of psychic crowding in Wordsworth's descriptions of London in book 7 of *The Prelude* represents a Romantic poetic consciousness. For Malthus and Wordsworth both, a Romantic consciousness emerges in reaction to the proliferation of other consciousnesses, or rather to the claims of other consciousnesses—for example, women's— on the individual. Solitude comes to be cultivated as a space for consciousness in which the individual is not answerable to others, and the waste landscape becomes the site of value because one can make it a peopled solitude, anthropomorphizing rocks and stones and trees, without encountering the pressures of a competing consciousness.

Insofar as this observation constitutes a critique of Malthus and Wordsworth, and in particular a feminist critique, it may be said to have been anticipated by Germaine Greer in her *Sex and Destiny: The Politics of Human Fertility*.[4] There Greer writes about population to suggest that the problem is not that there are too many people but rather that too many people believe that the world is overpopulated. Concluding the book with a passionate plea that the so-called developed nations not export their beliefs about population control, she calls for a reexamination of the allocation of resources. "If," she writes,

> we in the West think that only our kind of life is worth living, then clearly the numbers that the earth supports will have to be substantially reduced. The world could become a vast luxury hotel, complete with recreational space for us to hunt and ski and mountaineer in, but it must not be forgotten that our luxurious lifestyle demands the services of a huge number of helots, who cannot be paid so much that they can afford rooms in the hotel for themselves.[489]

Greer thus maintains that Western capitalism offers a most efficient variety of enslavement for the majority of the world's population and that Western views on the desirability of birth control translate into our commitment to cash in other people's necessities for our luxuries, viewing other people's lives as expendable, and seeing them as superfluities, just so much waste.

Overpopulation, from her standpoint, is a myth conceived in apology for Westerners being more concerned with a certain luxurious lifestyle than with the lives of other people. No one, she claims with some justice, knows "how many people the earth can support," and consequently no one knows if the earth is now overpopulated. Although she immediately affirms that "it is quite probable that the world is overpopulated and has been so for some time"(490), she moves from a hopeful discussion of redistributing the earth's resources to produce food for the many instead of luxuries—and even luxurious food—for the few to a vision of Western decline and fall. Like many of the eighteenth-century writers on population, she sees luxury as tending toward depopulation and the weakening of a society. And less interested in resource management than in the intrinsically moral aspects of the issue, she sketches with a certain relish an apocalyptic future in which Western nations are done in by the very luxury that they love: "Rather than being afraid of the powerless," she writes, "let us be afraid of the powerful, the rich sterile nations, who, whether they be of the Eastern or Western variety, have no stake in the future"(492).

Greer's defense of the reproductive practices of Third World nations thus does not merely claim that the "powerless" ought to be allowed what is very nearly the only power they have—the power to reproduce; she inverts the values that she sees in developed societies in her prediction of who will prevail. The populous powerless will live, the sterile rich will die. Thus, she ultimately recapitulates the narrative of scarcity that has animated the discussions of population for the last two and a half centuries. While first appearing to say that the rich nations should not impose their reproductive practices on poor nations so that all can live, she finally re-creates a world in which scarcity pits rich and poor against one another—but the difference between our present and her future is not that all will live but that the roles of living and dying will be reassigned.

Greer raises the issue of out-and-out scarcity to debunk it, suggesting that we probably have enough food to support a big population if we live lower on the food chain, but then she moves not just to an argument that we need to reallocate resources but well beyond to the argument that we need to eliminate rich people and rich nations. She thus restages the Malthusian battle for resources, suggesting once again the appeal of the scarcity argument from the time of its initial appearance in the eighteenth century in the work of James Steuart and, later, Malthus. The argument about scarcity, that is, emerges not just as an attempt to fit numbers of persons to quantities of resources; it also, and more importantly, is a very satisfactory mode of pitting groups of persons against one another, indeed of pitting one idea of what a person is against others. What is problematic about Greer's work— at least from a contemporary feminist standpoint—is that she relegates consciousness and individual freedom to the realm of luxury. Essentially advocating an agrarian system so "natural" or nontechnological as to involve all-consuming labor to produce subsistence living, Greer would eliminate the waste that she takes consciousness to be. This would of course produce equality—even though it would involve everyone's being universally enthralled to the production of mere sustenance, and Greer thus has no patience with accounts of women's acceding to consciousness in a way that might threaten Malthus.

The eighteenth-century debate about population likewise tended to emphasize the fitting of labor and resources rather than the relationship between population size and individualism. Thus, writers on population, looking around them and seeing work to be done and land to be improved, had first made the claim that the world was not overpopulated but the reverse. The land needed improvement, and people were therefore needed to improve it. Robert Wallace, in his *Dissertation on the Numbers of Mankind* of 1753,[5] said that no state could "be said to be populous, where there are great tracts of land uncultivated"(121) and went on to offer plans for promoting agricultural industry in Scotland. Writers on population frequently cited Montesquieu's *Persian Letters* to the effect that "there were fifty times in the world as many people in the days of Julius Caesar, the first Roman emperor, as are in it at present"; they might demur, with Wallace, that this was "certainly too high a proportion"(35), but they seldom differed with the basic premise that ancient nations had had more substantial populations than modern nations did. Godwin, writing in response to Malthus in 1820, stated categorically that "we live, as I have often had occasion to regret, in an unpeopled world."[6] Claiming that the world was empty rather than full, he indignantly wrote that "it is in this wreck of a world, almost as desolate as if a comet from the orbit of Saturn had come too near us, that Mr. Malthus issues his solemn denunciations, warning us on no consideration to increase the numbers of mankind"(486).

Population counts, these writers claimed, were more than a matter of neutral numbers. Those convinced that the modern world was "unpeopled," "dispeopled," or "waste" saw the superior populousness of ancient nations as yet another argument for the superiority of ancient governments over modern ones. As Wallace remarked in a footnote,

> The question concerning the number of mankind in ancient and modern times, under ancient or modern governments, is not to be considered as a matter of mere curiosity, but of the greatest importance; since it must be a strong presumption in favour of the customs or policy of any government, if, *ceteris paribus,* it is able to raise up and maintain a greater number of people.[7]

A good government, many writers argued, was a government that made people happy, and happy people tended to reproduce themselves.

These claims were easy to affirm—and equally easy to deny, because they were based on the flimsiest of data, including the various conflicting figures that ancient historians had offered about the numbers of soldiers whom various nations had sent to battle, along with modern census tables in a bewildering variety of arrangements. The debate about population proceeded as a series of conjectural histories with more powerful information about the symbolic value of population than about the actual numbers of human beings alive at any given time. The persistent and pervasive assumption was that populousness was a positive value, and that one could indicate the virtuousness of any cause by establishing a causal connection between it and an ample population—or the viciousness of anything that seemed to impede the growth of population. Thus, Benjamin Franklin boasted of extraordinary American fertility rates and stated that the people of America multiplied "by procreation, so as to 'double their numbers every twenty years.' " Franklin continued, " 'if in Europe they have but four births to a marriage, we may here [in America] reckon eight.' "[8] William Godwin, reading Franklin's claims with a jaundiced eye, found them less useful for establishing reliable information about the American population than about Franklin, whom he judged to have been always "eminently an American patriot," eager "to exalt the importance and glory of his country"(127). Similarly, Wallace provided less information about population than about his views on Catholicism when he maintained that the number of persons who had become priests and nuns "may justly be accounted one of the causes of the *scarcity* of people in all the countries under the pope's dominion"(88; emphasis added).

Given the pervasiveness of the assumptions that populousness in and of itself betokened happiness and civic virtue and that modern nations—particularly England—were woefully depopulated, Malthus's account of the inevitability of overpopulation in England was alarming not just because it constituted a dire prediction but also because it located danger in a hitherto unanticipated quarter. The production of people which had seemed desirable came to appear hazardous at best. Moreover, Malthus's mathematical ratios enabled him to make projections of population and food supplies which were both necessarily true because they were the result of an abstract technology for producing numbers and conveniently removed from any actual numbers of persons or quantities of farm produce. Because it is indisputable that a geometric progression quickly overtakes an arithmetic one, the only matter in doubt is whether the increase in agricultural production and the increase in population are appropriately tied to these respective ratios. And although Malthus's entire treatise revolves around the actuarial terror that the inexorable operation of these ratios is supposed to inspire, the treatise itself calls for the abrogation of this mathematical principle of population increase. Could the geometric progression not be altered, there would be no point in writing the *Essay,* which not merely laments the fate of the earth but also proposes strategies that would avert the onward march of the geometric ratio.

The dispute between Malthus and an opponent like Godwin thus first comes down to the question of the way to fit people to resources. Malthus, despite his writing to discourage population increase, figures reproduction as a mathematical process, the inevitable and essentially unvarying production of numbers from ratios of other numbers. Against this vision of the immortality of a mathematical body that replicates itself of necessity, Godwin sets one that argues the power of consciousness to intervene. Yet the power of consciousness is framed as much in terms of the weakness of the biological body as in terms of the force of human thought. Godwin would save humans from the inexorable operation of Malthus's immortal mathematical body by attributing to them a time-limited biological body, where individual foresight both imposes constraints on reproduction and appropriates the accidents of mortality to its own purposes.

Godwin thus maintains that population, insofar as it is a problem, is one that corrects itself. In example, he points to Sweden as a country about which "we have something approaching to authentic information" and firmly states "that if there has been any actual increase, it at least amounts to comparatively very little"(196). Malthus arrives at a terrifying account of population expansion, Godwin holds, by assigning to individuals a reproductive power in society that they could have only if humans were both immortal and so thoroughly incapable of reflecting on their circumstances that they never curtailed the size of their families (207ff.). Malthus uses a mathematical language of stability to maintain that food is subject to increase according to an arithmetic progression, that population is subject to increase in geometric progression, and that the "passion between the sexes" is "in algebraic language," a "given quantity" (52). The mind-limited body that Godwin imagines, however, checks population increase, so that the birthrate is high only in countries such as the United States which are societies that are "incomplete." While it obviously cannot forestall the possibility of future crop failure and scarcity, mortality, and so forth, it continually changes what Godwin, in scathing quotation of Malthus's language of mathematical function, calls their "values."

The question of freedom—as the freedom at least to plan—thus intrudes itself into even the actuarial debate in which Malthus and Godwin are engaged. The argument for connecting numbers with liberty and individual consciousness had been advanced by Hume in 1751, in his essay "Of the Populousness of Ancient Nations." Hume, specifically addressing himself to the issue of the relationship between ancient nations and modern ones, argued against what he saw as the cant of believing that the world was in decline, in numbers of people and in government (esp. 443). He wonders if it is "certain, that antiquity was so much more populous, as is pretended"(383). And his doubt specifically attaches to Rome and the institution of slavery. Without leaping to condemn slavery as morally reprehensible, Hume performs an economic analysis of it. Since, he reasons, it must have been more expensive to rear children in the city, where domestic slaves were most in demand, Roman slaveholders must have discouraged their slaves from procreating—to the point of establishing separate living quarters for men and women and forbidding their intercourse. Just as few cattle are bred "in all populous, rich, industrious provinces," where "provisions, lodging, attendance, [and] labour" are all dear (388), so economic disincentives work to check the increase in the number of children born to domestic slaves.

Thus, Hume refutes the claim of the supposed fertility of Roman slaves, concluding that the "human species would perish in those places where it ought to increase the fastest; and a perpetual recruit be wanted from the poorer and more desert provinces"(388). And he proceeds to argue that slavery and warfare were related ways of reducing ancient populations. In his account, slavery is a way of reading some people out of the count of reproducible persons, and warfare is a way of subtracting, since it eliminates some persons altogether (in killing them) and keeps others from reproducing (in consigning them to slavery). Observing that the ancient republics were almost perpetually at war with one another out of "their love of liberty"(400), Hume later remarks that "these people [the ancients] were extremely fond of liberty; but seem not to have understood it very well"(403). The ancient nations' imperfect understanding of liberty involves, of course, their commitment to their liberty as opposed to—and at the expense of— the liberty of others. Being dead means having no consciousness, and being a slave also turns out to mean having no consciousness, in that one is never at liberty to act on one's consciousness; and having no consciousness turns out to be the most effective check to reproduction. You must be a person to be allowed to reproduce, and liberty is the power not only to count but to have one's reproductive capacity counted in the ratios of population increase.

On Hume's account, material conditions determine fertility only insofar as they overlap with slavery or freedom. To be a slave is to have no choice but to attend to—or have someone else attend to—your market value, the cost effectiveness of your production. Malthus and Godwin, taking up the issue of freedom and slavery, continually argue about what condition approaches most nearly to slavery—the restraint that keeps someone from procreating out of an anticipatory fear of possible future dearth or the production of individuals who might be free only to starve.

Malthus and Godwin disagree, then, on whether or not there is a dearth of resources to support human life, on whether or not population should be checked, and on how effective individual decisions about procreation would be in limiting the size of a population. They agree, however, on one thing— that present governmental arrangements tend toward slavery rather than freedom. This agreement of course dissolves as soon as they begin to specify the features of government that are problematic. For Malthus sees government as delusive when it acts to disguise what he everywhere forbiddingly calls the operation of "Necessity"; Godwin, on the other hand, sees it as preventing the kind of equality and improvement among individuals that would bring an end to want. Thus, Malthus denounces the Poor Laws because they encourage a false security in offering such people as tenant farmers the illusion that they can be protected against want. Should crops fail, the small farmer with more family than food can know that society inter- venes to distance him and his family from starvation. Yet, Malthus argues, the Poor Laws, in appearing to distance the laboring classes from unex- pected sufferings, in fact institutionalize the sufferings of the poor by luring them into a false happiness that makes them think themselves free to pro- create, to produce more persons like themselves with whom they will have to share their portions. Thus, Malthus very sternly declares that "a labourer who marries without being able to support a family may in some respects be considered as an enemy to all his fellow-labourers"(40). This language would seem particularly melodramatic if it did not read the English Poor Laws as a way of reversing the drive toward independence that Malthus has seen civilization promoting. The insurance provided by parish aid, in his account, turns out not really to be protection against hardship that can be figured in terms of money or even food; rather it offers the only kind of insurance that he sees society able to provide—the security of the slave, the human whose need causes him, as in ancient nations, to cashier his inde- pendence.[9] Early in the *Essay* Malthus describes the progress of civilization toward increasingly efficient ways of supplying food and resources to peo- ple. And while it might seem to be a merely economic account of societies that supply their wants through hunting and herding to those that do so through agriculture and manufactures, the progress that he sees coincides with a decrease in slavery or virtual slavery, the property that people have in other people and their labor.

> The North American Indians, considered as a people, cannot justly be called free and equal. In all the accounts we have of them, and, indeed, of most other savage nations, the women are represented as more completely in a state of slavery to the men than the poor are to the rich in civilized countries. One half the nation appears to act as Helots to the other half, and the misery that checks population falls chiefly, as it always must do, upon that part whose condition is lowest in the scale of society.[27]

Women and children suffer, he says, as the women, "condemned as they are to the inconveniences and hardships of frequent change of place and to the constant and unremitting drudgery of preparing every thing for the recep- tion of their tyrannic lords"(27–28), cannot give the "necessary attention" to their labor-intensive infants. Moreover, even though one of the two car- dinal points of the *Essay* is that the attraction between the sexes is constant, he cites reports "that the passion between the sexes is less ardent among the North American Indians than among any other race of men"(27), as if to suggest that an extreme enough system of inequality begins to affect even the most basic and constant biological forces. The attraction between the sexes fails in the inexorable course it earlier apparently had, and consciousness in the form of unhappiness interferes with biological function.

The march of progress in Malthus's catalog of social organizations and the allocation of peoples and foodstuffs is one in which labor has constantly increasing returns and people impinge upon people to a lesser extent. Thus, herding represents an improvement over hunting: "The women lived in greater ease than among nations of hunters," and the men, united in groups that magnified their individual strength, "felt, probably, few fears about providing for a family"(29). This happiness, however, bred both contentment and children, which forced the tribe into migration and war in its search for food supplies. These were "bold and improvident Barbarians," for whom the response to scarcity was the sacrifice of the many to the conquest of "an Alaric, an Attila, or a Zingis Khan," and the exercise of "a power even, if distressed, of selling their children as slaves"(30).

Malthus's analysis of the way early societies fit people to resources has thus far concentrated on the way an individual's liberty has historically been the luxury that could be converted into necessities. Faced with starvation, earlier men could sell themselves or their children. The question of how many people the earth will support changes, he suggests, when it is a question of how many free people it will support. And Malthus's survey of civilizations clearly moves beyond the question of the mere satisfaction of food and the attraction between the sexes when he begins his account of an eighteenth-century man of marriageable age:

> A man of liberal education, but with an income only just sufficient to enable him to associate in the rank of gentlemen, must feel absolutely certain that if he marries and has a family he shall be obliged, if he mixes at all in society, to rank himself with moderate farmers and the lower class of tradesmen. The woman that a man of education would naturally make the object of his choice would be one brought up in the same tastes and sentiments with himself and used to the familiar intercourse of a society totally different from that to which she must be reduced by marriage. Two or three steps of descent in society, particularly at this round of the ladder, where education ends and ignorance begins, will not be considered by the generality of people as a fancied and chimerical, but a real and essential evil.[34]

Famine, plagues, and death in combat have all appeared as serious but conveniently remote perils of ancient forms of civilization in Malthus's conjectural history, but the thought of a woman unhappily married beneath her station also counts as "a real and essential evil." While the women of the hunting and herding societies had their misery reserved for them, it was rendered as a misery occasioned by excessive labor and inadequate visibility: they were always in danger of being absorbed into the production of the tyrant or the warrior hero. The woman who might be a suitable match for our young man of liberal education, however, is more visible than her predecessors precisely because she does not labor, because her produce is happiness or misery unmediated by any gainful employment. The very palpability of this imaginary woman's possible unhappiness suggests that she has a consciousness that counts, but the "idea of grief" that comes to Malthus as he contemplates her is the most effective prophylactic in the *Essay*. As marriage here, as elsewhere in the eighteenth and early nineteenth centuries, always stands for marriage-and-children, the young man who woos and wins her must be prepared to provide for several mouths if he is to ward off this unhappiness. And miserable as the single life may be, Malthus clearly paints it as preferable to acting on the attraction between the sexes so that one must confront the misery of scarcity not in the world but in the household.

The central fact about this example of misery is that it has nothing at all to do with the kind of misery involved in the prospect of imminent starvation. There is no way of remedying it by economizing on groceries or learning to eat lower on the food chain. And it epitomizes all that Greer loathes in its abject inability to see food and the attraction between the sexes as the only two simple and irreducible needs that are both necessary and sufficient for life. Particularly important is that Malthus stages it as the only account in his brief history of world civilization which attributes a consciousness to a woman, the only one, that is, that recognizes it might matter to anyone how a woman might feel about her lot in life. The passage, of course, registers its plangency mainly in terms that sound like "I hate it when women cry," but it also suggests the way the account of sustenance begins to shift if we are talking about creating a space for more than one consciousness, about whether there is room for two in these resources.

Godwin of course opposes the Malthusian model because he sees it as setting off a false alarm—seeing scarcity where there is none—and because he views it as a way of consolidating and exacerbating all that is wrong with English government and property law. Malthus would, he claims, derive property rights from the geometric ratio, would, that is, protect property against people—or against all but previously propertied people. In giving individuals priority to property, Godwin's *Enquiry concerning Political Justice* (1st ed. 1793, 3d ed. 1798)[10] and his *Of Population* (of 1820) articulate the most forceful argument against the Malthusian account of the pressure of population. Yet the irony is that Godwin begins to outdo Malthus as a calculator as he projects the possibility of realigning the relationships among food, human sustenance, and human labor. The earth can be improved to provide sustenance for more people—machines will bring "something like a final close to the necessity of manual labour" as ploughs are "turned into a field . . . [to] perform [their] office without the need of superintendence"(503). And people can be improved to need less sustenance or to find it in its most abundant forms: "no good reason can be assigned, why that which produces animal nourishment, must have previously passed though a process of animal or vegetable life"(500).

The argument that Godwin makes is one that makes infinite population increase look possible on the basis of increasingly efficient technologies for fitting people to resources. But if he presents it as possible, his *Enquiry concerning Political Justice* had suggested that it is anything but desirable. Yet while Godwin claims that the free human consciousness can alter even the material conditions of the world (look at recent advances in chemistry, he says), the consciousness of other people appears to him an even more dramatic form of slavery than it did to Malthus. For Godwin describes a society that would be composed directly out of individuals, that is, without any institutional mediation through government. He can thus speak of population as susceptible to infinite increase so long as society is merely the individual magnified, but the possibility of more than one person leads to the specter of inequality, and the idea of inequality leads to the ideas of imprisonment and slavery. "All formal repetition of other men's ideas, seems to be a scheme for imprisoning . . . the operations of our own mind"(2: 504). The institution of marriage is a monopoly whereby a man maintains exclusive property in a wife. Thus, common labor and cohabitation are undesirable, because society must be formed from individuals who are unconstrained by the influence of others. That is, this wreck of a world could contain more and more people, but they must never be in the same room, as the presence of more than one individual always threatens to produce the coerciveness that government embodies for Godwin. And Godwin finally concludes his defense of consciousness in *Of Population* with an argument for its restriction, for the kind of slavery that domesticity offers: a man's "children and his wife are pledges he gives to the public for his good behavior; they are his securities, that he will truly enter into the feeling of a common interest"(586).

In Godwin's account, the self is spread thin, particularly given the fact that his commitment to anarchy means that every reflecting individual is required to have a social policy. If human beings by dint of reflection are supposed to adjust to fluctuations in population to produce children as necessary, how will each individual know whether the society, like that of the

United States, is complete or incomplete? Against Malthus's anticipatory dread of the unhappiness of a woman who has married beneath her, Godwin sets the model of a self that must expand infinitely to become identical with the full population of the society while also remaining untouched by the presence of other consciousnesses.

Malthus can, then, admit—and forestall—the consciousness of the unhappy woman, so long as it is the *idea* of the unhappy woman; Godwin can introduce a wife and family as an individual's pledge to society, so long as society does not include any possibility of one consciousness being contaminated by the operation of other consciousnesses. And, as David Ferry has observed, Wordsworth learns from his love of nature a love of man that is a love of the *idea* of man—and that is, in turn, again a love of nature.[11] But if Wordsworth continually seeks out landscapes that are conspicuously "unimproved" (or undoes their improvements and manufactures so as to present them as unimproved), this solitary nature on which he will not tolerate previous marks keeps producing shadows of other people despite—or perhaps because of—his best efforts to suppress them.

Let "Lines written a few miles above Tintern Abbey, on revisiting the banks of the Wye during a tour, July 13, 1798" stand as an example of the negotiations among the individual, nature, and society in Romantic poetry.[12] As has been long and frequently observed, the poem initially appears a locodescriptive poem, "a summons to self-consciousness" in Geoffrey Hartman's phrase, in which the poet is alone with the landscape.[13] Seeing the same landscape twice on occasions separated by five years is like taking one's blood pressure at intervals: it enables Wordsworth to see which way he's going, to get his spiritual bearings.

Moreover, seeming to tell over to himself the story of his memory of the place and his present sense of it, he makes himself both teller and listener to this story that is so slight as to have almost no plot at all—just the merest "the place is much as I remember it." And the movement of description proceeds to link up the various elements of the landscape as if to say that their connection does not involve their encroachment upon one another. In fact, things in this natural scene are scarcely allowed to be what they are, in the effort to ward off the possibility of one thing impinging on another; the "orchard-tufts . . . lose themselves . . . among the woods and copses" and the "hedge-rows" are "hardly hedge-rows."

Now on one level Wordsworth is approvingly noting that the human intervention in the landscape blends in. The agricultural improvements, the "orchard-tufts" and "hedge-rows," do not "disturb / The wild green landscape." The only element that appears to exert any force on the landscape is that of the

> . . . steep and lofty cliffs,
> Which on a wild secluded scene impress
> Thoughts of more deep seclusion; and connect
> The landscape with the quiet of the sky.

And even though the pressure of the cliffs' intrusion palpably frames the landscape (so that one knows what Wordsworth means), the conundrum built into this landscape, this scene, is that one never quite knows when it is a landscape. How can the "orchard-tufts" and the "hedge-rows" not be part of the landscape, how can the cliffs not exactly count in the scene?

The point of all the exactitude of Wordsworth's description is that they do count—but not because they came together. Instead, the mention of signs of cultivation and the surmise about gypsies or a hermit function to indicate that they too have been subsumed in the landscape—not primarily, however, through natural agency but instead through the poet's molding of the scene. The ultimate mark of his seclusion, that is, is not that there are not any traces of other people in the scene but that he lays claim to seclusion by presenting himself as the only one who views the scene in this particular way. He is the only one who is humanizing nature by seeing at this angle the human elements in it naturalized.

It would be possible to see this pattern, with some recent critics, as involving a politically reactionary stance.[14] Wordsworth, in this view, sacrifices the reality of other people to an archaic vision of the land which continues his privilege and other people's suffering. And Wordsworth's account of "these forms of beauty" having sustained him in the "din / Of towns and cities" might well be read as simply a statement of the way an aesthetic memory can be used as a defensive weapon, a kind of shield to ward off a consciousness of the existence of other people. Yet a difficulty with that reading emerges when we remember—and when Wordsworth remembers— that Dorothy is there.

Or is she? One argument that has been advanced by some critics is that she only appears to be there and functions as a kind of optical illusion that enables Wordsworth to end by talking to someone other than himself. On this account, Dorothy appears as a function of the territorial imperialism of Wordsworth's ego, which incorporates people and things as it pleases. She is, then, not an independent consciousness but merely an epiphenomenon of his. But that model doesn't quite conform to the poem's odd premise— which is that Wordsworth must retreat into the landscape so that he can produce a sense of self, since he doesn't have enough selfhood for one person, much less two. Rather, that moment of remembering that Dorothy came with him is the unraveling of the imposition of solitude on the scene, the moment in which he implicitly backtracks from the reading of agricultural improvements, the marks of other people, as wasteland. It is his acknowledgment that the waste is always improved, that the self is already socialized.

But if Wordsworth appears more resigned to the existence of another consciousness than Malthus or Godwin, discovering that the self already is another instead of warily anticipating a possible encroachment, "Tintern Abbey" curiously insists that the presence of other people—even Dorothy—always appears as a kind of accident to the individual consciousness. The anthropomorphism that enables him to read the landscape as if it were a self that could endow him with a self effects its own curbs on the numbers of consciousnesses that can become visible. Malthus fears a reproachful consciousness of the unhappy woman at variance with his imaginary young man; Godwin shrinks from any contact between consciousnesses that might differ as he postulates the expansion of the individual into an identity with society; and Wordsworth defines a scene as wild, random, to proceed to make it yield meaning to and for his determining consciousness—only to have to rehabilitate the accident of another person's existence by imagining that she sees what he sees. The individual consciousness reading the landscape, that is, unlike the United States in Godwin's description, always takes itself to be complete.

Notes

1. My thinking on this subject has been particularly inspired by H. J. Habakkuk, *Population Growth and Economic Development since 1750* (Leicester: Leicester University Press, 1971), which presents a particularly thoughtful analysis of the economic conditions of population growth in the later eighteenth century in Britain, and by Catherine Gallagher, "The Body versus the Social Body in the Works of Thomas Malthus and Henry Mayhew," *Representations* 14:83–106, an essay that insightfully locates a shift from a labor-theory account of the value of the individual body to an exchange-theory account.

2. Hume provides a particularly clear account of these assumptions in his "Of the Populousness of Ancient Nations," in *Essays Moral, Political, and Literary*, ed. T. H. Green and T. H. Grose, 2 vols. (London: Longmans, Green, and Co., 1898), 1:381–443.

3. Thomas Robert Malthus, *An Essay on the Principle of Population*, ed. Philip Appleman (New York: W. W. Norton & Co., 1976).

4. Germaine Greer, *Sex and Destiny: The Politics of Human Fertility* (New York: Harper & Row, 1984).

5. Robert Wallace, *Dissertation on the Numbers of Mankind in Ancient and Modern Times,* Edinburgh: Archibald Constable and Co., 1809.

6. William Godwin, *Of Population: An Enquiry concerning the Power of Increase in the Numbers of Mankind, Being an Answer to Mr. Malthus's Essay on That Subject* (London: Longman, Hurst, Ree, Orme and Brown, 1820), 485.

7. P. 14. See also Malthus, 46.

8. Quoted by Godwin in *Of Population*, 126–27.

9. Cf. Wallace, *Dissertation*, 90.
10. William Godwin, *Enquiry concerning Political Justice and Its Influence on Morals and Happiness*, facsimile 3d ed., ed. F. E. L. Priestley, 3 vols. (Toronto: University of Toronto Press, 1969).
11. David Ferry, *The Limits of Mortality: An Essay on Wordsworth's Major Poems* (Middletown, Conn.: Wesleyan University Press, 1959), 104 ff.
12. William Wordsworth and Samuel Taylor Coleridge, *Lyrical Ballads: A Text of the 1798 Edition with the Additional 1800 Poems and the Prefaces*, ed. R. L. Brett and A. R. Jones (London: Methuen and Co., 1963), 111.
13. Geoffrey H. Hartman, *Wordsworth's Poetry 1787–1814* (New Haven: Yale University Press, 1971), 29.
14. See particularly Jerome J. McGann, *The Romantic Ideology: A Critical Investigation* (Chicago: University of Chicago Press, 1983), 81–92 and passim. An interesting example of this general view also appears in David Aers, "Wordsworth's Model of Man in 'The Prelude,'" in *Romanticism and Ideology: Studies in English Writing 1765–1830*.

6

In Search of the Natural Sublime: The Face on the Forest Floor

William Gilpin, in one of his numerous books of *Observations . . . Relative Chiefly to Picturesque Beauty,* steps aside from his descriptive excursion on the natural compositions awaiting the traveler to make a point about the appeals of certain dreary sites. The Edystone Lighthouse, he admits, has many drawbacks as a primary residence: its briny atmosphere makes breathing unhealthy; darkness and stench surround its living quarters; and stormy weather makes it impossible for boats to "touch at Edystone for many months" at a stretch.

> The whole together is, perhaps, one of the least eligible pieces of preferment in Britain: and yet from a story which Mr. Smeaton relates, it appears there are stations still more ineligible. A fellow, who got a good livelihood by making leathern-pipes for engines, grew tired of sitting constantly at work, and solicited a lighthouse man's place, which, as competitors are not numerous, he obtained. As the Edystone-boat was carrying him to take possession of his new habitation, one of the boatmen asked him, what could tempt him to give up a profitable business to be shut up, for months together, in a pillar? "Why," said the man, "because I did not like confinement."[1]

I shall be concerned here with the evolution of British travel literature in the eighteenth and early nineteenth centuries and with its recurrence to a particular set of contradictions—between intimacy with the domestic landscape and a sense of the confinement of society. The cultivation of the pleasures of a domestic and British—rather than Continental—landscape burgeoned, at the same time that very cultivation of the landscape presented itself as an escape from the society of other Britishers.

My argument here is that the Romantic discussion of landscape and the natural sublime absorbs and redirects anxieties implicit in the eighteenth-century conception of theatricality. Theatricality, as Michael Fried has compellingly traced it in his book *Absorption and Theatricality,* becomes less a vivid metaphor than a problematic as the mere consciousness of being beheld comes to be seen as a version of lying.[2] In the terms of this suspicion of theatricality, to be conscious of being seen is always to be in the position of mugging, putting on one's expressions for the sake of one's audience. Moreover, because works of art are inevitably made to be beheld, this eighteenth-century suspicion of theatricality poses a major challenge to the notion of art itself. Art thus looks like a deceptive practice not so much on the grounds of the maker's intention to deceive but on the basis of the more unsettling charge that the beholder's gaze renders it impossible for the artist to be anything other than deceptive. An apparent impasse about the validity of art objects thus installs itself at the center of discussions of art. Yet one of Fried's major claims is, essentially, that major French eighteenth-century painters converted an ontological problem into a strategic one; continually painting subjects who appeared so thoroughly absorbed in their activities as to have no consciousness of being beheld, these painters borrowed from their own subjects the authority of unconsciousness.

The impact of this line of thinking upon the genres of painting and upon the handling of particular examples of those genres is clear. Both history painting and portraiture, as Fried very convincingly shows, must reformulate their explicit claims to public attention. Moreover, such a reformulation is necessary not merely because painting should not reveal its designs upon its audience's attention but also because that attention itself comes to count as an assault on the painting, the gaze that makes it lie.

Kant's treatment of the sublime extends such an eighteenth-century obsession with the production of duplicity along with visibility by locating aesthetic pleasure in nature—outside, that is, of the question of design or intention. For if the process of trying to make one's consciousness present to another consciousness continually ends in the theatrical suspicion of deceptiveness, the sublime account of nature continually offers the possibility of an individuality that feels uncompromised. Against the theatrical fear of a diminution of consciousness produced by the very act of communication, the sublime establishes nature as the instrument for the production of individuality itself. The experience of pleasure in a nature that is, by definition, indifferent to your reactions, produces self-consciousness as a version of imagining where any kind of meaning might originate; the experience of pain or fear in nature, moreover, makes such self-consciousness look merely natural, like the forced product of nature's coercive force. From Burke's account of the self-preservative purposes of sublime terror to Kant's dynamical sublime, nature's might provides the model for an extraordinarily productive confusion. The theatrical world of society may make it appear that one cannot represent oneself even to oneself. The world of nature makes it appear that talking only to objects with which one shares no language guarantees individuality.

The function of guidebooks obviously shifts under this socio-aesthetic pressure. The ever-growing list of guidebooks in the eighteenth century describes for prospective travelers places to see, how to get to them, and what they look like. But these guidebooks also begin to describe the landscape in terms of possibility of on-the-spot constructions of sublime, beautiful, and picturesque views—what cannot be described because it has not yet been seen in exactly that way, from that spot, by that viewer.

Earlier, for Daniel Defoe writing his *Tour through the Whole Island of Great Britain* between 1724 and 1726, the obsolescence of the travel guide had seemed like a marketing opportunity (rather than a virtually formal feature for the dissemination of individuality). The work, Defoe writes, "itself is a description of the most flourishing and opulent country in the world."[3] As the country continually changes, so the descriptions must change, having already created an opening for Defoe's *Tour* and inevitably establishing future needs in that line: "Whoever has travelled Great Britain before us, and whatever they have written, though they may have had a harvest, yet they have always, yet they have always, either by necessity, ignorance or negligence passed over so much, that others may come and glean after them by large handfuls"(43). Even had there been travel writers more numerous and more diligent, Defoe says, there would still be room for further work, "For the face of things so often alters, . . . that there is matter of new observation every day presented to the traveller's eye." In sum, "the Fate of things gives a new face to things," and "new matter offers to new observation"(44).

The limitation of Defoe's guide is, thus, its proudest boast; its subject continually renews itself even as the description remains fixed. Its point as a document of the country's shape is to preserve the past as a standard by which to measure subsequent growth; it solicits the traveler to see how much things have changed—specifically, to see how much things have been *improved*—since the time Defoe made his observations:

> But after all that has been said by others, or can be said here, no description of Great Britain can be, what we call a finished account, as no clothes can be made to fit a growing child; no picture carry the likeness of a living face; the size of one, and the countenance of the other, always altering with time: so no account of a kingdom thus daily altering its countenance, can be perfect.[46]

The living face of Great Britain becomes on this account a large-scale version of the "garden of liberalism," in which the free growth of the face beyond its representation in the *Tour* becomes emblematic of its capacity to incorporate change, improvement, and the marks of human industry. Britain's face, moreover, is most natural when most populous, when marked by the presence of human settlements and commerce. He finds fault with Westmoreland for its desolation, describing it as "a Country eminent for being the wildest, most barren and frightful of any that I have passed over in England, or even in Wales it self," and proceeds to correct himself, to think more positively: "But 'tis of no Advantage to represent Horror, as the Character of a Country, in the middle of all the frightful Appearances to the right and left; yet here are some very pleasant, populous, and manufacturing Towns, and consequently populous."[4]

"Pleasant, populous, and manufacturing Towns, and consequently populous"—the word "populous" recurs with a startling insistence. We could, of course, relate its reappearance to the breakneck speed of Defoe's compositions and point out his tendency to get exemplary service from a corps of words that he continually presses. Yet the word "populous" does not merely echo itself, it also is called in to be a causal explanation for itself. Towns that are "populous, and manufacturing Towns" do not merely have population but also produce it. The logic can easily be made plausible: because one needs a certain number of people for manufactures, manufactures are drawn to populous towns, and manufacturing towns draw and retain populations by providing work for people to do.

As populousness becomes simultaneously cause and effect of itself, Defoe establishes a model that speaks feelingly not just about his preferences in landscape but about the nature of those preferences. Just as the words "new," "increase," "variety," "luxuriance," and "improvement" resound throughout his preface to the first volume, so here "populous" bespeaks a process of self-generation and self-extension that seems curiously disconnected from any description of what those populations might be—or even what they might look like. (Thus, Defoe in this preface begins with novelty before introducing examples: "If novelty pleases, here is the present state of the country described, the improvement, as well in culture, as in commerce, the increase of people, and employment for them"[43].) In Defoe's account of populousness producing populousness, we see an instance of his never allowing for a moment in which the type might have to be drawn from specific examples. He is, instead, calling upon types continually to demonstrate their typicality by manufacturing individual versions as merely more of the type. Manufactures, thus, operate exactly as nature does for him, as a process of replication that extends itself seemingly infinitely because it never links itself to individual identities that have any particular limitations in time.

For Defoe, then, it is not merely that nature looks most beautiful when it is, as in the Swiss Alps, relieved by the presence of human settlements and centers of commerce (549). It is also that manufacturing and commerce involve taking a lesson from his version of nature, in which the notions of exchange and self-replicating types and processes combine with more than a little indifference to individualities. His *Tour* functions less, that is, as a history than as a natural history (a description of natural process extended into a social and naturalized world). For even though historians have relied extensively on the *Tour* for information about eighteenth-century Britain, it not only announces bluntly that "the looking back into remote things is studiously avoided"(43) but also reveals a striking indifference to the project of getting the names of individuals straight. He seems, that is, unconcerned both with individuals and with the names and mortality that mark them as individuals.

Thus, Defoe's nature, like Defoe's commerce, makes theatricality look like a solution rather than a problem, because it never calls up a moment in which the typical and the individual, the general and the particular, are in any kind of collision or competition with one another. In fact, the *Tour* begins to look like a pretext for reading *Moll Flanders* as if it were not so much about the misrepresentations available in a world in which one must represent oneself to others as it is about a process of developing various self-presentations that, ultimately and additively, serve to make one typical.

What I am calling typicality here clearly underwrites a number of eighteenth-century rational enthusiasms for processes in which human systematization improves upon nature in a relatively impersonal way. Almost anyone (with the ironic exception of Arthur Young, the most active writer on scientific husbandry in the late eighteenth century) could learn and deploy scientific principles of agricultural management. Agricultural improvement, being a techne, had little discernible signature. Thus, Young sounds remarkably like Defoe when he catalogues the changes in the landscape that indicate human activity generically rather than particularly.

> [Once] all the country from Holkam to Houghton was a wild sheep-walk, before the spirit of improvement seized the inhabitants; and this spirit has wrought amazing effects; for instead of boundless wilds, and uncultivated wastes, inhabited by scarcely anything but sheep; the country is all cut into enclosures, cultivated in a most husband-like manner, richly manured, well peopled, and yielding an hundred times the produce that it did in its former state.[5]

The advance of the enclosure movement (accelerated with the passage of the Acts of Enclosure in 1801) had increased the amount of land that gave evidence of new ownership in new fences and hedges.[6] And while new fences clearly bespoke active owners, they also bespoke the relative interchangeability of the humans connected with the land through that ownership. The steady progress of enclosures in the countryside led to the rise of farming (and the concomitant decline of shepherding); and the proliferation of the steam engine after the 1775 patent of Boulton and Watt expired in 1800 promoted the accumulation of people in cities (as factories no longer needed to be built next to fast-running streams in mountainous areas but could instead be constructed in centers of human energy, population centers that became "consequently, populous"). The generic equivalence of one person's ownership and another's, of one person's technical knowledge and another's, and of one person's connection on one place or another produces the satisfactions of visible productivity.

Against the improved and improving landscape that will accommodate the pleasures of utility, the travel writing of a Gilpin or a Wordsworth sets an increasingly particular series of observations. And specific details about places and objects become less important for demonstrating that one has seen a particular place than for demonstrating that particulars do not lose themselves in types. The implicit claim staked for the individuality and specificity of natural objects, however, runs counter to an understanding of nature's capacity to be nature and endure by virtue of creating particulars as versions of the same basic type. The very notion of biological classification—along with Keats's "Ode to a Nightingale"—tends to stress the persistence of the type in terms of a relative indifference to the specificity of its examples. An oak, from this perspective, is less an individual than an exemplar of a class; a nightingale's song can be immortal because the species nightingale endures even as individual nightingales die. Yet Gilpin's travel writing reverses such an attention to the persistence of natural types by being careful of the particular.

In fact, Gilpin organizes his *Forest Scenery* as a progression that moves through various forests so that one can come to know the trees. The first volume, moreover, presents the various different genera of trees—the oak, the ash, the beech, the elm—in much the same way that a field guide to birds might, so that one will be able to recognize them when one sees them. Having divided trees into deciduous and evergreens, Gilpin begins with the oak, which he characterizes as having an especially strong grasp on the earth and as having unusually stout limbs. These comparatively invisible traits soon give way, however, to the oak's appearance to the eye:

> Examine the ash, the elm, the beech, or almost any other tree, and you

may observe, in what direct and straight lines the branches in each shoot from the stem. Whereas the limbs of an oak are continually twisting *huc illuc*, in various contortions. . . There is not a characteristic more peculiar to the oak than this.[7]

Now the Linnean system establishes classification on the basis of one's being able to discern that certain characteristics are peculiar to certain kinds of plants and animals. It claims, in other words, that all trees do not look alike. All of Gilpin's observations that I have cited thus far are perfectly consistent with the relatively straightforward taxonomies of natural science, in that they rely on distinctions between kinds of trees without insisting upon the individual trees.

Thereafter, however, through a process of almost relentless personification, Gilpin sharpens his distinctions. The oak may be, as the rubric attached to Gilpin's drawing (along with traditional hierarchy) declares, "the king of trees," but names become increasingly proper, as with the "Cheltanham Oak"(1: 123). These are "celebrated" individual trees, heroes of the vegetable kind. For the progress of the first book (of the three of *Forest Scenery*) is one in which Gilpin moves from considering trees as "single objects" to giving "the specific character of each" kind of tree to giving "a short account of some of the most celebrated trees which have been noticed." Trees, important for him as "the foundation of all scenery"(1: iii), first appear as "single objects" to suggest their usefulness for larger picturesque units, but ultimately the narrative returns to the individual (rather than the merely unitary) tree (1: iii).

Trees with names, these are trees with histories. Gilpin, that is, discovers everywhere the importance of age in trees. The oak's longevity gives it its particular distinction as the most picturesque tree. It endures long enough to become a vegetable contortionist. Trees as single objects, for Gilpin, frequently are trees that are freaks. Their idiosyncrasies develop, however, less as original natural lapses than as scars, signs of the accidents that a tree has sustained through time. Thus, although he maintains that "all forms that are unnatural, displease"(1: 4), he also demonstrates a particular fondness for many picturesque ideas that "are derived [not from utility] but from the injuries the tree receives, or the diseases, to which it is subject"(1: 7).

The tree as single object must be a tree that demonstrates that it has never been single, that shows its age less in terms of the rings to be discovered were one to do a cross-section of its trunk than in terms of its subjection to injury or disease. Longevity, that is, may give the look of singularity, but that look is produced by the tree's having been constantly in its own version of society, a confinement in which the tree's very identity has been determined by its incorporating accidental shocks into its development. The tree's organic wholeness and continuity with itself yields to its having a history, which is equivalent to its telling the history of things external to itself.

Old trees, "splendid remnants of decaying grandeur, speak to the imagination in a style of eloquence, which the stripling cannot reach: they record the history of some storm, some blast of lightning, or other great event"(1: 9). The incursion of other plants is even more important than the operation of weather in promoting picturesque effects. Gilpin relates, for example, that it is

> not uncommon for the seed of trees, and particularly of the ash, to seize on some faulty part of a neighbouring trunk, and there strike root. Dr. Plot speaks of a piece of vegetable violence of this kind, which is rather extraordinary. An ash-key rooting itself on a decayed willow: and finding, as it increased, a deficiency of nourishment in the mother-plant, it began to insinuate its fibres by degrees through the trunk of the willow into the earth. There receiving an additional recruit, it began to thrive, and expand itself to such a size, that it burst the willow in pieces, which fell away from it on every side; and what was before the root of the ash, being now exposed to the air, became the solid trunk of a vigorous tree. [1: 39–40]

The ash's "vegetable violence," the production of one tree's beauty (and mortality) out of the growth of another, culminates a series of discussions of beauty-inducing parasites, mosses, lichens, liverworts (along with near-parasites such as ivy and hops). These "tribes" of parasites, Gilpin says, "make no pretence to independence. They are absolute retainers. Not one of them gets his own livelihood, nor takes the least step towards it" (1: 16).

Parasites, neither productive nor beautiful in themselves, are the cause of beauty in others. They produce the individuality of trees by making trees look sociable, and by making society look like a process in which the independent becomes individual and beautiful by dying for the generations of trees. The commitment to producing individuality for trees by making their beauty generational, moreover, explains what might otherwise seem like Gilpin's almost insane commitment to natural forests rather than artificial plantings of trees. The artificial plantation sets all trees out simultaneously. And all plantation trees, planted equally, develop under conditions that are all external.

> When we characterize a tree, we consider it in its natural state, insulated, and without any lateral pressure. In a forest, trees naturally grow in that manner. The seniors depress all the juniors that attempt to rise near them.

But in a *planted* grove, all grow up together; and none can exert any power over another. [1: 31]

Gilpin's version of individuality, the visibility involved in picturesqueness, constitutes more than good design. For it rediscovers all the generational terms of society in what he repeatedly calls the tribes of trees. To make this argument, however, is to call attention to the process by which an apparent retreat from society becomes identical to a re-creation of it. Personification, it would seem, involves a substitution of unreal persons for real ones, a substitution that appears that much stranger or more disingenuous for the knowledge that senior trees do not affect junior persons in the way that trees affect trees, and persons, persons.

The process of translation through which trees and landscapes come to speak to humans introduces a new pressure for sequence into Gilpin's narratives. That is, Gilpin's emphasis upon foregrounds is not merely a technique for insisting that one can look at natural landscapes using exactly the same conventions that one has learned from looking at Salvator Rosa or Claude. Instead, it emphasizes the ways in which the recognition of objects has become increasingly externalized. The identity of this oak becomes dependent not merely on the regulative natural type oak, or even on the operations of one tree in the forest on another. Rather, it doesn't even count as a tree unless it has been personified by being seen in human perspective, with foreground.

It may be useful to recall Defoe by way of contrast here. For the *Tour,* as for *Moll Flanders,* the episodic format becomes the vehicle for typicality— if only because the episodic serves continually to make the representations of individuality seem superfluous. Thus, Defoe writes the *Tour* as series of thirteen letters that describe circuits of travel (based on "seventeen very large circuits, or journeys . . . taken through divers part separately, and three general tours over almost the whole English part of the island") that he can claim to have seen himself. And if he insists that "the accounts here given are not the produce of a cursory view, or raised upon the borrowed lights of other observers"(45), one of the striking things about the *Tour,* at least by comparison with later landscape guides, is that its narrative has very little specificity of direction. One sets out from London in one direction or another, observing the various sights and frequently interjecting comments about the relationship between one place and another, but one could, easily enough, follow one of Defoe's circuits in reverse. The firsthand testimony of the viewer makes the circuits of the guide marketable, gives them the freshness and topicality that Defoe is continually promoting, but it never suggests that the perspective of the viewer has any important role in constituting the sight.

This point is worth establishing largely for the extraordinary contrast it makes with the mode of later travel writing and all its emphasis on composition—in a curious revival of devotional "composition of place" that insists that one must compose even the natural scene that a writer like Defoe might merely have confronted. As is well known, a writer like William Gilpin composes his guides to picturesque travel as a way of reconciling nature with art, making the walking tour itself the near relation and opposite number to the eighteenth-century landscape garden. The reconciliation takes the specific form of finding nature recurrently incomplete, and in need of an observing eye that abandons the project of imitating nature for one of giving nature a finish that it would otherwise lack. As Martin Price has observed, "Gilpin does not expect nature to provide him with finished works of art," because nature is, in Gilpin's description, "always great in design, but unequal in composition."[8]

The picturesque becomes, on this account, what we might think of as a "grace beyond the reach of nature." Art may need nature in order to discern the elements of design, but nature needs art to compose it, to make its elements come together. Like perception that is half-creation, composition makes natural design look humanly comprehensible. Moreover, when Gilpin explains that nature "works on a *vast scale*; and, no doubt, harmoniously, if her schemes could be comprehended," his project sounds like one of mere translation, the adequacy of natural forms to human scale, "to adapt such diminutive parts of nature's surface to his own eye, as come within its scope."[9]

Picturesque travel recasts art with nature just as Gulliver recasts England with Lilliput and Brobdingnag, so that a formally composed foreground comes to seem as crucial to Gilpin as the idea of a telescope or microscope to Gulliver. Yet there is a difficulty with the adequation model. For Gilpin proposes that nature's deficiencies at composition come from skill at particularity—the design that renders individual shapes—*and* from hopeless inadequacy at rendering particularity—the "diminutive parts of nature's surface." Nature, working on a vast scale, is adept at the striking particulars that design singles out, but no good at all on composition if we understand that process as one of organizing particulars within harmonious relationships.

Composition, then, involves supplying a middle distance. And if the sublime aesthetic continually produces scenes in which the limitations of individual perception become tributes to the ability of human reason to think past those very perceptions, Gilpin's picturesque uses composition as a more routine way of insisting upon the centrality of the individual viewer. Mediating between nature's vastness and the particulars of nature's design, the picturesque traveler searches for composable scenes. Gilpin's recurrent complaint about numerous natural sites is that "there is no foreground"—an objection that can only be meaningful if one imagines that the process of composition is one of discovering, from the landscape's offering itself to painterly versions of perspective, the place in which the viewer stands.

The importance of the notion of composition lies, then, not so much in the idea of proportion or harmony. For what Gilpin discovers in his picturesque handling of landscape is not so much that landscapes can be pictured or that pictures can affect our viewing of natural landscapes but, more important, that painterly perspective on natural landscapes implies the necessity of the human gaze.

The process of composing, moreover, involves not just a process of giving the viewer a place to stand. It also particularizes the natural site by its very insistence upon approaches and foregrounds. The viewer is personified by this process, as someone to see in the human terms of artistic perspective becomes a demand of the landscape; and the natural scene is personified as the notion of foreground makes it appear that one needs to see a landscape from a particular angle—*as if it had a face*, a front and a back as human bodies do. When Gilpin judges one "great scene" in the English Lake District, "It was too extensive for the painter's use," he glosses that view by saying, "It is certainly an error in landscape-painting, to comprehend too much. It turns a picture into a map."[10] The map provides a perspective that no one ever has—or could have, so that it disappoints Gilpin's insistence upon the inclusion of the observer. Moreover, the map leaves a site looking schematic, like a mere element in a series; it is not, in short, a portrait.

If landscape painting traditionally used perspective to create a difference between foreground and background, portrait painting traditionally was all foreground.[11] The innovation of Gilpin's version of the picturesque was that it did not merely, as in Panofsky's account of perspective,[12] assign the viewer a place. Rather, it also insisted that its supplying a foreground enabled it to function as a version of portraiture—not mapping (with its "you are here") but portrait (with the process of foregrounding so conspicuously shifted to the picturesque tourist as to render the frame central by virtue of its absence, its needing to be supplied).

Gilpin, converting the likeness of the landscape from maps to portraiture, makes both landscape and observer singular—reciprocally singular. The viewer creates a singular nature by seeing a face in the landscape; the landscape creates the singular viewer as the projection of its perspectival movement. Yet this very insistence on the production of singularity obviously contradicts the guide's usefulness as a vehicle for introducing the traveler to specific places. For the kind of obsolescence that Defoe sees in his *Tour* is the kind of obsolescence inherent in any account that describes things at a particular moment in time (it cannot anticipate the future of things that are continually changing and being changed). The obsolescence of Gilpin's views cuts deeper, to suggest why guides kept being written and kept being denounced. Once the description came to involve both the mutability of grounds and the mutability of foregrounds, it became virtually irreplicable. The guide could only concern methods of seeing rather than objects of sight, because objects were picturesque—picturable and visible—only through an aestheticization that did not so much point out the similarities between nature and art as the singularities of the relationship between the object and the viewer.

For William Hutchinson, whose *Excursion to the Lakes in Westmoreland and Cumberland* was published in 1773 (as well as in 1774 and 1776 editions), and for Thomas West, whose *Guide to the Lakes* was published in 1778 (going through ten editions by 1812), the question of replicability revolves around the person of the guide.[13] Hutchinson chants a litany of abuse about the native informant, the person who would share his experience of a region with the uninitiated traveler: "so liable are strangers to be deceived and imposed on by their guides, on whose veracity they are sometimes obliged to rely for the information they obtain";[14] "this is a second instance, in this little tour, how little the relations of guides are to be depended on"(151). And the corruption of contested elections "exposes travellers to this reverse: a nasty, leaky fishing-boat, with an impertinent, talkative, lying pilot"(176). West, in fact, offers his guidebook as a substitute for the native informant; the book will "relieve the traveller from the burthen of those tedious enquiries on the road, or at the inns, which generally embarrass, and often mislead."[15]

It is, moreover, unclear whether the lying guide is worse than the truthful one, the one who continually prepares for one's confirming perceptions. The very justification for picturesque travel, for Gilpin and others, lay in the particularity of *what* one saw and in that particularity's enabling a reflexive sense of individuality in the traveler. The application of art to nature was, that is, a flight from the ways in which even art might issue not in particularity but in a kind of typical particularity—the mannerism of individuality, or signature. From Gilpin's standpoint, the advantage of nature over art was that it remained various. The "one great distinction between [nature's] painting and that of her *copyists*" is that "artists universally are mannerists in a certain degree. Each has his particular mode of forming particular objects. His rocks, his trees, his figures are cast in one mould; at least they possess only a *varied sameness*. The figures of Rubens are all full-fed; those of Salvator spare and long-legged: but nature has a different mould for every object she presents."[16]

The English Lake District, like any other watery region, creates problems for its guides, whether they be persons or books, because of its constant mutations. These problems become, moreover, the lakes' opportunities, their defeat of the mannerism of individual aesthetic perception. Lake scenery is, from one standpoint, "less subject to change" than forest scenery, because the water, like the forest land that could always become farm land, "remains unaltered by time."[17] The water, however, continually casts up different pictures of objects—pictures that are strangely causeless and disconnected from any original. "There is," Gilpin says, "another appearance on the surfaces of lakes, which we cannot account for on any principle either of optics, or of perspective. When there is no apparent cause in the sky, the water will sometimes appear dappled with large spots of shade"(106–7). If it is hard for any guide to represent himself or herself as typical, as seeing what others will see, the objects of sight in the Lake District have, without human agency, become even more singular than Gilpin's emphasis on perspectives and foregrounds could have predicted.

For if Gilpin's techniques of observation implicitly focus on the production of a face for nature and a reciprocal consciousness of the face of the observer whose perspective is itself put in the foreground, Wordsworth makes it difficult to locate the "speaking face of earth" that travel writing had seemed designed to produce. Publishing in 1810 his own *Guide to the Lakes,* Wordsworth writes to "reconcile a Briton to the scenery of his own country"(106). He writes, that is, to demonstrate the scenery as familiar, as personal. Moreover, with Gilpin and others, he describes itineraries in terms not merely of objects but of the approaches one should ideally make toward those objects. A "walk in the early morning ought to be taken on the eastern side of the vale" for the light, but on the western side "for the sake of the reflections, upon the water, of light from the rising sun"(98).

Directions for the tourist like these, however, give way to histories of unrecoverable sights—particular optical illusions he has experienced—in the "Miscellaneous Observations."

> Walking by the side of Ullswater upon a calm September morning, I saw, deep within the bosom of the lake, a magnificent Castle, with towers and battlements, nothing could be more distinct than the whole edifice;—after gazing with delight upon it for some time, as upon a work of enchantment, I could not but regret that my previous knowledge of the place enabled me to account for the appearance. It was in fact the reflection of a pleasure-house called Lyulph's Tower—the towers and battlements magnified and so much changed in shape as not to be immediately recognized. In the meanwhile, the pleasure-house itself was altogether hidden from my view by a body of vapour stretching over it and along the hill-side on which it

stands, but not so as to have intercepted its communication with the lake; and hence this novel and most impressive object, which, if I had been a stranger to the spot, would from its being inexplicable have long detained the mind in a state of pleasing astonishment.[108]

For Wordsworth, as for Gilpin, optical illusions epitomize the particularity of a particular sight. Their nonreplicability—or rather, the virtual impossibility of replicating them by manipulating the laws of optics or perspective—makes them even more distinctive than Gilpin's compositions that give natural objects faces that return, through perspective, the gaze of their viewers. One must approach from this angle, see in that light, at just that moment, for the illusory image to appear. The optical illusion, unlike the landscape above Tintern Abbey, does not remain, though changed, to be seen.

Wordsworth, meanwhile, has described a strange case of visual parasitism in this optical illusion. The tower, whose physical form occasions the reflection, is obscured from view even as the unreal castle is distinctly visible, so that the illusion arises as a curious competition between images. As with Gilpin's trees, the aesthetic perception revolves around the perception of one object's interfering with or suppressing another. While Wordsworth claims that the lakes provide "beautiful repetitions of surrounding objects on the bosom of the water"(107), the repetitions do not merely point to the ways in which a thing and its reflection can look alike but also, sometimes, insist upon the reflection taking precedence over an occluded original.

The hiding of the occasioning object is crucial, because it registers the optical illusion as a fundamental challenge to the project of achieving human translation of natural design. While Gilpin moves toward a version of landscape drawing as portraiture, which captures the distinctive face of a naturally designed object, Wordsworth depicts natural reflection as a likeness-taking that seems, quite literally, to take away the thing whose likeness it assumes. Natural portraiture, or, rather, the self-portrait by nature, thus achieves the kind of reconciliation between nature and art that Gilpin would have wished. It does so, however, by establishing natural art as a process of hiding causal connection (such as that between Lyulph's Tower and the castle in the lake) that no amount of supplementary perspectival framing can replace. The empirical connections between images and the objects that cause them (all that would be explained by the laws of optics) fail here, and the perspective that is Gilpin's instrument of practical idealism similarly fails to make it possible for a viewer to connect designed objects with their compositions.

Nature, by reflecting its own objects, creates its own art, one that is as varied and unmannered as Gilpin would have wanted. It takes the same thing (Lyulph's Tower) and makes it look different (like a castle in the lake). Nature, doubling images of objects, produces typicality as more of the same and particularity as the way that the sameness always looks like a variation. And while Gilpin would make nature complete by seeing its artistry, Wordsworth would see as nature sees—would see nature's self-doubling as marking out the only point at which nature identifies its perspective rather than relying on human composition. This project of natural seeing involves extrapolating the perspective that nature must have on its own images so far as to identify the place where the human viewer must stand. Instead, that is, of having the human perspective compose a scene that nature has designed but not put together, Wordsworth imagines the reflections as identifying an already composed perspective with which the viewer must align herself or himself.

Occupying nature's perspective is, in Wordsworth's *Guide,* substituting the mannerism of human guides for the leadings of nature itself. The human viewer, thus, does not merely approach from the west or the east, by way of this shadow-producing image or that impressive promontory. He or she moves from what looks like a human translation of natural production (Gilpin's perspective) to a site where no translation is necessary, where nature's artistry produces a standpoint. The only problem is that this location repeatedly turns out to be "the bosom of the lake." And Wordsworth, supplying only once a boat with which one might occupy the bosom of the lake, employs the phrase and the perspectival location persistently enough to suggest that it should guide one toward what he also persistently refers to as "tranquil sublimity."

This "tranquil sublimity" is sublime because it raises questions of individual identity, about one's ability to be particular and continue to exist as more than an optical illusion, a peculiar epiphenomenon of the ways that light falls on objects. And the strangeness of the anxiety about existence which is provoked here is that it occurs in what feels like a mere following out of the laws of experience. Kant's dynamical sublime plays empiricism off against transcendentalism as the terror that one feels at the implicit power of an imposing natural object yields to a consciousness of human reason's power that can supply that idea of might to nature. Wordsworth's tranquil sublime plays empiricism off against empiricism, as if the process of reconciling the split between your memory of what you have seen before (as someone who is not "a stranger to the spot") and the illusory image you now see were a process merely of seeing from the proper, the natural, standpoint. This is the place at which one cannot stand without, oneself, being absorbed into the steady bosom of the lake in a natural act of translation which discovers human identity and uniqueness as merely the variety that nature always lends to her types.

The drive toward particularity—the precipitation of individuality for observers and objects of sight—has moved from a substitution of the guidebook for the guide to the elimination of guidebook descriptions in favor of processes of composition, to the eradication of the viewer altogether. Nature, creating its own reflections, its own imaginary images, becomes its own best portraitist, as it produces objectless images that obscure real objects (such as Lyulph's Tower) for distinct unreality (the castle in the water). In this version of natural narcissism, the theatricality of representations is no longer an issue. Humanity is. For the process of occupying the best vantage point, not so that one can see nature in terms of art but so that one can see natural art, is the process of being received into the steady bosom of the lake. It is the process of becoming a part of nature's production of variety (which can vary even the same thing to image both substance and shadow). It is the process of becoming so particular and particularized that one becomes as typical as it is possible for a human to be—by dying into nature. Nature's variety, it turns out, depends on its not being composed, subject to the mannerism, the varied sameness, implicit in an actual human gaze, and in its according humans the same variation they have been seeking.

Notes

1. William Gilpin, *Observations on the Western Parts of England, Relative Chiefly to Picturesque Beauty* (London: T. Cadell and W. Davies, 1798), 228–229.

2. Michael Fried, *Absorption and Theatricality: Painting and Beholder in the Age of Diderot* (Berkeley: University of California Press, 1980).

3. Daniel Defoe, *A Tour through the Whole Island of Great Britain,* abridged and ed. Pat Rogers (Harmondsworth: Penguin Books, 1979), 43. I quote from this edition because of its general availability.

4. The Rogers edition silently eliminates "and consequently populous," the reading that appears in Defoe, *A Tour through the Whole Island of Britain,* ed. G. D. H. Cole (London: Peter Davies, 1927).

5. Arthur Young, *A Six Weeks Tour throughout the Southern Counties of England and Wales,* 3d ed. (London: W. Strahn, W. Nicoll, T. Cadell, 1772), 3–4.

6. See particularly Paul Mantoux, *The Industrial Revolution in the Eighteenth Century: An Outline of the Beginnings of the Modern Factory System in England,* rpt. (Chicago: University of Chicago Press, 1983). The chapters entitled "The Redistribution of the Land," 136–85, and "The Beginnings of Machinery in the Textile Industry," 189–219, provide an especially lucid survey of the economic reorganization that manifested itself in the land.

7. William Gilpin, *Remarks on Forest Scenery, and Other Woodland Views, (Relative Chiefly to Picturesque Beauty) Illustrated by the Scene of New-Forest in Hampshire,* 2d ed. (London: R. Blamire, 1794), 1: 31–32.

8. Martin Price, *To the Palace of Wisdom: Studies in Order and Energy from Dryden to Blake*

(Garden City, N.Y.: Doubleday & Co., 1965), 379. The Gilpin description comes from *Three Essays,* 1792, 70, cited in Price, 379.

9. Gilpin, *Three Essays,* 70.

10. Gilpin, *Observations . . ., Made in the Year 1772, on Several Parts of England; Particularly the Mountains, and Lakes of Cumberland, and Westmoreland,* 3d ed. (London: R. Blamire, 1792, 153–54).

11. I am grateful to Michael Fried for suggesting to me the importance, not to say the equivalence, of portraits and foregrounds.

12. See Erwin Panofsky, "Durer and Classical Antiquity" in *Meaning in the Visual Arts* (Garden City, N.Y.: Doubleday, 1955), 279–281; and *"Die Perspective als 'symbolische Form,' " Vorträge der Bibliothek Warburg,* 1924/25 (Leipzig and Berlin, 1927), 258–330.

13. See William Wordsworth, *Guide to the Lakes,* ed. Ernest de Selincourt (Oxford: Oxford University Press, 1970), note xi–xii.

14. William Hutchinson, *Excursion to the Lakes in Westmoreland and Cumberland,* 3d ed. (London: T. Wilkie and W. Charnley, 1776), 69.

15. Thomas West, *A Guide to the Lakes in Cumberland, Westmoreland, and Lancashire,* 4th ed. (London: W. Richardson and W. Pennington, 1789), 3.

16. Gilpin, *Observations on the River Wye, and Several Parts of South Wales, &c., Relative Chiefly to Picturesque Beauty: Made in the Summer of the Year 1770,* 5th ed. (London: T. Cadell Junior and W. Davies, 1800), 34–35.

17. Gilpin, *Observations . . ., Made in the Year 1772, On . . . the Mountains, and Lakes of Cumberland, and Westmoreland,* xiii.

7

Historicism, Deconstruction, and Wordsworth

I shall begin by isolating a largely indifferent instance, Wordsworth's, of a very general late eighteenth- and nineteenth-century phenomenon, the walking tour. Wordsworth, like many others in the latter part of the eighteenth century, occasionally toured the country—and did so on foot, either by accident or by design. In 1793, as Paul Sheats recounts it:

> Wordsworth and Calvert left the Isle of Wight in August, bound for the west of England. An accident to their carriage abruptly ended the trip; Calvert rode off on the only horse, and Wordsworth was left alone in the midst of Salisbury Plain. For the next three weeks he was once again a pedestrian traveler, as he made his way northward toward Wales along the valley of the Wye, where he viewed Tintern Abbey, met the little girl of *We Are Seven*, and walked for several days with the wild rover who became Peter Bell.[1]

I want to use this example to raise questions about sequence and personification as they have figured in recent Romantic criticism. For if the simple iterative gesture of putting one foot in front of another represents sequence for the walking tour, the questions that have loomed largest for the criticism are how—and whether—such a sequence can have faces attached to it.

It is easy enough to see that Wordsworth's walking tour, with its commitment to the accidental, or at least something like planned accident, has its affinities with the picturesque discovery of the motif in landscape. In painting and drawing, the notion of motif, through a geometrical reading of natural forms and their interrelationships, supplanted the notion of motive or motivation as an individual and psychological phenomenon. But if a natural motif instructed "the picturesque eye" on where to stand, in

Wordsworth's pedestrian tours the motif that provides a stance for the poet is the appearance of another person, someone whose words operate as the opening strokes of a linguistic geometry. Wordsworth's frequent use of conversations and dialogues in the poems associated with his pedestrian tours (poems such as "We Are Seven") thus might appear less as the excessively realistic gesture that Coleridge chided him for and more as a way of seeking a linguistic motif (understood not as a theme but as a formal perspective).

There are two problems with this suggestion, however. First, the treatment of language as assimilable to formal pattern raises different issues from those that emerge when natural objects are treated as assimilable to formal pattern; if found objects can become formal only in being supplied intentionality, "finding" human speech produces competitive intentionality. Second, one does not know how to determine the linguistic equivalent of pictorial perspective; grammatical structure, particularly its rendering of personhood as number (first, second, third, singular and plural), perhaps represents the closest approximation to perspective. Yet even a grammatical account of number provides only the sketchiest version of linguistic perspective, a positioning by virtue of having eliminated two or three other possibilities.

These problems—and their combined effect—have made it seem both obligatory and impossible to represent persons in literary works. Obligatory because of the moral discomfort aroused by taking literary works and their pretexts for granted, impossible because of the imperfect transmissibility of literary works and language. While one school of recent Romantic criticism tends to suggest that representations of other people constitute a means of suppressing them, the other claims that such representations essentially do not—and cannot—intersect with persons and could not suppress them even if they tried.

This problem of the presence—or absence—of other people seems to me the central one in Jerome J. McGann's account *The Romantic Ideology*, although he frequently identifies the issues rather differently—in terms of the Romantic desire for transcendence, the view that knowledge is an abstract rather than a social pursuit,[2] and the movement toward internalization which has been seen as characteristically Romantic. In his diagnosis, the "polemic of Romantic poetry . . . is that it will not be polemical; its doctrine, that it is not doctrinal; and its ideology, that it transcends ideology"(70). And although he repeatedly urges a critical criticism upon his readers, critique sounds less like a panacea when we realize that we can never know when we are standing apart from ideology and when we are merely instantiating it. The commitment to returning "poetry to a human form"(160) thus proceeds in terms of the assertion that "no adequate [literary] criticism can occur which does not force itself to take . . . into account" the reality that it is today "practiced under the aegis of very particular sorts of Ideological State Apparatuses" and the conclusion that "criticism must analyze, self-critically, the effect which those apparatuses have in shaping, and distorting, our critical activities"(159). On the one hand, ideology prevents the self from knowing itself: "for the cooptive powers of a vigorous culture like our own are very great"(2). On the other hand, the self that has been deluded is enjoined to move from its position of abject powerlessness to one of absolute power in being able to isolate and eject the alien power of ideology. The major problem is that the self can never know when it's done with this project of casting out ideology, and a subsidiary difficulty is that it is hard to see how the process of critique will not itself become a version of the very self-involvement it was designed to repudiate.

Thus, McGann sees the limits of Wordsworth's ideology becoming apparent in a poem like the Immortality Ode, of which he observes that "between 1793 and 1798 Wordsworth lost the world merely to gain his own immortal soul"(88), but he does not suggest that his own opposition between self and ideology might recapitulate the opposition between self and world that he has been describing. For in McGann's schema the only way to gain one's soul or oneself is to separate from one's world and its ideology. Critique is, then, consciousness imagined as an Archimedean lever; where ideology was, there ego shall be.

Far from eschewing a supposedly Romantic preoccupation with the self, thus, McGann recasts it in salvific terms. The chief difference between his version of self-consciousness and the Romantic one that he would repudiate is that he imagines a self-conscious self that achieves its transcendence through particularity. His "general argument," as he identifies it in his introduction to *The Romantic Ideology,* is that "artistic products, whatever they may be formally, are materially and existentially social, concrete, and unique." And he specifically labels his work in *The Romantic Ideology* (and in *A Critique of Modern Textual Criticism*) as part of a comprehensive project which seeks to explain and restore "an historical methodology to literary studies"(ix). This historical method would involve returning "poetry to a human form," seeing that what we read and study are poetic "*works* produced and reproduced by numbers of specific men and women," and McGann thus wants to distinguish between works of literature which "neither produce nor reproduce themselves" and texts, which do both, "which is merely to say that the idea of literature-as-text fetishizes works of art into passive objects, the consumer goods of a capitalized world"(160). McGann thus seems to encourage an historical criticism that would involve a recovery of the specificity of individual authors and their labor. And he explicitly claims that the process of categorizing literary products as "works" rather than "texts" is one aspect of the project of returning "poetry to a human form" and seeing "that what we read and study are poetic *works* produced and reproduced by numbers of specific men and women"(160).

Yet the particularity of individual poems emerges in a very peculiar way in an essay like "Keats and the Historical Method in Literary Criticism." For there it develops that McGann's version of historical criticism aims to confute a criticism that seems to be an amalgam of Paul de Man and scholarly editors who take the final author-corrected version of a literary text to be authoritative. McGann's view would counter the subordination of poet to poem that occurs when de Man, for instance, says, "In reading Keats, we are . . . reading the work of a man whose experience is mainly literary. . . . In this case, we are on very safe ground when we derive our understanding primarily from the work itself."[3] The dominant tendency of modern scholarly editors has been to denominate one version of a literary work as superior or authoritative because it represents the last or most recent representation of authorial intention. As McGann's readings of various Keats poems show, he would substitute an account of textual production for an account of texts. The social statements that a poem makes must continually be teased out by establishing contexts in terms of reference (the kind of enterprise that biographical criticism sets itself) and in terms of reception (the kind of approach that publication history may sketch out). Moreover, McGann's critic should identify his own context: "One of the principal functions of the socio-historical critic is to heighten the levels of social self-consciousness with which every critic carries out the act of literary criticism."[4] That is, the socio-historical critic has three sets of contexts to provide: that in which the poem originated, that into which the poem was received, and that in which the critic situates him- or herself.

On the face of it, this project sounds fine, in that it seems aimed at a literary version of truth in advertising. But only one of these contexts—that of a poem's reception very narrowly construed as the most basic facts of its publication history—can be delimited enough for one to say much of anything about it. And thus the multiplication of particulars that these very contexts provide does not so much enable us to recognize distance and difference from ourselves as insist upon the preeminence of difference as opposed to similarity. That is, McGann offers his method as an effort to avoid collapsing our contemporary views into those of Romantic poets in a disingenuous self-projection that hides behind the text, but this attempt to acknowledge differences—between then and now, authors and readers, and so on—challenges the very notion that any claim might be seen to apply to more than one case.

McGann's target, then, is any form of abstraction in which the terms of similarity (homogeneity) are allowed to obscure the differences among the individual works that have been grouped together. Thus, while generalizations about Romanticism rely on a process of abstraction from a collection of individual literary works, McGann would demonstrate the inadequacy of the generalizations to any individual case. On one level, he is of course right. Periodization and the counting that produces it do not personalize. The kind of operation that enables one to see things as part of a sequence or series does not preserve the distinct individuality of each individual or unit in the series. When one counts students, for example, one recognizes a basic similarity—their being students—that enables one to put them together for the purpose of making the count. But only by considerably exaggerating the claim being made by such a count can one suggest that such an operation involves taking the various terms to be identical—or even similar—in all respects. In other words, counting thirty students on some occasions does not mean that one cannot count fifteen women and fifteen men, or ten Asians, eight blacks, eight whites, and four Chicanos on others. Similarly, the literary periodization that we call Romanticism involves delimiting a literary period by making a count—juxtaposing a variety of heterogeneous materials so that one may count the literature of the years between the Augustan and the Victorian periods. In sum, the process of seeing that there is more than one of anything—simple enumeration—explicitly involves definition by extension, but it also implicitly involves definition by intension, by reference to some defining property. McGann, in repudiating the claims that appear to be made when one generalizes about the Romantics on the basis of a Wordsworthian model, does not in fact argue so much against that particular model as he does against the notion of any definition by intension, because he sees the fact of putting the various texts together as an illegitimate assertion of their identity. Thus, while he is most comfortable when defending Austen and Byron as distinct from Wordsworth, his argument becomes shakiest when he moves from Byron or Austen to the abstract "human face" of poetry. What McGann sees as the secondary "unmasking" of primary "illusions"[5] has plausibility then in so far as the "unmasking" constitutes the critic's prerogative not to understand something in the terms that he or she takes the poet or novelist to have provided. The "unmasking" does not, however, constitute a counterargument but rather the attempt to repudiate the very notion of abstraction or generalization, which for McGann is coterminous with formalism.

What he takes as formalism's hegemonic tendencies to elide differences thus yields a positive program of dispersion. Therefore, he criticizes not only literary critics who conflate themselves with the writers who produced the texts they read, but also editors who emphasize a definitive version of a text at the expense of other versions, who imagine that there is such a thing as Keats's "La Belle Dame sans Merci" in two forms rather than various essentially different poems. Arguing that the various poems that appeared under the title "La Belle Dame sans Merci" were not so much different versions of the same poem as different poems by virtue of their entailing different audiences, McGann essentially argues for removing an element from the counting series every time one can see *any* heterogeneous feature, whether in terms of the words on the page or the audience that read those words. And this tactic begins to suggest why it is that not even A. O. Lovejoy identified enough different Romanticisms to suit McGann.[6] It is not so much that one should engage in historical research in order to be able to acknowledge its difference from us, it is that there should be enough different Romanticisms, enough different poems, and enough different contemporary contexts to acknowledge every reader. Literature, that is, should be recognized as personalized, in McGann's account, so that it can be seen as different whenever the particular combination of writer, text, and reader changes. Personification is, on this account, not so much a trope deployed by poets in poems; it is the very function of literature and criticism—to make individuals of us all.

In adopting this version of personification, in which poems are, because of their didactic function, responsible for making people (and enabling people to make themselves the right way), McGann thus revives a time-honored account of the relationship between poetry and society. Poetry is, in this account, an antidote to the values of society, and McGann's only real variation on this essentially Arnoldian position is to claim that criticism can (or must) now assume the role that poetry used to achieve on its own. Now that it has been shown that poetry may itself represent (or be coopted into) the dominant values of the society, the critic must become a critical critic, identifying the values of poetry and choosing among them.

McGann clearly conceives his socio-historical approach as restoring the notion of individual choice to literary studies. And, in some sense, it does. By establishing so many competing genetic accounts, McGann continually leaves the reader free to choose. A multiplicity of contexts, poems, and readers ends up dissolving the question of how the words of a poem can come to seem like an expression of anyone's intention, because the very question of interpretation has been suspended by the commitment to taking a stand, to having the critic see the poem as an occasion for him or her to personify virtue. Thus, McGann rehearses a portion of Marjorie Levinson's argument about "Tintern Abbey"—that Wordsworth sets it up to be a poem that substitutes a landscape with social and political implications for an exclusively mental landscape. While "the ruined abbey had been in the 1790s a favorite haunt of transients and displaced persons," Wordsworth "observes the tranquil orderliness of the nearby 'pastoral farms' and draws these views into a relation with the 'vagrant dwellers in the houseless woods' of the abbey."[7]

What McGann and Levinson take to be the Romantic project of internalization becomes suspect in this schema, because Romantic internalization is equated with privacy, and specifically with a commitment to privatization which is willing to impose itself no matter what the consequences for other people. As soon as the homeless become the palimpsest on which the individual meditation is superimposed, the privacy of Romantic thought becomes clear—and clearly corrupt; the personal meditation comes to look like a willful refusal to see a world outside of oneself, an engagement of alternately weary and triumphant self-scrutiny when there are people with real problems. On this account, the poet's apparent isolation—not just from Dorothy but also from the homeless vagrants at Tintern Abbey—itself implicates poetry in a lethal attack on other people. The presence or absence of the representation of persons in a poem, that is, becomes the personal responsibility of the poet who did not put them in, or who edited them out. And it would clearly not be a satisfactory answer to say, "Maybe Wordsworth happened to be at Tintern Abbey on a day where there weren't any vagrants there, or maybe he was standing in a spot from which he could not see them." For the position that McGann and Levinson here adopt reenacts the solipsism that it claims to cast out by imagining that one's very perceptions lie within one's control.

The question of how a person gets into a poem thus seems, in McGann's version of historicism, to be essentially a thematic and quantitative issue. And in these terms, the autobiographical narrative continually reenacts the story of the suppression or oppression of other people that the *Lyrical Ballads* experiments in human suffering can be seen to have tried to avoid.

Against this effort to reclaim literature for the human, let us set Paul de Man's account, in his essay on Rousseau's *Confessions*, "Excuses," of the way persons enter literary texts.[8] Although McGann almost never mentions de Man directly, his dark comments about critics who have chosen to enter the prison house of language suggest that de Man ought to be one of his targets, whether he is, in fact, or not. The account of linguistic agency in "Excuses" gives particular scandal to McGann's position in both thematic and argumentative terms. There de Man analyzes Rousseau's description in the *Confessions* of his having committed an act of theft and then blamed it on someone else, Marion, a servant girl who worked in the household with Rousseau and of whom he was enamored. De Man's entire account rests on the argument that there is a difference between Rousseau's intentions toward Marion and the formal expression of those intentions which gets interpreted in such a way as to cause Marion harm. Thus, although de Man traces possible connective links between Rousseau's thoughts and his representation of them to those who have caught him with the ribbon, he focuses particularly on the moment at which Rousseau abandons—or attenuates—his causal explanations. That is, de Man patiently traces the metaphorical structures in which Rousseau's desire to possess Marion becomes substitutable for his possession of the ribbon and in which Marion becomes substitutable for Jean-Jacques in the reciprocal relationship that Rousseau equates with "the very condition of love"(283). He chiefly engages, however, Rousseau's explanation that his accusation was not intentional but rather accidental. Thus he points to "the use of vocabulary of contingency ('le premier object qui s'offrit') within an argument of causality" that allows "for a complete disjunction between Rousseau's desires and interests and the selection of this particular name"; "Marion just happened to be the first thing that came to mind; any other name, any other word, any other sound or noise could have done just as well and Marion's entry into the discourse is a mere effect of chance"(288).

The chief point here is that the existence of representations of persons is not coextensive with the empirical existence and actions of those persons—either those (such as Rousseau) who might appear to commit those actions or those (such as Marion) who might appear to be their objects. The entire drama rests on the difference between, on the one hand, taking names and persons as substitutable for one another and, on the other, recognizing names and persons as nonequivalent. Rousseau can thus say the name "Marion" in a way that implicates the actual person Marion in a criminal act that she did not commit and that he knows she did not commit. He can do so, moreover, without having meant it. Having a name thus far makes one hostage to the accidents of other people's uses of the name. But de Man describes two victims here. While Marion may be the incidental and accidental victim of Rousseau's act of naming, Rousseau is, in de Man's account, the victim of a misreading himself. Using someone's name is not itself an assertion of power (as it would be in the kind of Levi-Straussian analysis that Derrida demolishes in *Of Grammatology*). It is, rather, symptomatic of form being taken for content, of a name being read as if it had a necessary connection to the person who happened to bear it. The mechanical operation of the form thus dispatches two characters at once: Marion, whose control of her own fate has been definitively eliminated by the false personification of the reception of Rousseau's act of naming, and Rousseau, whose control of his own story has degenerated into a story of the implacable operation of reception to empty itself of original intention.

On de Man's account, Rousseau's personal feelings about an actual person begin to lose their relevance as soon as the text begins to operate upon the "actual event." And any interpretative gesture toward empathy or motivational conjectures may produce the "human face" that McGann calls for, but it does so only by insisting upon an abject projection of formal notions of persons upon the pure operation of matter. De Man's discussion thus far coincides with Kant's aesthetics in imagining form as continually enabling a movement in excess of experience precisely because of its ability to proceed beyond what can be empirically perceived. Yet, like Kant's account of the natural sublime, and unlike his account of the beautiful with its artificial objects, de Man's reading converts writing into a version of accident: as the formal reveals itself as material it becomes as unavailable for human purposes as nature. Thus, this procedure does not merely avoid anthropomorphizing nature. It also naturalizes the human, not by making it seem more normal but rather by making it seem unhuman. If nature is the more conspicuously nonhuman realm of accident, the mechanical reveals the accidental in the apparently human. While the register of the beautiful allows for the possibility of human producers of aesthetic objects and multiple readers (or viewers, etc.), the register of the sublime establishes its particular authority by situating the individual in a relation with nature that eliminates the practical (the communicative) uses of form by eliminating the possibility of anyone's having a privileged relationship to it. Because accident is always equally unintelligible to all persons, intelligible, that is, only when it happens to say "nothing" and therefore to coincide with a materiality that is itself not something but nothing, language might well be defined as prelinguistic rather than linguistic.[9]

This is to say that de Man analyzes ambiguity, the ability of language to be taken in more than one way, in order to read a multiplicity of meanings as annihilating the possibility of reconciling those meanings with one another. In doing so he is thus essentially challenging the basic assumptions implicit in the notion of ambiguity, which, along with allegory and irony, has been a basis for Romantic and post-Romantic claims about literariness itself. Whereas these terms once figured in Romantic and phenomenological arguments about the ambivalence of material form (and thus about the insufficiency of the material in accounts of meaning), de Man's point here (in what I take to be a repudiation of his well-known essay "The Rhetoric of Temporality" with its consideration of allegory and irony) is that seeing the stakes of naming is recognizing that neither allegory nor irony is genuinely possible. For ambiguity, like allegory, like irony, emphasizes the changes that can be rung on material equivalence. They depend, that is, on emphasizing the perception of identity even as it is transformed, made to look like difference. By contrast, the nominalism of de Man's position on naming is that not merely universals but names should exist genuinely in name alone—without the persistence that would make identity (even the identity imputed by auditors) a relevant issue. Once this position is really taken seriously, moreover, it becomes clear that referentiality (or nonreferentiality) is only the beginning of the problem of linguistic nominalism. Every word becomes a name. Thus, de Man's interest in the genealogies of Rousseau's excuses, which, on the one hand, emphasize a metaphorical substitution and, on the other, a narrative almost purely grammatical. (In the tropological exchanges of Rousseau's depiction of love, de Man observes, one can substitute "Marion" for "Jean-Jacques" and "Jean-Jacques" for "Marion"; in the motivational narrative, Jean-Jacques relates that he stole the ribbon *for* Marion. Marion for Jean-Jacques, Jean-Jacques for Marion.) The referent of the name "Marion" has, indeed, become obscure through multiplication; but, even more important, a word like "for" that looked as though reference was thoroughly beside its point has come to function as a name, as if language were so thoroughly unhomogeneous in its self-successiveness that it had to be continually restarted.

Whereas ambiguity, allegory, and irony revolve around the ability to mean different things with the same words, accounts of them have typically centered on reference, the names of things. De Man, however, emphasizes the nameness of names, in which the generalization of names lies not in their referring to things but in their being names that are incidentally rather than inherently repeated. The precise nature of this shift may become apparent if we compare de Man's account of the diverse meanings attached to the word "Marion" with a more traditional example of two diverse and even opposed names, "morning star" and "evening star," applying to the same thing. This case relies on having a referent as the focal point of a triadic relationship. While de Man sets up a similarly triadic relationship, he inserts the name (or word or "noise") "Marion" as the focal point. With such a shift, he is able to argue that there is a fundamental asymmetry in the relationship between language and things. That there always seem to be words that correspond to things does not apply in reverse; there are not always things that correspond to words. "Marion," seen from the standpoint of the persons interrogating Rousseau, makes sense in a referential system, but "Marion," from the standpoint of the contingent and merely contiguous series that de Man traces in Rousseau's narrative, makes sense as "nothing." Marion and "nothing" are, for de Man, equivalent in being terms that stand in equidistant relationships to "Marion" (just as "morning star" and "evening star" can be said to stand in equidistant relationships to the same physical body). While the convergence of two names on one object creates the paradoxical situation in which two such palpably different terms as "morning star" and "evening star" refer to the same thing while meaning different things, the convergence of one human referent and "nothing" on the name "Marion" yields a greater contradiction. For while the relative stability of the referent in the "morning star"–"evening star" example creates the possibility of continually arriving at "morning star" from "evening star" by way of the referent, de Man describes a case in which the fact of competing versions of the "same thing" is seen to bracket that thing as different from the various equidistant terms that would refer to it. That is, it functions in terms of pure positionality, having counted only to bring the other terms into proximity with one another. Thus, the account of the referential or cognitive—the connection between "Marion" and Marion—is juxtaposed with the performative—the connection between "Marion" and "nothing" which is laid out by the narrative. And the process of juxtaposing these two different meanings for "Marion" makes them look as though they resemble one another more than either of them resembles "Marion." Thus, the competing claims of cognitive and performative, epistemological and narrative, Marion and "nothing" are forced into a positional equivalence. The effort at equivalence (Marion = "nothing") quickly reveals itself as a *contradiction* (Marion ≠ "nothing") because de Man, having isolated the term that provided a rationale for each of the two divergent series, explicitly sees that term as self-dividing rather than a hinge between two different accounts.

The "morning star"–"evening star" case could be represented in numerical terms—as if you were to say that the number 7 could be represented as 10 if you were counting in a base of 7 and as 7 if counting in a base of 10. The apparent homology between the number 7 and its representation as 7 in a base of 10 counts neither as an absolute justification of the validity of this particular representation nor as a statement of the invalidity of other possible representations. Rather, it provides a context that enables the divergent procedures of representation to converge. It is, in other words, formal in imagining reference as a focal point for different explanatory systems. And it is precisely such a formal account of reference as a focal point that de Man is attacking. For in his account, the various ways of rendering "Marion" are put into a positional equivalence that relies upon the sense of identity but involves only the appearance of identity: that one could plausibly mean to be uttering a mere noise and that one could plausibly be understood to have named a thief by saying "Marion" does not mean (as it might in an extrapolation of formal idealism) that name is the linguistic equivalent of the *Ding an sich,* the unexperienced projection of the various possible versions of the experiential object. It means, instead, that name is the material unit of the illusion of succession.

The construction that de Man's deconstructive materialism would confute insists, that is, upon name specifically as name functions as an alternative to any notion of narrative sequence that emerges in an account of numerical series. While it is certainly the case that one can treat numbers as if they were names (according to the principle identifying randomness with non-heritability on which the access numbers for automatic teller machines are based), the question is whether the notion of sequence has really been defeated when one treats numbers as names. Whether, in other words, one can make all language be as conveniently performative as de Man would like. De Man, and Andrzej Warminski in exposition of him,[10] must resort to the claim that "zero . . . is heterogeneous to the number system" to make the operation of zero in numerical series look as though it is the (random) name upon which number depends. Yet this account of zero, which de Man and Warminski take from Pascal, treats number exclusively in terms of reference (toward things that might be counted) rather than in terms of system.[11] Now one can state with some confidence that the status of zero changed in 1888, when J. W. R. Dedekind declared, in the first of five axioms for the natural numbers, that "0 is a natural number."[12] When number was seen to involve the ability to produce another number by adding one to the previous number, zero could, like one, be recognized as a number. I introduce this information without any illusion that I am thereby clubbing Andrzej Warminski or Paul de Man with an ineluctable fact, an inescapable definition of what zero always is. I introduce it, rather, because the assumption that zero could have been—and was—incorporated into the number system indicates more clearly than any other specific example what is at stake in my doubts about de Man's account of materiality in general and zero in particular.

Three points concern me here: (1) that de Man and Warminski, in seeing materiality as necessary to language, mistakenly see materiality as exclusively constitutive of language, and make intention and systematization look like a mere imposition upon materiality; (2) that, even were materiality heterogeneous to tropological systems, my account of the role of systems provides a somewhat more—rather than less—defensible version of de Man's argument than Warminski's does; and (3) that de Man's presentation of arguments about Pascal's discussion of numbers and infinitude accords with a recurrent strategy in which operations that appear to involve human activity and effort are read (mistakenly, I would argue) as demonstrating the nonheritability of individual intention and formal intension in language.

As Warminski says, "zero in de Man's reading is heterogeneous to the number system—i.e., a tropological, transformational system—a 'foreign element' that is necessary for the system's self-constitution but that itself cannot be homogenized to that system." Similarly, materiality in de Man's reading is, in Warminski's phrase, "the heterogeneity of linguistic representation," and "the name 'Marion' read as a foreign element outside of the system of representation' (like 'zero' rather than a 'one')" instantiates this materiality precisely in the moment in which it is violated by the imposition of a meaning on an utterance "that innocently lacks sense." For de Man the sound of the name "Marion" (in "Excuses") and the look—the calligraphy or stenography—of allegorical writing (in "Pascal's Allegory of Persuasion") give a toehold to the production of meaning. Matter without meaning makes the production of meaning possible. As Warminski goes on to say, "*as* a (material) condition of possibility of meaning, *such* a condition is always necessarily its condition of *im*possibility."[13] Materiality—of which the sound of the name "Marion" and the zero "as inscription" are instances—is, then (or would be), formality without idealism, the stuff of language before it is appropriated to perception, to meaning.

Warminski takes me to be saying that de Man is absolutizing "the claims of language of or knowledge," in a mode that he characterizes (mistakenly) as pragmatist (the pragmatist argument against de Man has nothing to do with his supposed absolutism). I introduced the account of "ambiguity," "positional equivalence," and "self-contradiction," however, not to descry absolutism but precisely to give an example of the way de Man makes it look as if materiality might come to be an available notion. That is, I was interested in tracing de Man's interest in defeating any and all systematization and in his particular strategies for doing so. For ambiguity is a serious issue not because of there being different possible interpretations of the sound "Marion." De Man's account, rather, traces the systems that enable each of the announced meanings to produce an index to the distance between either meaning and the noise or sound "Marion." There is, in de Man's terms, a problem with presenting "utter contingency" as such, because "utter contingency" is not experientially available. It is a notion that is derived as a by-product of the incompatibility of competing systems. Thus, I take de Man not just to raise the possibility that a cognitive or referential account of meaning is supplanted by a performative account or even by any "entirely random" account but also to make a stronger claim—that the production of meaning does not become a more certain process when one piles various different systems on top of one another. Whereas an account like Roman Jakobson's holds out the possibility of producing meaning by creating a kind of grid out of semantic and syntactic systems, de Man's account puts those systems of explanation into competition and even contradiction with one another to insist upon their noncomplementarity, their inability to create, additively, more determinable meaning than either could individually.

Ultimately, de Man's argument here (as elsewhere) revolves around the question of agency. Speech-act theory might seem to offer the model of an individual's working on language to give it a meaning in the moment, in a context, through an acting out that does not rely on universal agreement or understanding, but de Man raises the issue of speech acts both to counter the idea that one might add the referential and the performative to one another and to suggest the distance between language and intention. That is, even as he presents speech acts as involving more of an attempt to incorporate individual intention than a referential account does, he also presents Rousseau's speech act, saying "Marion" when he meant "nothing," as a failed speech act, one in which Rousseau's auditors didn't catch his meaning. Thus, agency appears to be defeated once again even on the model of a description of meaning that insists upon the importance of agency.

Now it might look as though Rousseau's saying one thing and being apprehended as saying another were relatively trivial issues—on the order of saying that some sounds are heard and others are not. But the strategy that de Man employs is not merely to make the speech act the correction, or better version or an untenable referential account. It is, rather, to put the two systems into a contradictory relationship with one another precisely so that they cannot be translated into one another. For if the two systems did not conspicuously fail to converge, the very notion of materiality-as-heterogeneity would be both unnecessary and unavailable. That is, the contradictory relationship between referential and performative systems itself enables the claim that "Marion" is neither Marion nor "nothing," but noise. Without such contradiction, the mistaken but successful interpretation that the sound means the person Marion and the correct but failed account of "Marion" as meaning "nothing" would suggest only their inadequacy, and would not point to the noise "Marion" as the meaningless *trompe l'oreille* equivalence of a meaningful "Marion."

Thus, far from thinking, with Warminski, that de Man takes the cognitive and performative accounts of "Marion" to be part of similar tropological systems, while "Marion" as utter contingency stands outside that system, I would argue that de Man relies on the contradiction between those two accounts to produce a notion of heterogeneity as language's precipitation of otherness from within itself. Being unable to get from here to there within language thus becomes the justification for the notion of being unable to get from matter to form except through an imposition of meaning on "even utterances that innocently lack sense."

Indeed, that strategy of playing different linguistic relationships off against one another recurs throughout de Man's work, perhaps most interestingly in "Pascal's Allegory of Persuasion," in which propositional logic and modal logic, number and space, along with the infinite arrived at by multiplication and infinite arrived at by division, are seen as continually exchanging places, trying to become one another. De Man rehearses the claim that "the status of the one is paradoxical and apparently contradictory: as the very principle of singleness, it has no plurality, no number,"[14] but he continues that it "partakes of number, according to the principle of homogeneity." "*One* is not a number; this proposition is correct, but so is the opposite proposition, namely, that one is a number, provided it is mediated by the principle of homogeneity which asserts that *one* is of the same species as number, as a house is not a city, yet a city made up of houses that are of the same species as the city, since one can always add a house to a city and it remains a city." (Notice the resemblance, on this account, between the individual and the group, on the one hand, and the finite and the infinite, on the other. De Man is here recapitulating an astonishing tendency in late twentieth-century writing to treat the relationship between individuals and the classes that they make up as equivalent to the relationship between the individual and finite, on the one hand, and the unbounded and infinite, on the other. Thus, what began as a polemic against imagining that all the elements of all the individuals in a class were identical because they shared one term that enabled their collection into a class becomes a more sweeping argument for nominalism. In representing a skeptical conclusion about the application of empirical probabilities to individuals, this position imagines that it has also repudiated even the most formal account of causation implicit in the notion of there being any discernible relationship among the elements of a series.) For the case of one, then, de Man finds in Pascal's system "a great deal of dialectical contradiction (one can say $1 = N$ as well as $1 \neq N$), but one that guarantees intelligibility." Yet if the contradiction that one is and is not a number "guarantees intelligibility," the case that interests de Man is that of the zero, which "is radically not a number, absolutely heterogeneous to the order of number"(10). Pascal's cosmology, with its account of the coherence of number and space, he argues, is maintained by the inability of the language of homogeneity and infinitesimals to get to zero. That is, as Zeno's paradoxes suggested, one can never get to absolute zero when one starts dividing. The infinitesimal, like the zero, looks like the material residue of form.

For de Man the zero is outside the system of number but graphically necessary to it (as when one writes ten), and one is ambivalent (not a number because not multiple, a number because homogeneous to number). Yet the notion of homogeneity ultimately makes the opposition of singularity and multiplicity essentially irrelevant to the notion of number. What Dedekind announced, in his axioms of the natural numbers, was that zero and one were as solidly within the numerical system as any other numbers. As soon, that is, as one recognizes that numbers do not need to be multiples, one realizes that the grounds for having claimed that one was not a number have disappeared. It may not be intuitively obvious that one is a number if counting is the operation that seems to constitute number; one doesn't look like a number because the motive for counting doesn't immediately occur. But, even less intuitively obviously, zero becomes a number in exactly the same way that one does—by reinterpretation of the relationships among numbers that enables us to recognize that number needs *neither* to be a multiple nor to refer to a thing. One becomes a number when, that is, homogeneity becomes more important than multiplicity. Zero becomes a number when succession and heritability (traits that can be passed) become more important than a homogeneity that operates in terms of multiplication and division. And to insist that one is and isn't a number and that zero never is a number is essentially to imagine that you can never change the terms of a discussion, much less recognize that one kind of account consigns the other to mistakenness. It is, in other words, to stack the example so that a conception of number based on a formal perception looks as though it involved only the more contingent (and namelike) operation of counting. With such a procedure, it looks as though an analysis of the example itself has demonstrated that the formality of number—which is, most basically, an assertion of the claims of likeness to organize series—loses formality at the zero that borders it and recurs to the merely empirical operation of counting. For de Man's emphasis throughout is consistently on the referent, so that the absence of a referent looks like a loss of the notion of number, while the emphasis on the formality of number is precisely committed to making empirical reference less important than the question of whether one can discern the regularity of difference (the $+ 1$ that separates 0 from 1 and 1 from 2) as a likeness.

Of course, de Man is not responsible for Pascal's account of number, and I'm not faulting him for having failed to replace seventeenth-century mathematics with late nineteenth-century axioms for the natural numbers. The standings of one and zero in particular aren't so much the issue as de Man's commitment to operations in which human action has no effect—thus, his reading of Pascalian infinites and infinitesimals as if they indicated a truth about language. Multiplying (or adding, which is the same thing) involves getting to an account of infinity in which one's multiplying or adding doesn't make any difference; infinity doesn't get any greater when you add to it or multiply by it. Dividing similarly involves getting to an account of the infinitesimally small in which one's dividing doesn't make any—or enough—difference; there's always something left above and beyond the zero (because division doesn't have the same relationship to subtraction that multiplication has to addition). The principles of numerical succession and heritability make the extension of the series rely on intension; being able to supply the missing element of a series becomes possible through a formal registration of intention in which the system does not need empirical corroboration. You never need to count anything to supply 2 after 0, 1, or to supply a missing 5 between 4 and 6.

De Man, while certainly not subscribing to a Pascalian cosmology, is, from the moment he adapts his reading of Pascal to the purposes of his own account of language, in a peculiar position. For his lack of belief in a Pascalian cosmology can, in a continuation of the sublime logic of infinites and infinitesimals, make no difference to him. In having preserved the terms of Pascal's text intact, as if they said something about the truth of language, he has made textual form the ongoing repository of contradiction because the text preserves truths and falsehoods, accuracies and mistakes alike. One, having once looked as if it were simultaneously number and nonnumber, must continue to be treated as the bearer of such contradiction. And if the historical development of numbers might make it look like a mistake to say that one is not a number, what is most interesting about de Man's renunciation of history and agency is that it suggests that language continually resurrects irreconcilable contradictions by eliminating the possibility of the formal intention that would make it possible to see an account different from one's own as if it were not infinitely extended. This leaves him to suffer the terms of a text, its truth and its errors alike, and to discover meaningfulness and meaninglessness on the same plane.

De Man's position, while explicitly denouncing reception, in fact maximizes the importance of reception, by establishing the purchase of performative and cognitive accounts alike. (The greatest possible failure of intention to register itself in language can only be discernible as and through the greatest possible misunderstandings in reception.) This is as much as to say that the materiality of de Man's account of texts is infinite, because it is impossible, on the one hand, to delimit one correct interpretation (because it appears impossible to detach linguistic material from any meaning that has ever attached to it) and because it is impossible, on the other, for the adherence of any one meaning not to look adventitious (because it appears as the supervenience of form on matter). De Man's sense of materiality as infinite, and infinite because human agency is insufficient to add to or subtract from it, is, however, not merely a position about the relationship between linguistic and nonlinguistic materials. Indeed, although the point about singularity and plurality is couched (in the essay on Pascal) as an observation about what is linguistic and what is heterogeneous to language, perhaps the most telling part of the discussion is its move to describe plurality *as such* in the terms of infinitude (as if the point about cities being made up of houses were a point about the impossibility of determining the relationship between an individual and a collection because taking away a house would not make the city any less a city).

If McGann would present us with literary works that continually accommodate human form and purpose, de Man makes the literary the arena of the nonhuman, in that literature is asked to make only "natural" statements, that is, statements (in an intensification of I. A. Richards's notion of pseudostatements) in which linguistic matter is given a face by its utterer, but only to be given additional faces by its reception. But the drive to discount the merely personal, or the psychological motivation, oddly reinstates the personal as the occasion of an otherwise arbitrary connection. In de Man's account of Rousseau, the operation of naming began with a kind of panic reaction. To be confronted with other people's demand that you explain yourself is to have a panic reaction that causes you to blurt something, anything, out. And the substitution of the accident of apparently formed matter for the accident of other people's presence and pressure is therefore less than an out-and-out renunciation of knowledge. For it can claim to escape mistakenness only by insisting that there is nothing to be shared.

In this account (and in a line of argument that de Man develops more fully in "Pascal's Allegory of Persuasion"), number appears superior to name because the connection between numbers and the persons they correlate with can continually be reordered, reshuffled, and redirected. But de Man here insists upon a peculiarly naturalized version of number, in that he wants it continually to be detached from any of the operations performed with number and the inevitable directionality that those operations provide. For him to emphasize the claims of materiality and the progress of number toward name (the move he achieves with the zero and the one) is for him to delineate the aesthetic as the impossibility of aesthetic intersubjectivity by having made materiality look as though it were always, everywhere and equally, at odds with formality. Having created the illusion that language is essentially material and uninheritable because one can arrive at a word through different routes, de Man recuperates identity on the level of form that is no less form for its being presented as if it were matter. For in his reading of Rousseau's *Confessions* and in that of Kant's Third Critique ("Phenomenality and Materiality in Kant"), linguistic structures imitate the world they cannot represent only in aping their form, that is, in becoming just as material (and, thus, in his view as unintelligible) as the things they seem to (or seem to want to) represent.[15]

From McGann's standpoint, the multiplication of one's categories should continue infinitely so that one can register the variety of humans and their literary products; from de Man's, a nonphenomenal materiality represents the only possibility of recognizing that sequence and matter will never coincide. For McGann, there should be a name for everything; for de Man, names are names by virtue of looking simultaneously singular and infinite. And in the context of these positions, I should like to look at Wordsworth's treatment of counting in "We Are Seven," one of the poems that is connected with his walking tour of 1793.[16] The most frequently mocked poem by the most frequently parodied writer in English, "We Are Seven" notoriously depicts a standoff between a young girl and a man who is traveling through her village. She claims that she, together with her six siblings, makes up a family of seven children; he, for his part, tries to explain to her that one does not customarily count the dead. In other words, this poem takes up the question of personification, of the way persons appear in language, by staging a direct debate on the issue.

In the preface to *Lyrical Ballads,* Wordsworth distances himself from the personification of abstract ideas (on the grounds that "such personifications" do not "make any regular or natural part of" "the very language of men,"), and he goes on to assert that he wishes to keep his reader "in the company of flesh and blood."[17] But, of course, the interest of "We Are Seven" lies in the girl's being able by counting to personify persons—which in this case represent neither abstract ideas nor flesh and blood. Her personifications take their plausibility and their strangeness from the mere fact that they attempt to cancel out the difference between past existence and present existence.

Had the girl said, "We were seven," or some version of "my parents had seven children," her statement would have been unexceptionable, and her chance interlocutor would never have had anything to quiz her about. Seeing how easily their disagreement could have been avoided, one can see that perhaps the most curious aspect of poem is not how much the girl and the man disagree on but instead how much they agree on. From his question, " 'Sisters and brothers, little maid, / 'How many may you be?' " he establishes an equivocation about the relation between one person and many persons. The possibility for the word "you" to apply in the singular or the plural continues to operate unchecked and strangely undisambiguated, because his words conflate possession with existence, *having* sisters and brothers with *being* sisters and brothers.[18] Thus, the girl's apparent surprise in registering his question—" 'How many? seven in all,' she said / And wondering looked at me"—occurs almost as a question about the traveler's powers of perception. "How many are you?" receives the reply "We are seven" as if it were just a version of "I am seven." Her wonderment appears to revolve around the fact that her being seven in being one is to her as readily apparent as the fact that she has thick curly hair.

This equation between "we are seven" and "I am seven" becomes clearer by stages, as the child's ability to count her siblings first merely involves her ability to place them despite their physical absence from this place (" 'And two of us at Conway dwell, / And two are gone to sea' "). In this particular progression, death simply figures a distance greater than that from her to Conway, or from here to the sea. And yet the child cites the existence of her dead siblings' graves as proof of their continuing existence. Being farther away than if one were at sea reconciles itself with its exact opposite, its proximity: "Twelve steps or more from my mother's door."

The child can know that one sister and one brother are dead and can also claim the opposite—that they still live and therefore count so that "we are seven." And she can thus produce the possibility of speaking of absent things as if they were present by what looks like a simple development of the logic of naming. If names such as Jane and John—the names of the dead siblings—enable one to represent persons as existing even when they cannot be seen, they also enable one to insist upon the existence of those names beyond their loss of referents. In "We Are Seven," only the dead siblings have names (except for the speaker's "dear brother Jem," who appears in the first line of the first version of the poem). Their names hold their places. Ordinary enough, these names sound almost excessively like generic names when "Jane" and "John" follow upon "dear brother Jem." When the child cites these names, their familiarity—the familiarity of particular names made virtually general through frequent use—creates an opposition between the generic names and the particularized names, the man's and the girl's different apprehensions of these same words. For the girl, names function as if they could never lose their referents, their connection to persons who can be pointed to, even in the absence of their bodies. For the man, what is there now is what counts, and signs of persons—be they names or graves—bespeak bodily absence. Yet the importance of their conflict has tended to be obscured by criticism that has treated the poem on the plausible assumption that the poem, being a dialogue, enacts the exchange much as drama would. Thus, critics have tended to defend the child and abuse the man. The traveler, acting from a certain callowness, tries to force on the child a knowledge for which she is not prepared as he promotes efficiency with arithmetic in the best modern way. Or, in a development of such a position, he tries to impose his hegemonic system upon an innocent victim.

And from such a perspective, the traveler's explanation of his calculation sounds like a crude enough empirical distinction.

> "You run about, my little maid,
> Your limbs they are alive;
> If two are in the church-yard laid,
> Then ye are only five."

But his insistence upon counting what is there, what one can point to, and not to count what isn't, identifies not so much his world view as a crucial characteristic of numbers when they are used for counting. Counting, that is, always takes numbers to have references that are available to be pointed to. As Russell puts it, "The act of counting consists in establishing a one-one correlation between the set of objects counted and the natural numbers (excluding 0) that are used up in the process."[19] As the little girl of "We Are Seven" puts it, the act of counting consists in using number to preserve the integrity of the amalgam, the set of numbers that have been counted. And if William Wordsworth would say of his brother John's death in 1805, "the set is now broken," the girl of the poem speaks as if sets could never be broken. That is, she uses number as if it were name, as if it never counted down as it lost reference, as if none of the "objects" in the set could be exhausted.

Recalling the circumstances of the composition of "We Are Seven" in his notes to Isabella Fenwick, Wordsworth tells of having written the poem backward:

> while walking to and fro I composed the last stanza first, having begun with the last line. When it was all but finished, I came in and recited it to Mr. Coleridge and my Sister, and said, 'A prefatory stanza must be added, and I should sit down to our little tea-meal with greater pleasure if my task were finished.' I mentioned in substance what I wished to be expressed, and Coleridge immediately threw off the stanza thus:
>
> > A little child, dear brother Jem,
>
> —I objected to the rhyme, 'dear brother Jem,' as being ludicrous, but we all enjoyed the joke of hitching-in our friend, James Tobin's name, who was familiarly called Jem. . . . I have only to add that in the spring of 1841 I revisited Goodrich Castle, not having seen that part of the Wye since I met the little Girl there in 1793. It would have given me great pleasure to have found in the neighbouring hamlet traces of one who had interested me so much; but that was impossible, as, unfortunately, I did not even know her name.[20]

Wordsworth later deleted "dear brother Jem," that ludicrous rhyme, leaving the first line of the poem shortened by two feet. But the "joke of hitching-in our friend, James Tobin's name" counts as a joke, partially for demonstrating the ludicrousness of the accidents of rhyme and partially for demonstrating the accidents of meter. Like "I travelled among unknown men," "To the Cuckoo," and many other early Wordsworth poems, "We Are Seven" is cast in Common Measure, or ballad meter derived from the "split-up septanarius." That is, it has seven feet for every two-line segment. In this meter, "Dear brother Jem" makes seven, as form adapts name to the purposes of number.

The introduction of this detail risks suggesting that any formal ordering proceeds on its own, so that reference is ultimately either a matter of indifference or a private joke or pang. And on such a generally deManian account name is always on the verge of being assimilated to (one version of) number, which achieves its formality by virtue its indifference to retaining the specificity of its reference. But if Wordsworth decides that "Jem" makes one name too many, his other recollection about the hazards of naming involves having one name too few. He can't, when he revisits Goodrich Castle in 1841, seek out the woman who had been the eight-year-old girl in 1793 because he never got her name. That lack of a name, moreover, underscores an oddness of naming in the poem, that the only siblings who have names are the dead ones. Wordsworth never got the girl's name, that is, because she was there, because her being there to be counted seemed to render her name irrelevant.

The 1841 retracing of the 1793 walking tour thus throws into relief the importance and the limitation of counting as ostensiveness. The girl in 1793 needed no name because she was one, the one who could be pointed to. But her having been pointed to is no more useful to Wordsworth in relocating her than the multiplication of texts, contexts, and critical criticism is to McGann. It does not make it possible to relocate the girl any more than McGann's self-proliferating inventories would make it possible for him to show the way one gets from here to there in sketching out a genetic narrative that would humanize literary works.

That is, we can see McGann focusing on the sense of materiality that one derives from the empirical situation of counting, pointing to things and persons. De Man meanwhile has been pointing to the materiality of naming and number as their formal persistence directly establishes the irony of the notion of a memory of counting. McGann's socio-historical method would point to how one gets from here to there, or from Salisbury Plain to Tintern Abbey, but it can do so not by deriving a course from the things one can point to but only by a sudden act of definition: this poem is for human value. He can, that is, stipulate the value for people of literary works with a human face, but he can never show the way one could arrive at that value on the basis of an argument about how many things or people there are. And de Man, less interested in making literature serve society, continually dramatizes the implausibility of imagining that there is an explicable connection between persons—be they authors or objects—and their representations. What is, however, ultimately most interesting is that they both resolve interpretative issues in favor of an insistence on a more explicit (McGann) and a more covert (de Man) empiricism. McGann's nominalistic commitment to recognizing an ever-proliferating plurality and de Man's treatment of name and number as if they always involved (failed or limited) acts of reference—as if they were always a version of counting what there is—demonstrate the achievement of an empirical sublime, the ability to lose a sense of one in the process of producing yet more.

Opposed on everything else, they agree in seeing a fundamental conflict between the individual and collection, the specific number and the amalgam. "We Are Seven," in its pitting of numbering against number, does not so much invalidate their approaches as suggest that they move too far toward resolution of the conflict between what there may be and what may be represented. The traveler's initial direct question to the girl is "What's your number?" rather than "What's your name?" And this way of seeing it establishes the representation of persons as a conflict between a numbering that can say who is there and a conception of name and number that always treats the representation as an amalgam both more extensive and more untraceable than that empirical count. The opponents of a bill that would have inaugurated an English census in 1753 claimed that a count was " 'totally subversive of the last remnants of English liberty,' " that it would "reveal the weakness of England to her enemies, and that it concealed tyrannical schemes for compulsory military service."[21] As in Rousseau's account of the way metaphorical language precedes literal language, the proposal to say what there is—whether by naming or counting—appears as a threat. If naming a "man" like oneself first involves taking him to be a "giant," someone larger and stronger than oneself, fear of the census likewise takes self-enumeration as a potential disclosure of one's weakness. By 1800 the prospect of this count seemed at least unthreatening enough for a bill of census to be passed, for self-enumeration had come to be identified with the possibility of planning, of seeing other people as something other than accidents.

Numbering, that is, had come to be just another version of naming, not just a way of saying what there is, but largely a way of making it possible to anticipate one's future. It was, in that sense, simply the inverse of the process of numbering individual houses that had begun in London in 1764, an articulation that made it that much easier to retrace one's steps, because house numbers combine ostensiveness (a correlation between number and object) with the identification of a house as a part of a series. Thus, while counting is indifferent to sequence (in that it does not matter which of, say, seven things one counts first), an operation like the numbering of houses insists on the sequence of houses and numbers so as to enable various persons to arrive at a place (even by different routes). That is, it coordinates individual meanings by systematizing the notion of place.

The convergence of these uses of number in the late eighteenth century suggests the possibility of reading a poem like "We Are Seven" in terms of a more general movement to coordinate meanings among individuals. For however much an individual number may slough off reference, the narrativizing of numbers in such projects as the numbering of houses represents a process of developing names as if they could function like numbers (with the heritability and successiveness that involves a regular interval between one term and the next). This coordination of meanings in numbering thus allows for representational divergence that can, for all its difference, be registered as comprehension. That is, despite the divergent arithmetics that yield "one" and "seven" for the problem of how many "you" are, the poem is less about the girl's incorrigibility or the man's obtuseness than about reconciling numbers to unity, or understanding another way of conceiving persons. Where modern criticism sees a gap, that is, the understanding of mathematics that I have associated with Kant sees an interval. And that sense of interval epitomizes the way in which Romantic formalism rescues language from a fundamental empiricism, by making it clear that the relationship among the terms supplements empirical reference. Just as the natural sublime comes to stand for an experience of something that does not already exist, the interval represents the formalist discovery of the patterning of language as at least as important as its ostensible referents. The problem of "We Are Seven" is that the girl speaks what ought, on an empiricist or crypto-empiricist account, to be an incomprehensible language. Yet what I take to be the chief point of the man's abandoning the exchange and walking away is to acknowledge that he understands what the girl has said. The poem is, then, a representation in miniature of the spirit animating paraphrase, an exchange of what you mean for what I would say, and in which the coordination of meaning counts neither as oppression nor as formal accident.

Notes

1. Paul Sheats, *The Making of Wordsworth's Poetry: 1785–1798* (Cambridge, Mass.: Harvard University Press, 1973), 83.

2. Jerome J. McGann, *The Romantic Ideology: A Critical Investigation* (Chicago: University of Chicago Press, 1983), 5.

3. McGann, "Keats and the Historical Method in Literary Criticism," *MLN* 94 (1979), 989.

4. McGann, "Keats," 994.

5. See Clifford H. Siskin, *The Historicity of Romantic Discourse* (New York: Oxford University Press, 1988), 62 ff., for a particularly cogent critique of McGann.

6. See McGann's discussion of Lovejoy and Wellek in "Distinguishing Romanticism," *Romantic Ideology*, 17 ff. The original debate was established by A. O. Lovejoy, "On the Discrimination of Romanticisms," *PMLA* 39 (1924), 229–53; and René Wellek, "The Concept of Romanticism in Literary Scholarship," *Comparative Literature* 1 (1949), 1–23, 147–72.

7. McGann, *Romantic Ideology*, 86. See Marjorie Levinson, *Wordsworth's Great Period Poems* (Cambridge: Cambridge University Press, 1986). Although McGann's book appears three years before Levinson's, he summarizes the argument of her unpublished work.

8. Paul de Man, "Excuses (*Confessions*)," *Allegories of Reading* (New Haven: Yale University Press, 1979), 278–301. My exposition of this passage coincides with, and relies on, that of Steven Knapp and Walter Benn Michaels in "Against Theory," *Critical Inquiry* 8 (Summer 1982): 134.

9. The prefatory note "Wordsworth and the Production of Poetry" that Cynthia Chase and Andrzej Warminski wrote for *Diacritics* 17 (Winter 1987), 2–3, may serve to indicate my fundamental agreement with Chase and Warminski over what de Man said (and to localize the disagreement over its value). Although they first attribute de Man's position to Wordsworth, claiming that Wordsworth's importance lies in that "his poetry maintains the priority of the poem's production over its understanding or reception" (2), they proceed to describe de Man's 1967 lecture "Time and History in Wordsworth" in terms of the notion of production. Even if their descriptions of Wordsworth's and de Man's 1967 avant-gardism amount to descriptions of what Kantian formalism achieved ("For it is only in language that the complex 'temporal structurizations' of the Boy of Winander, for example, can take place: that is, it is only in language that the unimaginable event of one's own death can be reflected on as though it were an event in the past," 3), however, their emphasis on production suggests why I call de Man's later work prelinguistic rather than linguistic. For the "Excuses" essay is not merely a statement of nominalism, the view that universals exist in name only, it establishes an account of the performative as idealist nominalism (as Chase and Warminski would say, a "performative of a sort—a gesture that acts to constitute an entity, rather than cognizes [sic] an entity already there, is the condition of the emergence of signs and figures, and of the phenomenal world," 2).

10. For a somewhat different version of this debate between Andrzej Warminski and myself, see Frances Ferguson, "Historicism, Deconstruction, and Wordsworth," *Diacritics* 17 (Winter 1987), 32–45; Andrzej Warminski, "Response," *Diacritics* 17 (Winter 1987), 46–48; and Frances Ferguson, "Response," *Diacritics* 17 (Winter 1987), 49–52.

11. See Paul de Man, "Pascal's Allegory of Persuasion," *Allegory and Representation*, ed. Stephen Greenblatt (Baltimore: Johns Hopkins University Press [English Institute], 1981), 1–25.

12. See the discussion in H. Behnke, F. Bachmann, K. Fladt, W. Suss, eds., *Fundamentals of Mathematics* 3 vols. (Cambridge, Mass.: M.I.T. Press, 1986), 1:72, which includes an accidentally interesting remark on naming: "The best-known system of axioms for the natural numbers is due to Dedekind (1888) but is named after Peano (1889)."

13. Warminski, "Response," 47.

14. "Pascal's Allegory of Persuasion," 9.

15. See Paul de Man, "Phenomenality and Materiality in Kant," in *Hermeneutics: Questions and Prospects,* ed. Gary Shapiro and Alan Sica (Amherst: University of Massachusetts Press, 1984), 121–44.
16. Elaine Scarry, in her introduction to *Literature and the Body: Essays on Populations and Persons* (Baltimore: Johns Hopkins University Press [English Institute], 1988), writes wonderfully about counting as an operation that is simultaneously the most and the least referential of activities.
17. William Wordsworth, *The Prose Works of William Wordsworth,* ed. W. J. B. Owen and Jane Worthington Smyser 3 vols. (Oxford: Clarendon Press, 1974), 1:130.
18. This conflation has its point, because *having* brothers and sisters is bound up with *being* a brother or sister oneself.
19. Bertrand Russell, *Introduction to Mathematical Philosophy* (London: Allen, 1963 [1919]), 16–17.
20. William Wordsworth and Samuel Taylor Coleridge, *Lyrical Ballads,* ed. R. L. Brett and A. R. Jones (London: Methuen and Co., 1963), 280.
21. Quoted in Paul Mantoux, *The Industrial Revolution in the Eighteenth Century: An Outline of the Beginnings of the Modern Factory System in England,* rpt. (Chicago: University of Chicago Press, 1983), p. 342.

Index